"In this lively and intelligent report, Danny Goldberg reminds us once again how the battle for freedom of expression needs to be refought every day. I don't know for sure if God is on Goldberg's side, but after reading this book, I sure am."
—Eric Alterman, author of *Liberal Media? The Truth About Bias and the News*

"What was the Sixties? It was 'I am the Walrus' blaring from the record store in Chapel Hill.It was hearing some guy yell 'No pictures!' at an anti-war meeting. It was the smell of trampled grass on the Washington Mall during the March on the Pentagon. It was hearing the word fascist spoken in regular conversation. It was the zip in the air knowing the draft was coming to get you. It was seeing *Hair* your last day in New York on the way to Africa and the Peace Corps. If you want to get a feel for the '60s, in fact if you want to keep the spirit alive, just read *Dispatches from the Culture Wars*."
—Chris Matthews, host of CNN's *Hard Ball with Chris Matthews*

"*Dispatches from the Culture Wars* is a riveting report from the front-lines. Whether you stand to the left, right or center in America's culture wars, Danny Goldberg's book is a must-read for anyone who cares about civil liberties, the First Amendment, and rock and roll."
—Anthony Romero, Executive Director, ACLU

"Danny Goldberg has spent 30 years fighting for your rights."
—Paul Begala, co-host, CNN's *Crossfire*

"Danny Goldberg's memoir contains the powerful reflections of the most progressive activist in the recording industry. His candor, vision, and sense of humor are infectious. It is required reading for those concerned with transforming America into a genuine democracy."
—Cornel West

"This is the history of the world that I have lived in all my life; the planet where the atmosphere is composed of equal parts: politics and art."
—Steve Earle

**DISPATCHES
FROM THE CULTURE WARS:**
*How the Left Lost Teen Spirit*

# DISPATCHES
# FROM THE CULTURE WARS:
## *How the Left Lost Teen Spirit*

Danny Goldberg

MIRAMAX BOOKS   NEW YORK 2003

for information address:

HYPERION, 77 WEST 66TH STREET

NEW YORK, NEW YORK 10023-6298

ISBN 0-7868-6896-1

The author and publisher gratefully acknowledge permission to reprint
the following previously published material:

"Love Me, I'm a Liberal" by Phil Ochs © 1965 Almo Music Corp.

on behalf of Barricade Music, Inc. All rights reserved. Used by permission.

"John Walker's Blues" from *Jerusalem* by Steve Earle © 2002 published by Sarangel Music

(ASCAP) and administered by Bughouse, A Division of Bug Music, Inc.

All Rights reserved. Used by permission.

"The River" by Bruce Springsteen. © 1979 by Bruce Springsteen (ASCAP).

All rights reserved. Reprinted by permission.

Excerpt from "The Ballad of the Skeletons" from *Death and Fame: Last Poems 1993–1997*

by Allen Ginsberg © 1999 by The Allen Ginsberg Trust.

Reprinted by permission of HarperCollins Publishers Inc.

10   9   8   7   6   5   4   3   2   1

For Rosemary,
Katie, and Max

# CONTENTS

## ACKNOWLEDGMENTS

I first would like to thank my partner in Artemis Records, Michael Chambers, whose vision and friendship have given me a home in the record business during the years that most of this book was written. Without the vocation that he and I work so hard on together, I'm not sure I would have had the confidence to embark on this project.

Similarly, I thank my colleagues at Artemis including Michael Krumper, Sage Robinson, Ken Walsh, Adrian White, and especially Daniel Glass.

Jack Newfield for years bugged me to write a book such as this and his encouragement was, and is, indispensable. He's a great writer and a great friend.

Andrew Wylie, my agent, not only shopped and sold my proposal but has been an extraordinary source of support in all ways. Andrew is a cosmic grand master at his craft. He has been a great friend as well as an agent during this process. I thank him from the bottom of my heart.

At Miramax Books I want to thank Susan Mercandetti, whose initial leap of faith is something I will never forget. JillEllyn Riley has led me through the process with care, attention to detail, and support the likes of which have continually delighted and surprised me. I also want to thank Tina Brown, whose blessing was so helpful, and Harvey Weinstein, whose blessings remain essential. And especially I thank John Burnham for welcoming me into his world.

JillEllyn introduced me to Harper Barnes, my editor. Harper worked tirelessly on the structure and narrative. To the extent that the book has a coherent structure, much of the credit belongs to him. In places where it rambles on too much, it's probably because I failed to take his advice.

Several people spoke to me at length about the themes of this book, and I thank especially Harry Belafonte, David Fenton, Tom Hayden, Gary Hart, Paul Krassner, Norman Lear, Michael Lerner, Jack Newfield, William Schneider, Marge Tabankin, Jack Valenti, and Dr. Rosalyn Weinman.

I appreciate the feedback on an earlier draft from Michael Des Barres, Victor Goldberg, Patrick Goldstein, Robert Greenwald, Jack Newfield, Earl Katz, and again Marge Tabankin.

My assistant of many years, Robin Klein, has been helpful in countless ways, and no expression of appreciation can possibly suffice.

I have been blessed with many cheerleaders, makers of contacts, confidants, and partners in political mischief. Among that number I especially thank Stanley Sheinbaum, Ken Sunshine, and Chuck Blitz.

In developing the confidence to write I am grateful to several editors over the years who have given me the space to express myself in opinion pieces, including Michael Lerner, Victor Navasky, Katrina Vanden Heuval, Bob Kuttner, and especially Allison Silver.

These books were of particular help in clarifying my thoughts:

Edward DeGrazia, *Girls Lean Back Everywhere: The Law of Obscenity and the Assault on Genius*

Jib Fowles, *The Case for Violence on Television*
Marjorie Heins, *Not in Front of the Children*
Jack Newfield, *Somebody's Got to Tell It*
Eric Nuzum, *Parental Advisory: Music Censorship in America*
Paul Slansky, *The Clothes Have No Emperor*

Thanks to musicians and to the music business, for giving me a place in the world.

My political consciousness was born in my childhood. I thank my parents, Victor and Mimi, for their inspiration and love and my sister, Rachel, brother, Peter, sister-in-law, Lola, and nephew, Benjamin, for constantly setting an example for me to live up to.

Thanks to Hilda Charlton, whose blessings I am grateful for beyond description.

Love to my kids, Katie and Max, who graciously put up with my disappearances to the basement.

More than anyone I am indebted to my wife, Rosemary Carroll, who not only has encouraged me in every way imaginable and led me through many dark passages, but also read every draft and version and gave me continual notes and comments, without which this work would have been infinitely more embarrassing.

**DISPATCHES
FROM THE CULTURE WARS:**
*How the Left Lost Teen Spirit*

# Introduction
## Rock, Rap, Reactionaries, and Liberal Snobs

IT MAY SEEM a little ridiculous for someone like me, a guy in the music business, to be criticizing the Democratic party and the American left, but I'm sick and tired of watching the ideas that I believe in lose political ground. Like other people in my field, I've been able to meet many of the intellectual and political leaders whose beliefs I share. I usually come away inspired by their policy ideas and deeply depressed by blind spots that doom those ideas. A political ideology whose purpose is to help and empower ordinary people is often directed by leaders and strategists to whom the public is an alien beast and to whom young people seem to be, astonishingly, irrelevant.

*It's always the young that make change. You don't get these kind of ideas when you're middle-aged. The young have daring, creativity, and energy— they have impatience. So you take your young legs and your eagerness and your natural feelings for justice and peace and a better deal for our planet and you go out and you make tomorrow better than it is today.*

—Abbie Hoffman at age fifty, speaking to a college audience

Even though majorities of the American public regularly tell pollsters they want national health insurance, tighter gun control, better pay for schoolteachers, energy independence, and stronger environmental regulation, advocates for these causes seem unable to translate this public support into political results. Not only has the Democratic party grown considerably weaker over the past few decades, but mainstream Democrats have moved steadily away from progressive causes. The 2002 election was merely the latest example of Democrats walking away from millions of their supporters and potential supporters, supposedly for politically pragmatic reasons, but with toxic political results.

The weirdest thing about the political shift to the right is that it has occurred during a time when virtually every cultural battle in America has been won by the left. People who have fought for abortion rights, free speech, gay and lesbian rights, and racial equality can look at a country transformed in their image. Yet most leaders in the political left and the Democratic party have profoundly mixed feelings about their cultural allies.

People in the entertainment business, especially the music business, are linked in the public mind with profound cultural changes over the last several decades. So, without ever planning it that way, I've become an enemy in the "culture wars," not only in the minds of conservatives but to many Democrats and others on the left whose policy goals I passionately support.

I have been in the music business for more than thirty years as a PR guy, a personal manager, and for the last decade as a record company president and owner. I have worked with rock legends such as Led Zeppelin, Neil Young, KISS, REM, and Nirvana, with pop icons such as Diana Ross and Madonna, with politically committed musicians like Joan Baez, Bonnie Raitt, Jackson Browne, Bruce Springsteen, and Steve Earle, and with gangsta rappers, singer-songwriters, boy bands, heavy metal icons, classical tenors, country divas, jazz masters, and critical darlings, as well as with such counterculture icons as Allen Ginsberg, Timothy Leary, William Burroughs, and Cornel West.

I am fifty-two years old, a "baby boomer" and an "aging hippie." I am also a businessman. I live in New York now, which is where I was born, but for most of the 1980s I lived in Los Angeles, and when I visit there I am still a "Hollywood liberal," working at times with such conservative targets as Norman Lear, Barbra Streisand, and Jane Fonda.

My wife, Rosemary Carroll, and I are parents of a girl and a boy, which, contrary to conventional wisdom, hasn't made us any more politically conservative. We have hosted fund-raisers for, among others, liberal Democrats like Hillary Clinton and Ted Kennedy, and worked with such independent voices as Jesse Jackson and Ralph Nader.

I've met with foreign leaders, such as El Salvador's Jose Napoleon Duarte, Nicaragua's Daniel Ortega, South Africa's Nelson Mandela, and several Israeli prime ministers, and with every Democratic candidate for president in the last decade. I've been on the boards of many organizations, including Amnesty International, the American Jewish Congress, and, especially, the American Civil Liberties Union (the ACLU).

I am an activist as an avocation. Except on issues that pertain to my business, I am certainly no expert. People in the entertainment business who support causes do so primarily as cheerleaders, sometimes as fund-raisers, and occasionally to help frame and transmit messages for their side.

What exactly is "my" side? In previous eras there were more clear-cut definitions of what "left" and "right" were. Today there are dozens of variations. On economic issues I'm a typical liberal.

Having run my own businesses and having worked for big corporations, I have a basic belief in capitalism, but I think that government, representing the collective will of the citizens, has a special obligation to balance out the excesses of the marketplace. I wouldn't mind paying higher taxes to have national health care, better paid schoolteachers, smaller class sizes in public schools, and more jobs programs to help get people out of poverty and help average-income people deal with their lives more easily. It seems to me that many Western European countries have been better at supporting people on the low end of the economic spectrum than Americans have, and the extent of poverty in America seems immoral to me given our country's wealth. Although I've never been a member of a labor union, I believe they should be stronger. Corporations have so much power that it seems healthier to me for there to be a strong counterweight on behalf of workers. I also think our country should be more generous with foreign aid given the immense poverty around the world.

Conservative rhetoric that implies that private charities can replace government doesn't ring true to me. I know that governments tend to be inefficient, but there are some things that only government can do, such as build highways, protect the environment, provide police protection, etc. The environment is an area where it's particularly important for government to enforce the public interest when it clashes with the economic interest of businesses. And by the way, there's plenty of corruption and inefficiency in the business world as well. I'm fascinated by the antiglobalization movement and I suspect that important moral leadership will emerge from there, but I'm not particularly sophisticated about many of the underlying issues.

Although some of the artists I've worked with have been involved with a wide array of issues and I try to read on a variety of topics, my primary interest is American culture and my primary field of activism has been about individual rights. It drives me crazy, for example, that the United States has so many of its citizens in prison, most of them for nonviolent crimes. Many of the people I know both in the business and in the political worlds would have spent time in jail if these laws were enforced against everyone.

I am an ardent civil libertarian and have been an officer of the ACLU since the mid-1980s. The ACLU was started in the 1920s as an advocacy group for the Bill of Rights with special emphasis at that time on the right to unpopular criminal speech in the wake of people who opposed World War I. During World War II the ACLU defended Japanese Americans who were interned by the Roosevelt administration. The ACLU has been involved with many landmark legal cases, including the court decisions that legalized abortion, that banned prayer in public schools, that gave accused criminals the right to remain silent and the right to an attorney, and virtually every case in which the government has attempted censorship of the arts.

It was the latter area that drew me to the ACLU when the music business was attacked, but I soon found myself enthralled with the organization's deeply idealistic vision of democracy, and it's the one political place where I've been involved as a participant as well as a supporter.

A belief in progressive economic policy doesn't automatically go with a commitment to civil liberties. For example, there are many left-wing Catholics who favor making abortion illegal. There are progressive college professors who favor "speech codes" on campus. There are members of "identity groups" representing the interests of gays and lesbians, feminists, African Americans, Jews, and so on who support boycotts of media offensive to some members of their groups.

I am an absolutist on free speech. I believe strongly in protections for those accused of crimes. I am against the death penalty, I am pro-choice, and I am in favor of affirmative action to get racial minorities and women into positions that have been historically closed to them.

Having been associated with the ACLU as an officer since the mid-1980s, I am often getting into arguments with progressive friends who disagree with the ACLU on one issue or another, none more than the organization's belief that many campaign finance laws such as McCain-Feingold interfere with freedom of speech. (The ACLU supports complete public financing of political campaigns as the solution to this problem and I agree.) Paradoxically, there are numerous conservative libertarians who agree with the ACLU on these issues but with whom I personally disagree on a wide array of economic issues.

Similarly, foreign policy in the post–Cold War period does not lend itself to traditional left-right divisions. I don't know much more about foreign policy than what I read in the newspapers, so I'm not inclined at this juncture to give a shopping list of every superficial foreign policy opinion I've ever had, but growing up during the Vietnam War has certainly made me suspicious of convoluted government rationales for military action. However, I am not a pure pacifist and I agree there are rare occasions when killing people with the military is the least bad course of action.

There are millions of people who share this set of beliefs. My lament is that the political culture whose role it is to advance the progressive agenda has grown increasingly elitist, snobbish, and removed from huge chunks of the American people, including most young people. This cloistered retreat is responsible for twenty years of regression for progressive policies after decades of progress during most of the twentieth century. There is no one reason for the disconnect between progressive politics and young people and much of Middle America, but I think that my own experiences in walking between the worlds of politics and entertainment can shed light on some of the neuroses that have made the political left far less popular than the ideas it champions.

Although I've supposedly been in the middle of one, I've always found the phrase "culture war" bizarre, especially as it applies to entertainment. No one ever talks about a culture war in the music business. We talk about "great records" and about "hits." We talk about "artists" and about "fans," and we talk about the ways to connect those two groups: radio, record stores, TV, concerts, press, and recently a lot about the Internet, CD burning, and new economic models.

And we talk about how much money everyone risks and everyone makes. We don't think of ourselves as being at war with anybody, except maybe metaphorically with one another. We just want to get our ideas and products out. If people don't like them or want to criticize them, no problem. No one has ever suggested passing a law mandating exposure to dirty movies or rap music or beatnik poetry, nor boycotting retailers that choose not to carry R-rated videos, nor "shaming" people in bow ties who want to return to the culture of the good old days.

Having been a teenager during the Vietnam War, I have connected rock and roll with politics as long as I can remember. By the 1970s, after attaining enough success in the music business to be able to help political causes I believed in, I began by working with rock artists who did benefits for environmental groups. I later got involved in efforts to prevent a Reagan-era war in Central America.

It never occurred to me that the way I made my living would itself become a political issue, but in 1985, when I read of Tipper Gore's efforts to intimidate record companies into instituting a ratings system for lyrics, I felt compelled to defend my colleagues in the music business and the adolescents who loved and helped create the culture that was under attack. Since then, a substantial amount of my activist avocation has focused on the intersection between popular culture and politics.

This book is a memoir based on fifteen years of experience at that intersection. At every place in the ideological spectrum, from moderate Democrats to movement radicals, again and again, in dozens of different ways, my experience is that the left avoids reaching out to large masses of Americans. For example, as I was finishing this book, journalist Jack Newfield told me he had just had lunch with a senior Democratic campaign advisor whose clients had included Senator Charles Schumer. When Newfield referred to Eminem, whose rap album is by far the most successful recording in the United States this year and is filled with political references, the political maven look puzzled and confessed he had never heard of Eminem. Similarly, I was recently on the phone with one of New York's most progressive congressmen who had never heard of Russell Simmons, the rap producer who has become one of New York's leading black activists. If one is a classics professor or art critic, there is nothing wrong with having tunnel vision and an aesthetic or philosophy that ignores popular taste and trends. Such independence of thought can be a virtue in those professions. But for the vocation of politics, the goal of which is to move majorities to support policy goals, such parochial myopia is outrageous. Without mass public outreach, politics, especially progressive politics, cannot succeed.

The phrase "culture war" is itself deceptive. It seems to me that several different culture wars have been going at the same time.

I. THE REVENGE OF THE CULTURAL CONSERVATIVES

The "culture war" most commonly described is driven by attacks on popular culture by conservative cultural critics. Cultural conservatives believe that American society reached its moral zenith in the early 1950s. Then a supposedly dreadful decline began with the advent of the beatniks, hitting bottom in the late 1960s with the hippies and the antiwar movement.

One archetypal cultural conservative is Jerry Falwell. After September 11, 2001, Falwell joined fellow conservative Christian Pat Robertson on *The 700 Club* and blamed gays, feminists, and the ACLU for the tragic attacks in New York and Washington, claiming that left-wing libertines had driven an angry God "to remove his protection from America." Even President George W. Bush criticized Falwell's remark, but there's no denying that Reverend Falwell spoke for a certain constituency that remains part of America's cultural mix.

Similarly, George Will, Lynne Cheney, Pat Buchanan, William Bennett, Robert Bork, and Norman Podhoretz all talk about a "coarsening" of American culture since the fifties. Their opposition to pop culture has been perfectly consistent and can be traced back to attacks on early rock and roll and Beat poetry by conservatives in the fifties, and to Vice President Spiro Agnew's demonization of the Beatles in the sixties.

Cultural conservatives like Bennett claim that high divorce rates, drug addiction, and teen violence are all the result of modern culture. They want a return to the authoritarian America of the 1950s, when the Catholic Church could make books "banned in Boston" and J. Edgar Hoover and the acolytes of Senator Joseph McCarthy could marginalize and terrorize any kind of unorthodox political or cultural thought. Not surprisingly, cultural conservatives frequently bemoan the state of the popular entertainment culture. It was ever thus.

## 2. THE ASCENDANCE OF THE LIBERAL SNOBS

Most of my own battles, however, have been with liberals and Democrats, many of whom I've supported in political campaigns. Starting in the mid-1980s, Democratic politicians and left-wing intellectuals began agreeing with cultural conservatives about the supposedly negative effects of popular culture.

The Democratic party's commitment to culture bashing was exacerbated during the Clinton era and reached a new pinnacle with the national ascendance of Senator Joseph Lieberman of Connecticut. But it's not only so-called New Democrats who have embraced attacks on pop culture. So have important voices on the political and academic left, including, at times, Ralph Nader and Rev. Jesse Jackson.

Most liberal snobs are from my own generation, the so-called baby boomers. Cultural conservatives want their children to grow up like they did; liberal snobs are afraid theirs will.

Conservatives attack pop culture going back to the turn of the last century. Liberals will extol the virtues of pop culture well into the sixties and conveniently claim that "something changed" shortly after they themselves came of age.

Liberal snobs tend to focus on violence and bigotry, cultural conservatives on sex. There are virtually no Democratic voices sticking up for youth culture. Although conservative Christians are a vital part of the national Republican coalition, many Republicans are actually more open-minded on the issue of free speech and pop culture than many Democrats, and I'm not just talking about libertarian conservatives such as P. J. O'Rourke and Ann Coulter.

President George W. Bush was seen on magazine covers with U2 lead singer Bono following a meeting about debt relief in the third world, and Bush cracked jokes while welcoming rock/reality-TV star Ozzy Osbourne to a White House dinner. There are no policy implications to any of this, but politically it sends a message that Bush is a "regular guy," whereas Democrats, whose actual agenda is far more relevant to young people, come across as uptight, preachy elitists.

One problem seems to be that many members of my generation, the generation now in power, have a basic resentment toward young people. This is a particularly foolish position for people to the left of center, since no progressive change has ever occurred anywhere in the world without the energy and inspiration of young people, who traditionally have provided the shock troops for the left.

Liberal snobs and cultural conservatives alike often are what free-speech activist Marjorie Heins calls "metaphorically challenged." Usually educated in law, journalism, political science, or sociology, politicians and pundits spend decades viewing human behavior in a linear, literalistic way. They frequently interpret art and entertainment as if they were devoid of metaphor, humor, irony, or Aristotelian catharsis. Looked at through this lens, neither fairy tales nor Greek tragedies nor classic opera would pass moral muster.

### 3. THE WASHINGTON DOMINANCE OF TONE-DEAF MAVENS

The same snobbery and insensitivity to young people that drives culture bashing has created a Democratic party and a public-interest left whose leaders appear unwilling or unable to communicate with the "unwashed" masses who do not read newspaper op-ed pages or watch public television. This isn't exactly a culture war so much as a disconnect between progressive political leaders and the culture of the people they want to lead.

By tone-deaf mavens, I mean the self-insulated consultants and pundits who have enormous influence on American politics and who, for the most part, are much more tuned in to other mavens in Washington than to what Americans are really thinking.

Conservatives, who control far more media than left-wingers, are clever enough to promote the spokespeople who have "working class" styles, like talk show propagandists Bill O'Reilly and Sean Hannity. The mystery is why so few progressives do the same cultural homework. The obvious exception is Michael Moore, whose populist style has created an enormous audience for his progressive views despite the media bias.

The fact that academics with radical new ideas no longer reach out to a mass audience was lamented as long ago as 1986 by Russell Jacoby in *The Last Intellectuals*. By contrast, he cited Galileo, whose "crime" was not to have revolutionary thoughts about the solar system, but to publish them in colloquial Italian instead of academic Latin. Most progressives today express themselves in language that might as well be Latin. And it's not just Democrats like Al Gore using incomprehensible insider jargon like "Social Security lockbox."

When I interviewed Gary Hart for this book he speculated that American politics was less progressive now because more of the public was "less compassionate" than they had been in the 1960s. If this were so, Republicans would have increased their share of eligible voters. Instead, the big increase has been among nonvoters, and more recently, Nader voters.

If Hart were correct, George W. Bush would not have described himself with the poll-tested phrase "compassionate conservative." The moral lessons of the 1930s and 1960s have been ingrained in the majority of the public. There is a consensus against racism and for fairness. The debate that conservatives have cleverly constructed is not about compassionate goals but about whether or not progressive programs actually work. The failure of progressives has been their inability to explain to average Americans why their particular solutions are better or even how their ideas are different. On the weekend before the 2002 election, the *New York Times* published the results of a poll of Americans in which they asked people about their sense of the vision of each major political party. Forty-two percent felt that the Republicans "had a clear plan for the country," if they gained control of Congress. Only 31 percent felt that the Democrats did.

Organizations on the far left are even less likely to communicate in the cultural language of mass America. "The left likes to talk to itself," says my old friend David Fenton, whose PR firm Fenton Communications has represented a Who's Who of progressive organizations over the last twenty years, from Greenpeace and Amnesty International to the NAACP Voter Fund.

"The do-good sector," says Fenton, "is filled with wonderful people who don't have business backgrounds. So they haven't had to think about mass audiences and mass communications and affecting mass behavior. I think that there's a cultural antipathy toward the mass market, a cultural alienation from television and other forms of mass communication.

"How many groups do you know, who, when you ask them about themselves, will hand you a video?" Fenton adds in frustration. "For young people, videos and computers are the dominant form of communication and it's not like that's a new phenomenon."

Many on the left blame their communication breakdown on the vast sums of money behind right-wing media such as Rupert Murdoch's Fox News or Rush Limbaugh's widely syndicated radio show. But the right wing has always had huge amounts of money and powerful media allies, like Henry Luce and William Randolph Hearst. In ages past, the left wing trumped reactionary media ownership with charismatic and creative populist messages.

Bill Clinton had personal charisma, but he used it more for defense against the right wing than for the advancement of progressive issues or for party building. Otherwise, the image of the Democratic party on the national stage for the last few decades has been as dull as dishwater. Jack Newfield asked me rhetorically, "How did we get these fucking zombies as our candidates? If you put Mondale, Dukakis, and Gore next to each other, they couldn't utter an interesting sentence between the three of them."

A big part of the problem for Democrats is that they keep narrowing the spectrum of political debate, fearful of alienating anyone. In 2000, Democratic pollster Stan Greenberg urged Democrats to run a campaign stressing moral and religious values, because he said that the Monica Lewinsky scandal had "again associated Democrats with sixties-style irresponsibility." This argument ignored poll after poll showing that most Americans were not as offended as Washington pols and pundits by Clinton's sexual misconduct.

This sort of advice helped persuade Al Gore to choose culturally conservative moralist Joe Lieberman as his running mate, and to run a shambles of a campaign that reduced the Democratic margin of young voters (ages eighteen to twenty-four) from 19 percent in 1996 to zero in 2000. It was as if the Democrats had written off the young vote, so important to them in the past. Because of the shibboleth that "young people don't vote," younger voters are rarely included in the focus groups that drive campaigns. This has created a vicious cycle of self-destructive thinking by the Democrats: Young people don't vote, so don't bother with issues and techniques that might attract young votes.

In 2002, the experts hired by Democratic politicians told them to focus on the need for affordable prescription drugs. This is certainly a morally and politically viable issue. But it is not the only such issue. Prescription drugs are particularly important to older voters and less important to younger ones. The mavens didn't see any need for Democrats to have an issue that mattered to young people. The same mavens told Democrats not to criticize President Bush after September 11. This certainly made moral and political sense for the first month or two. But the Washington geniuses extended their noncriticism of Bush for fourteen months, until the 2002 election. There was no fierce scrutiny of the systemic breakdowns that allowed the September 11 attack to happen, nor criticisms, nor call for resignation of any senior or junior staff in any security agency, nor any vocal Democratic calls for greater funding of security of harbors, train stations, and so on. Most notably, there was barely criticism of Bush's radical shift in American foreign policy.

Another vicious cycle was created. Bush gains popularity as a figurehead after a national tragedy. Democrats don't criticize him for fourteen months. Bush, uncriticized and unchallenged, remains popular. Bush uses that popularity to defeat Democrats.

It's not just the loss of younger voters that should concern Democrats, it's the loss of youthful energy and innovation—the loss of teen spirit, embodied in a popular culture that almost inevitably is created by the young and then spreads into the rest of the population. It wasn't just voters from ages eighteen to twenty-four who were turned off by the sanctimonious yet wishy-washy Gore-Lieberman campaign. Millions of Americans who believe in free speech and who want universal health care and gun control and higher public school teacher salaries and tougher environmental regulations were not convinced that the Democrats agreed with them, because the party's message was so cautious and muted and clumsily presented.

Given the intricacies of public policy, it seems trivial to some of my political friends that I spend so much time and energy worrying about "packaging" instead of "substance." But in a democracy, politics without communication is like the proverbial tree falling in the forest without a witness. The unseen and unheard message might as well not exist.

During most of American history, liberals and progressives understood how to communicate with average people through popular culture. The legendary American radical Emma Goldman once said, "I don't want to be a part of any revolution I can't dance to."

Harriet Beecher Stowe's melodramatic popular novel *Uncle Tom's Cabin* was one of the catalysts that galvanized Northern white support for the opposition to slavery. Lincoln, upon meeting the diminutive novelist, is supposed to have said, "So you're the little lady who started the big war."

Upton Sinclair's muckraking novels helped launch reforms of factory conditions. Woody Guthrie's music was intertwined with the growth of American labor unions.

Franklin Delano Roosevelt, the architect of modern liberalism, calmed American fears after the Great Depression and sold his New Deal program through his mastery of a relatively new medium, the radio, with his fireside chats. John Kennedy was elected in large part because of his mastery of another relatively new medium of popular culture, television, and his popularity soared as a result of his casual, youthful energy, his sense of fashion, and his relaxed and witty televised press conferences.

Martin Luther King was a master of media strategy as well as the most compelling orator of the second half of the twentieth century. King knew exactly how Bull Conner's police dogs attacking children in Alabama would play on television and prick the conscience of mainstream America. At the March on Washington in 1963, King's famous "I Have a Dream" speech followed performances by Mahalia Jackson, Bob Dylan, and Joan Baez.

It is impossible to imagine the civil rights movement, the labor movement, the protests against the war in Vietnam, the environmental movement, the women's movement, and the struggle for gay and lesbian rights without the powerful catalysts provided by the energy and inspiration of the young and their popular culture. The Democratic party and the left will either heed that message or find themselves doomed to more decades of cultural victories and political defeats.

"If you remember the sixties," rock icon David Crosby said only half jokingly, "you weren't there." Crosby was in part alluding to drugs, but his remark also captures the intensely personal way that Americans experienced the kaleidoscopic and tumultuous events of the sixties. It is hard to find any facet of contemporary politics and culture that does not in some way reflect that decade. Yet no single version of that rich, contradictory, and sometimes incoherent era can ever feel fully authentic to most of us who were there.

Ironically, many who claim to remember the era clearly and well—and this includes most Washington politicians and pundits—don't remember it at all. What they remember, or pretend to remember, is a cartoon of the sixties.

Chronologically, I am defining the sixties as the decade that began with President John F. Kennedy's assassination on November 22, 1963, and ended in 1974 with the resignation of President Nixon.

Subjectivity aside, there is no doubt that the following changes were achieved or powerfully set in motion during that period:

- The civil rights movement stirred the conscience of millions and spurred legislation that put the force of law behind black demands for equal treatment in schools, employment, housing, and public accommodations, at least cracking open the doors of the American Dream for millions of African Americans.

- The women's movement inspired new legislation and fought for the enforcement of existing laws forbidding discrimination on the basis of gender in the workplace and in other key areas of society.
- Widespread availability of birth control pills and legal access to abortions gave women much more choice about when and if they bore children, making it much less difficult for them to pursue careers and enter professions, and introducing an era of freer sexuality.
- Court decisions virtually eliminated government censorship of the arts, and books and movies that used frank language and explicit images to portray life realistically were embraced by most Americans.
- The war in Vietnam spurred hundreds of thousands of Americans, most of them young, to become active in a massive peace movement that ultimately made Vietnam the nation's most unpopular war and forced politicians to end it.
- Gay activists, long limited in influence to relatively small bohemian subcultures, brought gay men and women openly into mainstream American life.

In the world of popular music, "the sixties" is definitely a positive reference, a time when creativity exploded and profits soared. Rock music, stimulated by the explosion of FM radio and multi-track recording technology, produced the soundtrack to many sixties lives. We still feel the influence deeply: Modern recording artists sample or emulate Jimi Hendrix, Sly Stone, the Beatles, and the Motown sound. Until the death in 1995 of Jerry Garcia, the Grateful Dead was the most popular touring band in America.

Today, classic rock radio stations draw millions of listeners and remain immensely profitable by playing the music of the sixties. In national polls, that quintessential sixties happening, the Woodstock Festival, shows up along with the moon walk as the most significant event of the era.

In the political world, however, the phrase "the sixties" is used almost exclusively as a negative. The prevailing political images of the sixties are of the "hippie" protesters at the 1968 Democratic Convention and the disastrous George McGovern presidential campaign of 1972. Conventional wisdom has it that sixties protesters ruined the 1968 convention on the outside and the 1972 convention on the inside—too many women, blacks, gays, longhairs, and showbiz types turned off moderate voters and gave the federal government to Republicans. The Democratic presidential vote declined from 61 percent in 1964 to 44 percent in 1968 to 40 percent in 1972.

Virtually all of today's Democratic political figures entered politics in the wake of those losses and of the Watergate scandal. Former president Bill Clinton and presidential aspirants Al Gore and Richard Gephardt, among others, were first elected to political office in 1976.

The myth that these Democrats and their media allies thrust upon us today is that their party was able to regain parity only when it embraced traditional politics and rejected the idealistic fervor of the sixties. The myth ignores the potent role in the Democratic presidential victories of 1976, 1992, and 1996 played by the pro-choice movement, the women's movement, the environmental movement, the civil rights movement, and minority voter registration spurred by Jesse Jackson's presidential runs. And it closes its eyes to the staid, conventional, un-sixties personae of Democratic candidates like Walter Mondale and Michael Dukakis. But because the myth reinforces the cultural prejudices and the political authority of powerful Democratic politicians and their allies in the media elite, it prevails.

"The sixties still haunts politics," CNN political editor William

Schneider told me one summer afternoon in 2001. "I used to call it the thirty-year war, but at the rate things are going it could be the forty-year war. Most of politics today, in one way or another, is a reaction to the sixties. Republicans and conservatives explicitly offer themselves as a contrast to the sixties."

That's true. Ronald Reagan made his national reputation as governor of California in great part for cracking down on campus peace demonstrators. Marilyn Quayle reminded the 1996 Republican Convention that "not everybody dropped out and took drugs in the 1960s." George W. Bush cited *The Dream and the Nightmare*, Myron Magnet's excoriation of "the sixties culture," as a key inspiration for his successful 2000 campaign.

But many Democrats also seem to show revulsion for the culture of the sixties. As a result, those millions of voters who supported the civil rights and antiwar movements, and who embraced the profound cultural changes associated with the sixties, are torn between choosing the lesser of two evils, supporting third parties, or joining the vast and growing ranks of those who simply don't vote.

To me, and to many other so-called baby boomers, the sixties stirred the collective American psyche and soul in ways that defy conventional political analysis and that included a spiritual dimension, a search for unconventional and nonmaterialistic kinds of freedom that inspired millions of people—and clearly turned off millions of others.

The movie that best depicts the period is *Easy Rider*, which embraces the mind-expanding potential of psychedelia but harshly condemns mind-numbing hard drugs. Not coincidentally, *Easy Rider* was the first Hollywood film to use rock music successfully as shorthand for emotions. Its soundtrack featured then-current songs like Steppenwolf's "Born to Be Wild" and the Band's "The Weight" as metaphors for the quest for freedom.

*Easy Rider* captures something crucial in an exchange between the long-haired hippie Billy (Dennis Hopper, who also directed) and the short-haired lawyer George (Jack Nicholson):

BILLY: People think we're gonna slit their throat or something. They're scared of us.

GEORGE: Oh no. They not scared of you, they're scared of what you represent to them.

BILLY: All we represent to them, man, is someone who needs a haircut.

GEORGE: What you represent to them is freedom.

BILLY: What the hell's wrong with that? Freedom is what it's all about.

GEORGE: That's what it's all about but talking about it and being it— that's two different things. I mean its real hard to be free when you're bought and sold in the marketplace. 'Course—don't go telling anyone they're not free cause then they're gonna get real busy killing and maiming to prove to you that they are free. They talk and talk and talk about individual freedom but when they see a free individual, that's gonna scare 'em.

Sadly, since at least the mid-1980s, the Democrats and the left seem to be the ones who have been running scared. Meanwhile, the Republicans and the right win most of the races.

Tom Hayden, one of the few authentic sixties protest leaders to have entered electoral politics, says, "The Democrats who got elected to office in the seventies were catering to a market of protest voters, but they themselves were not a part of either the civil rights movement or the antiwar movement in any significant way, with rare exceptions such as [Georgia congressman] John Lewis. You've got a lot of careerists who never inhaled the sixties so, of course, they have no perspective on what it was all about."

In Washington, it is an article of faith that Bill Clinton is a "sixties" guy. CNN's Schneider looked at me like I'd lost touch with reality when I even questioned the notion. "He was the first president who grew up in the sixties, he smoked pot, he avoided military service in Vietnam," the affable pundit reminded me.

To me, it is mind-boggling that Bill Clinton is considered a symbol of the sixties. I can't imagine him sitting around a campfire sharing a joint and talking about freedom with Billy in *Easy Rider*, nor hanging out with the Yippies of Paul Krassner. He was not at Woodstock, nor at any American antiwar rallies. His musical hero is Elvis Presley, not Dylan or Hendrix. He plays the saxophone, not the guitar. His erotic posture resembles that of the macho fifties "rat pack" that entranced his hero John Kennedy, not the sexual liberation of the sixties. Clinton is a brilliant type A careerist, driven to escape the poverty of his upbringing and always focused on conventional achievement, in many ways more influenced by the culture of the fifties than the sixties.

While conservatives thought Clinton was being disingenuous when he said he had smoked marijuana once but "did not inhale," I along with many former hippies feared that Clinton was telling the truth. As *New York Times* columnist Frank Rich says, "Calling Bill Clinton a sixties person is like calling Dick Clark the voice of rock and roll."

The 2000 Democratic ticket was overtly anti-sixties. When Al Gore named cultural reactionary Joseph Lieberman as his running mate in the 2000 election, one of my friends protested to liberal Democratic senator Barbara Boxer. She snapped, "Don't get stuck in the sixties."

Attacks on popular culture and in particular the lyrics of popular music by Lieberman and other Democrats, including Tipper Gore and her censorious coterie (the late Frank Zappa called them "the Mothers of Prevention") were the original inspiration for this book. Tom Hayden explains this ultimately self-destructive syndrome by saying, "It's like a rite of passage to prove that the sixties is totally out of your system. It's like a drug test, as if they're saying 'I'm clean. I have attacked those lyrics.'"

But is the denunciation of the sixties really necessary, or even productive? Immediately after an election in which both parties implicitly ran against "the sixties," Capitol records released a collection of number one singles by the Beatles, a band once excoriated for all the supposed sins of the sixties, from long hair, wild clothing, and loose living to experimentation with mind-altering substances, making drug references in their songs, and even allegedly slandering the name of Jesus Christ.

The Beatles' *One* collection sold 10 million copies and was easily America's best-selling album—some thirty years after the Beatles had broken up, long past the time when most Americans supposedly had become completely turned off by the sixties—at least, according to the tone-deaf mavens of American politics.

Of course, the continuing popularity of the Beatles and other bands of the sixties does not mean that everyone who bought the *One* album also bought John Lennon's egalitarian political ideals or George Harrison's meditative spirituality. But for many millions of baby boomers who were there, and millions of younger people who wish they had been, the sixties was a good time, a time of hope, idealism, exuberant youthful rebellion, and sheer fun. Countless national advertisers try to hook into those good vibrations to sell products to people who want to feel young and hip, co-opting even politically edgy songs like Lennon's "Revolution" (Nike) and, perhaps most astonishingly, Creedence Clearwater Revival's scathingly bitter antiwar anthem, "Fortunate Son" (Wrangler).

It should go without saying that there were plenty of negative aspects of the sixties, including drug abuse and senseless radical violence. The popularity of sixties culture indicates that a large portion of the public views the positive elements and constructive changes of the sixties as having been more significant in their memory. It seems perverse that the Democratic party and the left in general shy away from using the same favorable public feelings about the sixties to promote progressive ideas while advertisers have no qualms about using those collective emotions to sell running shoes.

# CHAPTER 1

# The Sixties

## The Cartoon
## vs. the Realities

IN 1963, WHEN I WAS THIRTEEN and the Beatles' recordings made their first invasion of the United States, I was already in love with the sixties, even if the decade was just beginning to define itself. I had few friends and lived vicariously through the media. My biggest source of inspiration was *Mad* magazine, whose sarcastic and sometimes outrageous parodies of pop culture and politics fed the restless imaginations of teenage baby boomers across America, but I also loved the gleaming, inspirational image of youthful President John F. Kennedy. I bought books con-

*There's this saying, "May you live in interesting times." I always thought—"Hey that's great. It could be my mantra."*

*But then I learned it was a Chinese curse. Well maybe it's a curse to the ruling class. But to people who would rebel against the ruling class, living in interesting times is a blessing not a curse.*

—Paul Krassner,
editor of the *Realist*,
and co-founder of
the Yippies

taining his speeches and taped photos of him above my bed. When President Kennedy was assassinated, my parents, my brother, and I were devastated, and we watched television coverage obsessively for days in a deep emotional connection with the tragedy and with the rest of the country.

My younger brother, Peter, and I grew up in a liberal household. Our father, Victor, was a textile executive and our mother, Mimi, was a poet and protégé of William Carlos Williams. My parents had both worked on the Henry Wallace campaign in 1948 and our household was always filled with talk of current events. When our youngest sister, Rachel, was born in 1963, the civil rights movement was crusading through the American South.

Our family enthusiastically followed the efforts of Martin Luther King's Southern Christian Leadership Conference (SCLC) and other groups fighting racial segregation. I particularly admired the Freedom Rides organized by the Congress of Racial Equality (CORE), with blacks and whites risking their lives by traveling together on buses through the most segregated parts of the South.

I also reveled in the triumphs of a brash young boxer named Cassius Clay. One day, early in 1964, a junior high school friend named David Simon told us he had seen Clay on the subway and had gotten an autograph.

We looked over his shoulder and saw a name we'd never heard before: Muhammad Ali. We thought David had been duped by an imposter and called him "simple Simon" for a few days until we read in the newspaper that Clay had indeed become a Muslim and changed his name. My adulation of Ali only increased as the years went by, particularly in the light of his idealistic opposition to the Vietnam War and his extraordinary comebacks.

In the summer of 1965, between tenth and eleventh grades, I

attended a weeklong Quaker workshop in nonviolence. At that point, the burgeoning black power movement and the rising tide of street demonstrations against the war in Vietnam were creating a schism on the left between people who trusted the traditional political structure to produce change, and people, most of them young, who impatiently pushed for more radical action.

Sitting around a campfire I heard one of the older teenagers play and sing a song with the following opening verse:

I cried when they shot Medgar Evers, the tears ran down my spine
I cried when they shot President Kennedy, he was like a brother of mine
But Malcolm X got what was coming, he got what was coming this time
So love me, love me, love me, I'm a Liberal.

The subsequent verses of "Love Me I'm a Liberal," written by Phil Ochs, continued to draw the distinction between mushy, middle-of-the-road liberals and committed, leftist radicals.

The sadly debased word "liberal" originally referred to the anti-Communist left as epitomized by Eleanor Roosevelt, people committed to equal rights for minorities and women and to government help for those left out of free-market success. But by the middle 1960s, self-described liberals were the leading proponents of the Vietnam War. The distinction between liberals and radicals was crucial, and I thought—and still think—that Ochs nailed it. I discovered that music could mirror my own feelings and magically make me feel more powerful and less alone.

By the late sixties and early seventies, the word "radical" had been equally debased by violent fringe groups like the Weathermen. Remaining uncomfortable with the Vietnam era connotations of "liberal," many on the democratic left switched to the word "progressive," which is what I currently call myself, although it seems like a bit of a mouthful.

I saved my allowance money to buy Ochs's two albums, *I Ain't Marching Anymore*, and *All the News That's Fit to Sing*.

Later in the summer of 1965 I volunteered in the ultimately unsuccessful mayoral campaign of New York congressman William Fitts Ryan, a passionate left-wing Democrat who outspokenly opposed the Vietnam War, rare at that point for an elected official. For me, a high point of the campaign was the afternoon I sat in a sound truck next to James Farmer, the leader of CORE, whose booming bass voice had inspired millions in his television appearances talking about the Freedom Rides. The memory of sitting next to and talking to such a great man would get me through many dark, angst-ridden periods of my teenage life, particularly because Farmer had been so accessible and friendly. At his suggestion, he and I actually took turns on the microphone exhorting listeners to vote for Ryan.

Later that same year I went to Washington for a peace march and was transported when SDS leader Carl Oglesby spoke of how Lyndon Johnson's cold warriors "broke my liberal heart." I became an ardent fan of the counterculture, although at that point mostly through the media. I listened fervently to New York's free-form listener-supported radio station, WBAI-FM, and loved the trenchant wit of Abbie Hoffman and Paul Krassner on the all-night "Radio Unnamable," hosted by Bob Fass. I devoured books by James Baldwin, Rachel Carson, Michael Harrington, and Marshall McLuhan, and I grabbed copies of Krassner's fearlessly radical satirical journal the *Realist* and any underground newspaper I could get my hands on.

I didn't agree with everything I read or heard. Some of the more radical and apocalyptic leftist rhetoric, even then, grated on my sense of proportion and view of reality. I loved the idea of trying to break through the materialistic, narrow-minded, Cold War status quo. But I thought John Lennon was right on the mark when he sang to radicals in his song "Revolution": "If you're talking about destruction, don't you know that you can count me out."

Music had always provided an emotional connection to the world in my house. My parents loved folk music and my childhood years were filled with Pete Seeger, Odetta, and Burl Ives. Then came the folk revival of the early 1960s, with musicians like Peter, Paul, and Mary, Judy Collins, and Joan Baez setting a standard of political credibility that would influence musicians for generations to come, and my own work as well.

In my earlier teen years, I also developed a love for classical music, but Beethoven and Bach and all the rest were put on hold when I started eleventh grade and passionately embraced rock and roll.

More than thirty years later, I can vividly remember my record collection from that time. The first Beatles album I bought was *Rubber Soul*. The first Stones album was *The Rolling Stones Now*. I cherished the Lovin' Spoonful, Muddy Waters, Mississippi John Hurt, Howlin' Wolf, Junior Wells, Tim Hardin, Simon and Garfunkel, the Holy Modal Rounders, Arlo Guthrie, Dave Van Ronk, the Fugs, Tom Rush, Judy Collins, Joan Baez, the Young Rascals, Country Joe and the Fish, Blue Cheer, the Velvet Underground, Tom Paxton, Big Brother and the Holding Company, Donovan, Cream, Steppenwolf, Jefferson Airplane, everything by the Beatles, everything by the Rolling Stones, everything by Jimi Hendrix, everything by Phil Ochs, and, most especially, everything by Bob Dylan.

I still recall the afternoon during eleventh grade when an older kid named Paul Mintz pulled me aside in a school corridor to play Dylan's "Ballad of a Thin Man" on his portable record player. I was transported when I heard Dylan sing the chorus line, "Because something is happening here, but you don't know what it is, do you Mr. Jones?" Mintz and I weren't friends, he was just so excited about the song he had to play it for somebody that very instant. Like a lot of young Americans, I was to spend a significant amount of energy over the next decade trying to ensure that I was nothing like the clueless Mr. Jones.

Over the next several years, a close and deep awareness of these rock albums became a cultural code for many baby boomers. A teenager could go to someone else's house and immediately feel a sense of kinship from looking at the record collection piled on the floor. I always thought it was an auspicious sign if there were blues albums alongside the rock and roll. And I could bond immediately with a stranger who quoted key Dylan lyrics intelligently.

The carefully detailed political position papers that radical groups labored over so strenuously paled in comparison to the visceral power of songs that made manifest shared political beliefs, songs like Dylan's "Only a Pawn in Their Game," about the murder of civil rights leader Medgar Evers, and the Buffalo Springfield's "For What It's Worth," which described the ominous police presence at a protest march in Hollywood.

Rhythm and blues, gospel, and other kinds of black music had been intertwined with the civil rights movement since the late fifties. No one personifies the musical artist as activist more than Harry Belafonte, who in the fifties had been one of the biggest pop stars in the world as the result of such hits as "Jamaica Farewell" and that staple of sports arenas "The Banana Boat Song (Day O)." Belafonte was also one of Martin Luther King Jr.'s closest advisors.

Belafonte recalls that on the night of Dr. King's historic march from Selma to Montgomery he asked for a concentration of artists in Selma to "lift the spirit of the troops." Mike Nichols, Elaine May, Billy Eckstine, Leonard Bernstein, and Sammy Davis Jr., among others, joined Belafonte for the event, which took place on the grounds of St. Jude's Catholic School, "the only place in Selma we could rely on to be safe." Belafonte told me, "Because the ground was rain soaked we made a stage out of eighty empty coffins. Artists stood and sang and Dr. King gave a speech about the importance of culture—people were tired and wet as they waited for the push into Montgomery the next morning."

Aretha Franklin and others worked with Belafonte to support Dr. King all over the country. At the March on Washington it was Belafonte who organized the entertainment that helped draw the crowd for King's "I Have a Dream Speech."

Because of the international contacts Belafonte had made in his travels as a performer he was able to expand Dr. King's network at a crucial time when money was needed to keep the organization going and the first wave of American donors was tapped out as the result of unrefunded bail money. Many of Dr. King's advisors counseled against taking the civil rights struggle out of the country, including King's influential father, Martin Luther King Sr. "Daddy King was upset," Belafonte recalls. "The argument was that it was a mistake to put our dirty laundry out in public." Dr. King ultimately took Belafonte's advice and authorized the singer to stage an event at the American Church in Paris. When the U.S. State Department pressured the church to withdraw sponsorship, Belafonte flew to Europe and organized a private event with help from European actors Peter O'Toole, Simone Signoret, Yves Montand, and Melina Mercouri, as well as leaders of the French labor movement. The result was a sold-out event at the Palais Du Sports, the city's biggest arena. Shortly thereafter he organized a similar event in Sweden with the king of Sweden as the event's chair. "That was before he got the Nobel Prize," says Belafonte. "It helped set him up for the prize. Artists did that."

These events not only raised money and raised the spirits of the "troops," they also raised the visibility of the civil rights movement so that the moral message could be seen and heard by millions of whites who hadn't been paying attention. "We struggled to get attention in the civil rights movement," I was told by the Reverend Jesse Jackson. "When Harry brought down Tony Bennett and Marlon Brando and other entertainers, that's [when] the coverage of demonstrations started getting on the news."

At the same time, less overtly political artists such as Ray Charles appealed to Middle America and humanized the black experience to a depth previously unknown by many white Americans.

"People say that art is a reflection of reality, but the R&B of the late 1950s and early 1960s was really pushing society," Georgia congressman and civil rights hero John Lewis told NPR. "It was like a headlight, not a taillight, with the rest of society trying to catch up."

Black music crossed over to the young white audience, with the greatest impetus coming from Detroit's black-owned Motown Records. Under the leadership of Berry Gordy, Motown launched the careers of the Supremes, Smokey Robinson and the Miracles, and the Temptations, who turned out Top 40 hits and made repeated appearances on national TV shows such as *American Bandstand* and *The Ed Sullivan Show*. Berry Gordy was criticized by some political leaders for not involving his artists more overtly in civil rights marches. However, Motown released recordings of Martin Luther King's speeches and was the label that effectively integrated American musical culture.

Later in the sixties, many R&B artists became more politically outspoken, including Curtis Mayfield ("People Get Ready") and, most notably, Marvin Gaye, who wrote the compelling antiwar song "What's Goin' On" in honor of his brother's return from Vietnam.

Experimentation with psychedelic drugs was woven into the fabric of dozens of songs, like the Jefferson Airplane's "White

Rabbit" and Jimi Hendrix's "Purple Haze." Later, George Harrison's discovery of meditation as a more profound alternative to drugs inspired me and millions of other rock fans. It is hard to imagine the subsequent birth of the New Age movement without the influence of rock musicians such as Harrison, John McLaughlin, and Carlos Santana.

Foreshadowing schisms that would haunt the political left for decades to come, many lefty folk music fans felt betrayed by Bob Dylan's 1965 switch from acoustic folk to electric rock music and his radical change from linear political anthems like "The Times They Are a-Changin'" to impressionistic and surreal personal songs such as "Like a Rolling Stone." I was young enough that I discovered and embraced his first half dozen albums, folk and rock, political and personal, all at the same time. To me, the purists who didn't like the electric Dylan were left-wing versions of Mr. Jones.

During 1965–67, while I was in eleventh and twelfth grades, I was much more of a spectator than a participant in the sixties culture, but the would-be hippies I hung out with at the progressive Fieldston School in New York were an interesting and intense bunch. Among my best friends were Peter Kinoy and his sister, Joanne, who were the children of noted civil rights lawyer Arthur Kinoy—his clients included Martin Luther King Jr. and Adam Clayton Powell. My best friend, Joel Goodman, was the nephew of counterculture icon Paul Goodman, whose book *Growing Up Absurd* was ubiquitous on college campuses. Joel and his older sister, Rachel, had recruited me to join them in protesting air-raid drills in 1962. Although we got into trouble, we noticed that the school stopped having the drills the following year.

Another friend was Gil Heron, later to become famous as the brilliant political songwriter and jazz/R&B/poetry artist Gil Scott-Heron. Even in high school, Gil had an uncanny ability to express himself and would come into class with intricate autobiographical short stories that dwarfed anything the rest of us could write, and he played the piano seemingly effortlessly while the rest of us were agonizing over our lessons. Another high school friend Susan Solomon married the drummer of Country Joe and the Fish, "Chicken" Hirsh. (Susan later married journalist Paul Goldberger.)

Much of the controversy about rap and rock music over the years has focused on the way teenagers process song lyrics. I certainly knew as a teenager that songs could carry powerful messages, but I can say definitively that my friends and I never took lyrics literally. The Rolling Stones' great song "Satisfaction," for example, would lead you to believe that Mick Jagger was not getting laid. Yet my friends and I assumed quite the opposite. We felt he was expressing a feeling from his past and telling his male fans that it was okay to be lonely and frustrated when you're young. If a rock god like Mick could have once felt that way, we could deal with our (hopefully) temporary lack of satisfaction as well.

More to the point, we understood lyrics impressionistically and metaphorically. I didn't know any daughters of royalty like the character in "Play with Fire," and I certainly had no idea what the culture of "Knightsbridge" was. But I loved being able to sing along with the chorus "Don't play with me cause you're playing with fire." His projection of strength compensated for my feeling of weakness.

On the other hand, I always was uncomfortable with Jagger's anti-female lyrics (we didn't know the word "misogynistic" in those days) in songs such as "Stupid Girl" and "Under My Thumb." I just tuned them out or skipped over them so I could focus on the songs I loved. I think teenagers, then and now, can appreciate the work of an artist without buying the whole package.

Deeply felt songs also give young people vivid insights into lives far different from theirs. I loved Woody Guthrie's song "Hard

Travelin'" and Big Bill Broonzy's blues classic "If You're Black Get Back." As a comfortably middle-class white kid, I had nothing in common with the poverty and prejudice reflected in those songs, but through the alchemy of art, an emotional connection was made. I assume that today's middle-class kids, white and black, connect with the emotions of ghetto-inspired hip-hop in the same personal way.

Listeners interpret songs very subjectively. In the film *In the Name of the Father*, the Irish protagonist (played by Daniel Day-Lewis) plays Bob Dylan's "Like a Rolling Stone" on the jukebox. As with many of Dylan's lyrics, the literal meaning of the words is a torrent of venom, in this case clearly aimed at a woman, a former lover. Yet the Lewis character's joy in the song is utterly unconnected to feelings about women—or to anger. The chorus, "How does it feel!!?" drives him to pump his arms in exhilaration. Somehow the fact that Bob Dylan can scream above his pain gives us the courage to feel we can overcome our own and rejoice in that recognition.

Even at this most political of times, explicit "message" songs like those of Phil Ochs or the early Bob Dylan were the exception. Poetic and musical expressions of angst were more common. A friend of mine interviewed that most politically earnest of sixties artists, Joan Baez, for his school newspaper, and she talked about how much she loved The Rolling Stones' angry impressionistic rant "19th Nervous Breakdown."

We all felt that the rock artists we followed were different from other people exposed in the mass media. Rockers, we imagined, were a lot like us. In San Francisco, local hippies freely mingled with the Grateful Dead and the Jefferson Airplane. My own brush with hippie immortality came one Saturday afternoon in high school. A few friends and I were sitting in sunny Central Park feeling very "summer of love" and playing a silly kissing game when Joan Baez herself walked over with a boyfriend and hung out with us.

Her famous long brown hair had recently been cut to shoulder length, but that did nothing to diminish her stunning beauty, and fame had not spoiled her unpretentious nonchalance. She was not on a star trip, and it was strictly first names only. We were all simply enjoying a spring day together in the new world of the sixties.

I got a chaste kiss on the cheek from the queen of folk music before she sauntered away. My friends and I were all way too cool to make much of a big deal about it, but we shared quick delighted glances.

My academic career was a huge disappointment to me and my parents. I dropped out of the University of California in Berkeley after a single week in the fall of 1967. In the Bay Area, where I continued to live for a while after I dropped out, I befriended a group of Vietnam vets who had become druggies in Vietnam and had great connections for every sort of illegal substance. (One of the lies implicit in the cartoon version of the sixties is that hippies hated the guys who fought in Vietnam, which couldn't have been further from the truth. It was the politicians we blamed.) I had started smoking pot in my junior year of high school, begun taking LSD in earnest in my senior year, and in Berkeley and Oakland I did just about every other drug that existed at the time.

The first time I went to Winterland was also the first time I saw Janis Joplin perform, with her band Big Brother and the Holding Company. As I watched Joplin's passionate performance, a young woman in a diaphanous white dress with flowers in her long blonde hair came walking through the audience and handed me a white tablet from a stash of free samples. It was "White Lightning" LSD, manufactured by the notorious Bay Area chemist Owsley, who had borrowed a marketing technique from the mainstream.

For a brief period, outward symbols such as long hair on males, the lack of brassieres on women, the peace sign and symbol, and energizing injections of hippie slang into meaningful conversation created a genuine sense of community. And then, it seemed, it was over almost before it had begun.

Quickly, the fashions and language became absorbed by the mainstream media, and charlatans, from cult con artists getting rich off converts to the murderer Charles Manson, exploited the very sense of trust that the outward symbols conveyed. Various forces, including the invasion of hard drugs and the inevitable process of aging, obliterated much of the complexity, vision, and sense of community that had inspired millions of young people.

The outward trappings of hippiedom quickly became just part of the cartoon, a caricature of pot-smoking airheads wearing bell-bottom trousers and love beads and using words like "man" and "dig" in place of coherent sentences. As the Vietnam era grew uglier in the late 1960s, particularly in the wake of the King and Robert Kennedy assassinations, the mainstream media focused on the tiny coterie of radicals who engaged in violence.

Films and novels about the period have generally failed to capture the communal spirit and the lively diversity that endures in the memories of many of us who were there. One of the few things that survived with its soul intact is the period's music.

To walk around the Bay Area in 1967–68 was to hear the same songs broadcast on the "underground" (but commercial) radio station KMPX-FM pouring out of every store and apartment. Rock music was a soundtrack for the lives of millions of people across America, and it proved a heartier cultural artifact than fashion, slang, or rhetoric. The power of the music has endured, especially the more obscure album cuts that haven't been overused as source music in movies or for TV commercials.

Many of us saw a glimmer of hope for a better world, and hearing the music brings back that feeling, not just for baby boomers but for younger people eager to recapture something they have read and heard about. I know I am not the only one who plays old records behind closed doors to get myself re-energized for the battles of day-to-day life.

For young people in the sixties, the feeling of connectedness and freedom was real and unforgettable, but for me and many others, a reliance on drugs began to sour the spirit of the times. One afternoon in the early spring of 1967, I went to the San Francisco airport to fly home and visit my parents. I was barefoot, as I often was in those days, and I was informed by the authorities that I could not board a plane without shoes. With the heady confidence of the era I looked around the airport and my eyes fell upon a young man with longish light brown hair who had that "sixties" look.

It turned out that he had just landed and was on his way home. After hearing my dilemma, he promptly offered me his shoes and gave me his address so I could mail them back. My exhilaration at having been protected by the hippie universe soon turned to mortification when I lost his address. I suspect that millions of such spaced-out incidents shortened the communal spirit of the sixties, and I still regret my inadvertent betrayal.

Nine months after having moved to Northern California, and six weeks before my eighteenth birthday, I was arrested in Berkeley on assorted possession charges after having asked policemen for directions while I was virtually nodding out on Seconals.

Back in New York, after the expensive lawyer my parents hired got me released into their custody, I attended group therapy sessions that convinced me that my attraction to drugs was self-destructive. Still inspired by rock and roll, I listened carefully to

George Harrison's songs and began a long devotion to meditation and Eastern spirituality as an alternative to drugs.

Despite my new straightness, I had no interest in going back to college, which still felt alien to the rhythms beating in my head. I had an extremely high number in the selective service lottery, which meant I would never be drafted. In the fall of 1968, through an ad in the *New York Times*, I got a clerical job at *Billboard*, the music business trade magazine. It turned out that my job was in what was called the "chart department." Prior to my first day on the job I had no idea that there were "charts" showing which records had sold the best the previous week.

The first week that I called stores for information, one of the singles on the checklist was "Piece of My Heart" by Janis Joplin and Big Brother. I inserted several extra checkmarks next to the song. I liked to tell myself that the single went Top Ten because of my secret help.

I was transported the first time I saw an actual issue of *Billboard*, filled with color advertisements for albums, some by my favorite rock bands and some by country and western, R&B, or pop artists I'd never heard of. It hadn't previously occurred to me that rock and roll was part of a business. The idea that the business was big enough to justify putting out a thick color magazine blew my mind. (There were actually three weekly music trades at that time, the others being *Cashbox* and *Record World*.)

I quickly learned the names of all of the record companies and discovered that getting radio stations to play the records was the most important route to a hit. This, too, was news. My main sources for learning about new rock musicians had been my friends and the music section of the *Village Voice* and *Rolling Stone*.

Radio stations around the country used the *Billboard* charts to choose which records to play, and many stores stocked records based on them. So the charts had a huge effect on sales. One after-noon, James Brown himself called to check the chart position on "Say It Loud, I'm Black and I'm Proud." It was number twenty with a bullet (moving up) on the pop chart that week.

What Brown really wanted to know was how well his song was doing with white "pop" audiences. It was already number one on the R&B charts.

Although black musicians were the prime force behind the cre-ation of rock and roll, and Motown had made huge strides in merg-ing pop and R&B, there were still a lot of racial barriers in the music business. There would not be a black president of a pop label until the 1980s. A few black musicians such as Jimi Hendrix and Sly Stone had substantial white audiences, but rock would remain dominated by white musicians until the late nineties, when rap conquered the predominantly white-male rock audience.

Every week at *Billboard*, the staff would listen to all of the new singles that were submitted for review and rate their hit potential. One of my assignments each week was to call the influential tip sheet editor Bill Gavin with the list of our predictions. Gavin was shocked when I told him we had picked "Give Peace a Chance" by the Plastic Ono Band as a future Top 20 hit.

"You're kidding," he said. "There are hardly any instruments on it, no one knows the name Plastic Ono Band, and as far as we can make out there is some bad language. Radio stations aren't going to play it."

Biting my lip and speaking as tactfully as I could, I explained that as important as radio was, the underground and rock press were also very influential. Beatles fans knew that it was a John Lennon record. His fans would accept the unorthodox production and the song was clearly about ending the war in Vietnam, a com-pelling topic to many young record buyers.

Gavin was correct that the powerful Top 40 radio stations, for the most part, didn't play "Give Peace a Chance." And I was right that it didn't matter. The single indeed went to the *Billboard* Top 20 and became one of Lennon's most famous records. And by then, in cities across America, innovative stations like WBCN in Boston were hiring young, hip DJs and letting them choose longer and less-publicized songs from albums by artists like Dylan and the Beatles. Within a few years, these album-oriented rock stations came to rival Top 40 stations for market dominance.

One of the fascinating things about working on the charts was that it seemed as if all of America were present. This was 1968, a year in which the country was famously divided on political and cultural issues. Yet through the prism of the record business, one could see pro-military country records, antiwar rock records, Christian music, R&B, classical, and jazz all coexisting. For the music business, America was one big record store.

I soon discovered that there was a job at record companies called "promo man" (they were all men in 1968). These guys, made semifamous in 1965 when the Rolling Stones sang snidely about an "Under-Assistant West Coast Promo Man," didn't look anything like hippies. The older ones wore expensive suits and carried themselves like gangsters, and the younger ones had self-consciously styled longish hair and weird, pseudo-hip clothes that seemed to exist solely for their profession.

Shortly before Christmas 1968, Lew Selener, a promo man from Capitol Records, paid our department a visit. Lew, probably in his early thirties at the time, seemed far too old to me to "get" rock and roll, but there he was, sporting an early version of the blow-dried haircut, wearing an all-white jumpsuit, and handing me a free copy of the just-released and much-coveted Beatles *White Album.* I think my jaw literally dropped. A free Beatles album, exactly on the release date! Clearly being in the music business wasn't a normal job. Thirty-three years later I still marvel at my good luck in stumbling into it.

Despite my joy at getting free records, I was too much of a hippie to fit into the promo world. I discovered that another section of the *Billboard* office housed music journalists, people who not only got free records and free tickets to concerts but actually got paid to review them. There was one writer on staff, Ed Ochs, who liked rock music and was reputed to have actually met the members of Steppenwolf.

The older editors avoided rock concerts in favor of nightclub performances, where they could get free drinks and dinner, and they assigned me to cover the rock shows that Ochs couldn't get to, including some at the Fillmore East auditorium and at rock clubs such as Unganos and Steve Paul's The Scene. One evening, while walking down the stairs at a club called Salvation, I actually passed Jimi Hendrix, who was walking up the same staircase. "Hi," I mumbled. "Hi," he replied.

I felt as if I had stepped through the looking glass.

There have been countless arguments—and even books written—about when innocence was lost in rock and roll. I can tell you for certain that by the time I started at *Billboard* in 1968, rock music was a business.

The communal group the Diggers had staged "The Death of Hippie" in San Francisco in 1967 to blame the mass media for destroying the intimacy of experimental culture in Haight Ashbury. Some rock purists went back a year and pointed a finger at the Monterey Pop Festival, when Columbia Records president Clive Davis signed Janis Joplin, and Mo Ostin of Warner Bros. signed Jimi Hendrix. Others blamed Dylan and Joplin's manager, Albert Grossman, for introducing high-pressure, big-bucks bargaining into sixties rock, or Columbia Records for running much ridiculed print ads headlined "The Man Can't Bust Our Music." Some even went back to the fifties and blamed Elvis's manager, the huckster Col. Tom Parker.

My own theory is that there was never pure innocence in rock and roll. It was always about money and only sometimes about art. John Lennon used to tell the early, poverty-stricken Beatles they were going to the "toppermost of the poppermost." Jimi Hendrix himself had the idea of playing guitar with his teeth to get attention. A volatile brew of art, spirituality, and commerce is built into the genetic code of pop music and always has been, and the contradictions exist not only in the guts of the business but in the hearts of the audience and the souls of the artists as well.

Ten months after my first day at *Billboard*, I went to the 1969 Woodstock Festival in a limo commandeered by press agent Jane Friedman. No one else on the magazine's staff had any interest in going. Barely nineteen, I had a hotel room nearby and a backstage pass to the climax of sixties rock. I wrote a long, starry-eyed review of Woodstock, and *Billboard* ran it on the front page. Although I was drug-free and gainfully employed, I was still deeply inspired by the communal spirit of the audience. Even though I was able to go backstage and gawk at Joe Cocker and Joan Baez, I was much more interested in roaming through the vast, unruly audience, exchanging smiles and cosmic one-liners with my fellow hippies.

Although a lot of the counterculture had been developed as a result of shared enemies—parents, police, the government, people who just didn't like long hair—the spirit at Woodstock had almost nothing to do with any sense of antagonism toward the straight world. The townspeople, cops, and other "straights" were, in fact, quite pleasant and considerate to the invading horde of freaks, and the hippies, for the most part, were genuinely full of love and good feeling for the world outside, as well as for each other. We felt a sense of community in our musical tastes, clothes, and culture, but not to the exclusion of the rest of the world. The feeling is captured beautifully in Michael Wadleigh's feature film, *Woodstock*.

The spirit of mutual love and freedom emanating from upstate New York via TV news was just the sort of evidence of a cultural upheaval that terrified the Nixon administration and other parts of the political establishment, who fought back bitterly in that period.

Vice President Spiro T. Agnew became the first major national political figure of the period to attack rock and roll, castigating the Beatles for the allegedly pro-drug content of the lyrics to songs such as "Lucy In the Sky With Diamonds" and "With a Little Help from My Friends." The FBI, which had targeted all anti-war and civil rights groups under its now notorious COINTELPRO program, relentlessly investigated John Lennon, and the government attempted to deport him.

Paul Krassner reflects, "People who were rebelling were rebelling not just politically but spiritually and economically. They shared automobiles. They used a lot of candles instead of electricity. They didn't have insurance policies. They were becoming more tribal. They made their own clothing. They didn't get addicted to cosmetics. They got interested in Eastern religions of liberation rather than Western religions of control. They were a threat and I still would love to see whatever files there are. How the think tanks extrapolated the hippie lifestyle."

But not all of the destructive forces that attacked the counterculture came from establishment opposition. A few months after Woodstock, an ill-conceived deal with the Hells Angels to provide security for a rock festival in Altamont, California, headlined by the Rolling Stones, led to the stabbing death of a fan. By then, illegal drug use had degenerated from the daring experimentation of intellectuals such as Timothy Leary and Ken Kesey into wide-spread abuse of amphetamines, barbiturates, heroin, and that old standby, alcohol. Jimi Hendrix, Janis Joplin, and Jim Morrison all would soon kill themselves with drugs, all at the age of twenty-seven. Millions of less famous young people developed drug and alcohol problems.

The Black Panthers, whose organization began with legitimate complaints about police attitudes toward blacks in Oakland, California, and several of whose members were killed by police in various cities under suspicious circumstances, soon degenerated into a drug-dealing thuggish culture. And the Weathermen, a radical offshoot of the Students for a Democratic Society, were always a fringe group with a tiny following, but their violent actions darkened the image of the predominantly nonviolent antiwar movement.

"Their very name gave them away," Paul Krassner recalls, still amazed after all these years by the obtuseness of their choice. "They were trying to co-opt rock fans so they named themselves after a Dylan lyric—but they obviously never listened to the song. They took lyrics that said you don't need leaders and used it to declare *themselves* the leaders." (Dylan's "Subterranean Homesick Blues," which contains the line "You don't need a weatherman to know which way the wind blows," later admonishes, "Don't follow leaders.")

Not long after returning from Woodstock, I switched to a competing trade magazine, *Record World*, where I wrote a weekly column. I met the rock critics of the time at an endless series of press parties and concerts. One of my first columns praised a concert by the MC-5, a raucous, politically left-wing Detroit band that I had seen in Queens. I got a phone call from Danny Fields, who had signed the band to a recording contract at Elektra and then had taken them with him to Atlantic Records. He had coined the phrase "company freak" to describe his role at Elektra as the liaison between the traditional executives and artists like the Doors and Judy Collins. Danny was later to discover and manage the Ramones.

Danny introduced me to Gloria Stavers, editor of *16 Magazine*, who had been one of Lenny Bruce's lovers and close friends with Jim Morrison. I also met Australian journalist Lillian Roxon, who had just written the *Rock Encyclopedia*, and club owner Steve Paul. These four elders—Danny, Gloria, Lillian, and Steve—became my mentors, as they did for other young New York rock writers, including Dave Marsh, Lisa Robinson, Nick Tosches, Richard Meltzer, Lenny Kaye, and Lester Bangs.

Because of Danny's blessing, I was welcomed in the back room of Max's Kansas City, a restaurant with a music stage upstairs. Max's was run by the curmudgeonly Mickey Ruskin and was originally a hangout for New York artists, many of whom paid their bar bills with paintings. Max's proximity to Andy Warhol's studio, the Factory, helped make it the nighttime home for an assortment of drag queens, poets, actors, and uptown celebrities looking for an edge.

The music people who were part of Max's scene were mostly cynical, bitter, and possessed of an acute and ironic sense of the zeitgeist. Alice Cooper, David Bowie, Janis Joplin, Leonard Cohen, and many others spent hours trading one-liners with the back-room crowd. Max's was my entry point into the New York seventies rock scene, and it was there that I developed friendships with Patti Smith, members of the New York Dolls, and others.

The rock writer from our clique besides myself who would enter the high-octane commercial music business was Boston's Jon Landau. At the time, he was the most respected *Rolling Stone* writer and soon became editor of its highly influential record-review section. He later became the personal manager for Bruce Springsteen and Shania Twain, among others.

I wrote sporadically for *Rolling Stone*, the *Village Voice*, and *Craw-*

*daddy*. During those years, I was one of about fifty New York writers who would go to editors and publishers and explain that we "understood" the new rock music because we had long hair and were the right age. Although I was a relatively low-level rock writer, I was nonetheless invited to significant events, like Bill Graham's legendary Thanksgiving dinners at the Fillmore East, where the guests sat at long tables on the Fillmore stage next to Graham favorites like members of the Jefferson Airplane.

I was still emotionally connected to aspects of the political agenda of the counterculture. In May 1970 I joined yet another antiwar march on Washington with Danny Fields. Danny knew writer Stu Werbin, one of the organizers of the event, so we were welcomed into the fenced-off backstage area. This was before the era of slickly produced plastic laminated backstage passes. If you got backstage, you stayed there.

I was astonished to see my hero Phil Ochs, who had walked out into the crowd, trying to convince one of the young antiwar-movement security guards to let him back into the stage area. I rushed over and yelled at the guard that Ochs was part of the program. The guard acquiesced immediately, since I was on the right side of the fence and had conviction in my voice. Ochs waved appreciatively.

It was to be my only face-to-face encounter with my hero.

In retrospect, I realize that the confrontation between Ochs— with his populist instincts and his expansive nature—and the insecure security guard, binding himself with ill-defined rules of turf and an arbitrary pecking order, was an ominous symbol of a sad but stubborn fact: Political activists don't always respect or understand artists, even politically committed artists. And the resulting failure to communicate has haunted progressive American politics since the sixties.

# CHAPTER 2

# The Sixties II

## Culture vs. Politics

L ONG AFTER BOB DYLAN went electric and the openly political songs of Phil Ochs and Tom Paxton were superseded by psychedelic rock, politically charged music could still ride high on the rock charts. In November 1969, the Jefferson Airplane released their most fiercely political album, *Volunteers*. ("Up against the wall, motherfucker," they screamed at reactionaries in the song "Volunteers of America.")

The "supergroup" Crosby, Stills, Nash, and Young created a powerful and hugely successful anthem and eulogy with "Ohio," released within weeks of the killing of student antiwar protesters at Kent State Uni-

*During the past few years, I have straddled the line between "the movement," and "the community," between "the left," and "the hip," between the world of "the street," and the world of "the media." I have doubts I can go on balancing these forces in my head much longer.*

Abbie Hoffman
in *Woodstock Nation*,
1970

versity in 1970. The governor of Ohio vainly tried to ban airplay of the song in his state, claiming more violence would result from lyrics such as the dirge-like refrain, "Four dead in Ohio."

Graham Nash had a solo hit in 1971 with "Chicago," about the Chicago Eight conspiracy trial of Abbie Hoffman, Jerry Rubin, and other leaders of protests at the 1968 Democratic Convention. ("Is your brother bound and gagged?" Nash angrily asked, referring to the judge's actual treatment of defiant defendant Bobby Seale of the Black Panthers.)

Still, gulfs between left-of-center politics and the increasingly popular alternative culture kept yawning open. The political left had mixed feelings about the counterculture from the beginning, and those doubts and tensions led to the cultural/political fragmentation that drives me crazy today.

The person who most successfully walked the tightrope between the doctrinaire political left and the chaotic, exploding baby boomer culture was Abbie Hoffman, who had a brilliant sense of how to use the mass media. But even Abbie occasionally stumbled, most famously at the Woodstock Festival. Tripping on acid, he made the mistake of grabbing the microphone during a set by the defiantly anti-establishment British rock band the Who.

Hoffman began lecturing the crowd about the imprisonment of John Sinclair, and guitarist Pete Townshend literally kicked him off the stage. Years later, in a *Rolling Stone* interview, Townshend said that he felt in retrospect that Hoffman had been right to try to focus the crowd on a political agenda, but another opportunity for détente had been lost.

The conflict goes back practically to the beginnings of the sixties counterculture. An early battle came in the San Francisco Bay Area in the fall of 1966, while I was still in high school back in New York reading the *Realist* and listening to Bob Dylan. Thirty-six years later

I discussed what happened with three of my elders: Allen Ginsberg, Paul Krassner, and Berkeley leftist Michael Lerner.

Ginsberg, Timothy Leary, the Diggers, and others planned a "be-in" in Golden Gate Park to celebrate the burgeoning counterculture. The phrase "be-in" echoed "sit-in" and "teach-in," confrontational tactics used by civil rights and antiwar groups. But the full name of the event—"Gathering of the Tribes for a Human Be-In"—hardly suggested a confrontation.

Assuming that any large coming-together of longhairs had a political subtext, a group of Berkeley political radicals, including Lerner, his roommate Jerry Rubin, and a friend named Stew Albert, set up a meeting with the San Francisco hippies. Also at the meeting were members of the Jefferson Airplane and Country Joe and the Fish.

One of Lerner's political cohorts asked the hippies, "What are the demands going to be?" The response was laughter. "Demands" were made at demonstrations—this was going to be a be-in, a gathering. Michael Lerner still burned with frustration as he recalled what he sees to this day as a missed opportunity:

"Jerry Rubin, Stew Albert, and I were hoping to build a mutually respectful alliance between the counterculture and the political antiwar movement...with the hopes of creating a be-in like our teach-ins, but including not only politics but also the spirit of the counterculture. We were perfectly prepared to have music be the major part of the day but we also wanted to have political content articulated and taught. The musicians and their friends acted as though we were crazy to want that. They said, 'Hey man, this is a gathering of the tribes.' And we said, 'Well, our tribe likes to communicate not only with music but also with words.' But...the countercultural people could not imagine any sharing of the space. It was to be music and nothing else."

In fact, both the Jefferson Airplane and Country Joe were intensely political in other contexts. I don't think the rock and hippie culture ever wanted to control political debate. They simply insisted on not being dictated to by lefty politicians at what were essentially musical and cultural events. They were not going to toe a party line, or have the poetic spirit of cultural events transformed into political rallies.

The Human Be-In drew 20,000 people, a huge number for a counterculture festival at the time, and featured music by the Airplane, the Grateful Dead, and the Quicksilver Messenger Service, and poetry from Allen Ginsberg, Gary Snyder, and Lenore Kandel. Krassner recalls, "Ed Sanders and his sense of theater greatly propelled such events."

Jerry Rubin was one of the few political radicals who spoke. In *A Long Strange Trip*, a history of the Grateful Dead, Dennis McNally says that Jerry Garcia was completely turned off by the anger in Rubin's speech. From that point on, the Dead were studiously apolitical in their songs, although they would perform at many benefit concerts for progressive causes over the years.

One year later, Hoffman, Rubin, Krassner, and a few others formed the so-called Youth International Party—the Yippies. The immediate goal was to inject some creative counterculture fervor and a pointed sense of the absurd into the deadly serious protests planned by left-wing political groups for the 1968 Democratic National Convention in Chicago. Jerry Rubin, formerly a conventional left-wing politician who had actually run for mayor of Berkeley, had become a self-appointed spokesman for the very hippie culture he had once thought lacked seriousness.

In the aftermath of the madness of the 1968 convention, both inside the hall and outside in the streets, many liberal Democrats blamed the Yippies for creating the sense that the party was unable to control the chaos in its midst. And that sense of chaos, they maintained, led to Richard Nixon's narrow victory over Democratic candidate Hubert Humphrey.

After Chicago, Rubin and especially Hoffman became the best-known opponents of the Vietnam War. With the timing of a Las Vegas stand-up comic and an intuitive understanding of mass media unrivaled at the time, Hoffman was completely at home in the hippie culture. He was among the Yippies who created media theater with a sharp political edge through events such as throwing dollar bills onto the floor of the New York Stock Exchange.

In 1970, A. J. Weberman convinced various New York political radicals including, sad to say, Abbie Hoffman to picket Bob Dylan's house on MacDougal Street in Greenwich Village on the occasion of Dylan's thirtieth birthday. The pickets demanded that Dylan resume writing "political" songs instead of "personal" ones like those on his then-current album *Nashville Skyline*. Dylan was in Israel at the time and his creative dynamic proceeded according to his own internal rhythms, presumably unaffected by the protesters, who looked like idiots to the very constituency they wanted to "educate." Ultimately, the radical left pushed the culture away, not the other way around. Hoffman later expressed regret for the Dylan picketing.

Hoffman wistfully hoped that the trial of the Chicago Eight would open a dialogue between hippies and radicals, and he arranged for Judy Collins and Allen Ginsberg to testify.

Rubin and Hoffman understood television better than anyone on the left. "You can't be a revolutionary today without a TV set," Rubin wrote in his book *Do It*. "It's as important as a gun. I never understand the radical who comes on TV in a suit and tie. Turn off the sound and he could be mayor. The words may be radical but...television is a non-verbal instrument. The way to understand TV is to shut off the sound. No one remembers any words they hear; the mind is a Technicolor movie of images, not words."

For all of the foibles and limitations of the Yippies—and at times the loose-knit organization seemed little more than a PR umbrella for the activities of its founders—they were unique among their peers in figuring out how to actually communicate with and move a mass constituency. Their efforts were a major factor in bringing hundreds of thousands of Americans into the streets to protest the Vietnam War, a level of protest against a war Americans were fighting unheard of in our history.

By 1971, at the advanced age of twenty-one, I was already slightly older than the core audience for rock music. As managing editor of *Circus* magazine, I decided to embrace the next generation by being the first editor to put the newly popular Grand Funk Railroad and Alice Cooper on the cover. A few of the more intellectual critics excoriated me for the Grand Funk cover, but I was convinced that to stay relevant we had to stay open-minded about what younger kids liked. This philosophy formed the basis of the rest of my career, and has also informed much of my criticism of the political left.

Aging is apparently not a problem for the best rock critics, as writers such as Robert Christgau, Jon Pareles, and Robert Hilburn have proven with their brilliant, up-to-date writing over the past thirty years. I, however, had another problem that doomed my career as a journalist. I hate to criticize musicians. As someone who had never learned to play the guitar, I tended to put musicians on a pedestal and felt guilty when I gave them too hard a time. At *Billboard* I had reviewed a concert by the Rascals and included a line dismissive of the guitar playing of Gene Cornish while lauding the band's star vocalists Eddie Brigati and Felix Cavaliere. I was mortified when Cornish called me and complained.

I was in my early twenties and mainly interested in having a good time. I went through four jobs over the course of eighteen months, including one with Albert Grossman's music publishing company. I idolized Grossman, who worked with great artists and seemed to be able to combine being a wealthy businessman with a knowing embrace of hippie culture. I got to know him quite well in later years, but this time around I had only a few brief audiences with him. One day, though, Janis Joplin came into the office and I got to shake hands with her. "I work here," I said nervously. "So do I," she wearily replied.

I found a cabinet in Grossman's office with pristine copies of the legendary and unreleased "basement tapes" of Dylan and the Band and made copies for a few of my friends, including Patti Smith, who was then a clerk at Scribner's bookstore. Copies of the basement tapes had already started circulating, but they were hard enough to get that they still had some cachet.

Patti reciprocated by stealing me a copy of the *I Ching*. Soon thereafter I was able to get Patti a job at a minor publication called *Rock* magazine, which is where she first was published, before launching her extraordinary career as a poet and rock singer.

Finally cutting the cord with rock journalism, I got a job as director of publicity for a collection of labels called the Famous Music Group. The highlight of my time at Famous was publicizing an album by the band Detroit. It starred Mitch Ryder, a great singer and an authentic rock and roll madman best known for his performance of "Devil with a Blue Dress On."

Detroit's manager was John Sinclair, who had been the leader of the White Panthers, a radical left-wing group in Michigan around which the MC-5 developed. In late 1969, Sinclair had been arrested for possession of two marijuana cigarettes and given a ten-year jail sentence. The injustice spawned a protest movement and a concert and rally in late 1971. Allen Ginsberg read, and John Lennon and Yoko Ono wrote and performed a song that began, "It ain't fair, John Sinclair, ten for two for smoking air."

Four days later, helped by the publicity, Sinclair was released. Fresh out of jail, Sinclair took a while to come to grips with the rapid mainstream assimilation of previously underground symbols. He naïvely told me he was optimistic that America would change radically because so many more people now had long hair.

Other Famous Music releases I worked on included Melanie's biggest hit, "Brand New Key," and Billy Joel's first album, *Cold Spring Harbor*, but my primary contribution to innovative rock culture during this period was to introduce our head of A&R (Artists and Repertoire) Marty Thau to the seminal music of the New York Dolls. Marty went on to become their manager and a significant figure in early New York punk rock music.

At this stage of my life, I was ill suited for the corporate world. Constantly restless and reckless, I was shown the door at Famous Music after a year. I occasionally sold a freelance piece to the *Village Voice* or *Rolling Stone*, but I was unemployed for several months and really depressed.

Then Gloria Stavers turned me on to a radio lecture by Baba Ram Dass, and later introduced me to him. Ram Dass, who had previously been Richard Alpert, Tim Leary's LSD cohort, had turned to Eastern spirituality. Through him I met a nonsectarian yogini named Hilda Charlton. I began attending her weekly meditations, which, among their many virtues, focused me more seriously on work.

In 1973, I was hired by Lee Solters, the venerable Broadway press agent whose clients included Frank Sinatra, Barbra Streisand, and the Ringling Brothers, Barnum and Bailey Circus. My job was to be the longhaired guy who could communicate with rock bands and the writers who covered them.

Solters taught me a crucial lesson in PR. I had thought that my job was to use relationships with writers to get coverage for our clients. He correctly explained that this approach limited the results: How many favors could a writer do for even his closest friend? The key, he explained, was to give the writers a good story.

One of the first clients I was assigned was jazz saxophonist Stan Getz, who was between records and had an engagement coming up at the Rainbow Grille. Getz was a shy man who would rather play Ping-Pong than discuss PR angles. I told Lee that there just wasn't anything interesting about the guy except that he had a birthday coming up. Pulling a classic PR chestnut out of his hat, Lee told me to contrive a birthday party for him. We got a few of his friends to agree to come, and one afternoon at the Rainbow Grille Stan Getz's birthday was observed by jazz legends Zoot Sims and Dizzy Gillespie; Louis Armstrong's widow, Lucille; Stan, his wife, his high school band teacher, me... and four TV news cameras! The lesson—create a good story and you don't need a favor—has helped me ever since, and has important relevance to politics as well as music.

I was able to convince Steve Paul to give us his clients Johnny Winter and the Edgar Winter Group. And I got a huge break when Led Zeppelin became a client of Solters.

Lee knew they were big, but he hated their music, so he had me accompany him to Paris, where he signed them. The group's stars, singer Robert Plant and guitarist Jimmy Page, were fascinated by the American hippie era and liked that I was a little younger than them and had long hair but could still communicate with people in suits. Working with Led Zeppelin would be the turning point in my career.

By 1973, the conventional wisdom on George McGovern's landslide defeat by Nixon the year before had been set in concrete—McGovern lost because of the sixties, including the highly visible support he got from feminists, left-liberal movie stars, and even Yippies.

It's easy to forget that the Democrats staged a stunningly inept campaign, beginning with the fiasco over the quick departure from the ticket of vice presidential candidate Thomas Eagleton, who hastily withdrew after it had been revealed that he had received electroshock therapy for depression, not the greatest way to launch a campaign. Of course, McGovern was running against a still relatively popular incumbent. And the Nixon campaign, we learned later, wasn't playing by the rules. The Watergate scandal, which brought Nixon down less than two years later, originated in a burglary of McGovern's campaign manager's office.

In any event, as CNN's William Schneider has told me more than once, the Democrats have never gotten over their misinterpretation of McGovern's defeat.

Schneider recently reminded me of the Nixon campaign's caricature of McGovern's platform: "Acid, amnesty, and abortion." Yet a year after that election, abortion became legal, a decision supported by a majority of the American people, and a few years after that President Carter granted amnesty to Vietnam draft evaders, a decision applauded by most Americans. And the earnest George McGovern, a decorated Air Force pilot, the son of a Methodist minister, was about as far from an acidhead as you could get. So what explains the intensity of the mainstream Democrats' reaction against "the sixties"?

"The sixties," explains Tom Hayden, "didn't produce any lasting figures or institutions to carry the banner, to carry the flame, and to keep the soul of the sixties alive. It was too anarchistic for that." Into the vacuum, Hayden says, stepped "Democrats who got involved with politics in the early seventies and had no background at all in the civil rights movement or the Vietnam protest movement.

"There was a quest for power by the people who came out of the sixties but were not of the sixties," he told me. "They opened the door to the black middle class. And to women. And they withdrew from the embarrassing exposure in Vietnam. They gave the eighteen-year-old the vote. So they created a niche for working within a reformed system. Which gave people who had been on the outside a lot of mileage for a while . . . It led to McGovern, it led to Carter, it led to environmental laws being passed in the eighties. But these Democrats ran out of steam because there was no longer a culture behind them."

The new Democrats were scared of sixties culture, even though much of it had been embraced by a wide cross section of American society. And conservatives helped widen the gulf by intimidating Democrats into distancing themselves from a huge chunk of their natural base. Millions of people who were inspired by the nexus of politics and culture in the sixties, members of the so-called Woodstock Generation, people like me, would increasingly find themselves without a political home.

**CHAPTER 3**

# The Real
# Seventies Show

THE VIETNAM WAR officially ended in 1973. In August of 1974, Richard Nixon was driven from office by the Watergate scandal. The sixties were over.

Nixon was replaced in the White House by Vice President Gerald Ford. As a Republican Congressman and Speaker of the House, Ford had been a true-blue conservative, supporting Barry Goldwater and urging the impeachment of Chief Justice Earl Warren, a perennial right-wing target. Ford had ascended to the vice presidency in 1973 after the archenemy of sixties pop culture, Spiro Agnew, resigned as a result of his own scandal due to alleged financial improprieties during his time as governor of Maryland.

However, in his half term as president, Ford was an affable moderate, and his administration was culturally neutral. Ford's son, Jack, and daughter, Susan, liked rock and roll. When I read in *Peo-*

*ple* magazine that Susan Ford's favorite band was Led Zeppelin, I contacted White House photographer David Kennerly, who was also a friend of the Ford family, to see if the Fords wanted Zeppelin to visit. The visit never worked out, but the fact that I could have a normal conversation about such a thing with someone in a Republican administration was a radical change from the embattled atmosphere between the White House and the world of popular culture during the Johnson or Nixon administrations.

Most significant, Betty Ford was like a sea change from the previous First Ladies, Pat Nixon and Lady Bird Johnson. Betty Ford would talk openly about her own past drug abuse and made it clear that she had not lectured her kids about avoiding premarital sex.

Some of the dreams of the sixties were coming true. In 1973, the Supreme Court legalized abortion in the *Roe v. Wade* decision, and another Supreme Court decision aimed at rolling back free speech had unintended consequences. Warren Burger, Nixon's replacement for Earl Warren as Chief Justice, wrote the majority opinion in the Miller decision, which held that "obscene" speech had no First Amendment protection. But the ruling allowed local "contemporary community standards" to be one of the tests of prosecutable obscenity.

The Miller decision was an invitation for local prosecutors to roll back liberal court decisions that went back to the mid-1950s and had opened the door to widespread use of profane and obscene language and frank sexuality.

In 1956, newly appointed Supreme Court Justice William J. Brennan had written in the Roth pornography case that literature, art, and ideas "having even the slightest redeeming social importance—unorthodox ideas, controversial ideas, even ideas hateful to the prevailing climate of public opinion" were protected by the First Amendment.

Allen Ginsberg's "Howl" provided the first major test of the new standard. The "Howl" obscenity trial in 1957 produced this classic exchange between metaphorically challenged prosecutor Ralph McIntosh and literary critic Mark Schorer:

MCINTOSH: You understand what "angelheaded hipsters burning for the ancient heavenly connection to the starry dynamo in the machinery of night" means?

SCHORER: Sir, you can't translate poetry into prose. That's why it's poetry.

MCINTOSH: In other words, you don't have to understand the words.

SCHORER: You don't understand the individual words taken out of their context. You can no more translate it back into logical prose English than you can say what a surrealistic painting means in words because it's *not* prose. I can't possibly translate, nor, I am sure, can anyone in this room translate the opening part of this poem into rational prose.

Judge Clayton Horn, who taught a Bible class in Sunday school, dismissed the case. He cited Brennan's doctrine, writing that "Unless the book is entirely lacking in 'social importance' it cannot be held obscene." Ginsberg had used words like "fuck," "cock," "ass," and "cunt," Horn stated, because "he believed that his portrayal required them as being in character... An author should be real in treating his subject and be allowed to express his thoughts and ideas in his own words."

Allen Ginsberg was one of the few heroes of the Beat Generation of the fifties who remained a significant figure in the counterculture, not just into the sixties but until his death in 1997. In his last years, Ginsberg told me of a maddening conversation he had in the mid-nineties with Federal Communications Commissioner

James Quello, who might have benefited from going back and reading Judge Horn's decision.

" 'Howl' is a very good poem," said Quello. "If only you could change a few of the words, I wouldn't have any objection to it being broadcast."

Despite Chief Justice Burger's worst intentions, local prosecutors across the country reacted to the Miller decision by apparently deciding that voters in their communities didn't want a rollback in free speech. The effect was to lock in a level of legal free speech in the arts that would have been unthinkable even a decade earlier.

The loosening of restrictions on profanity also received unlikely and inadvertent help from President Nixon. The Watergate-related release of Nixon's taped White House conversations showed that behind closed doors the president had cursed incessantly, so much so that almost every sentence in the edited mainstream press version of the transcripts seemed to contain the phrase "Expletive deleted."

The seventies climate of freedom and plain speaking produced a golden age in American movies as directors such as Martin Scorsese, Robert Altman, Hal Ashby, Michael Cimino, and Francis Ford Coppola reinvented the motion picture with more realistic portrayals of sex and violence. Their works were quickly accepted by worldwide audiences.

The war in Vietnam was reimagined via Ashby's *Coming Home*, Cimino's *The Deer Hunter*, and Coppola's *Apocalypse Now*. All three films, and others to come, focused on the humanity and pain of veterans and led to greater empathy and understanding between the vets, their families, and the American people, particularly those who had opposed the war. More-populist entertainment also embraced free speech, as tough guys Clint Eastwood and Charles Bronson, among others, appeared in hit movies featuring violence, profanity, and sexual frankness that would have been unthinkable a few years earlier.

In comedy, the brilliant social satirist Richard Pryor and hundreds of comedy club followers used the freedom Lenny Bruce had fought and died for—Bruce's all-consuming legal battles left him broke and in despair, contributing to his death in 1966, but shortly afterward a federal court decision on one of his appeals extended First Amendment rights to the performing arts.

On television, *Saturday Night Live* debuted in 1975 and began a tradition of satirizing American presidents, starting with Chevy Chase's slapstick version of Gerald Ford constantly slipping and falling down. Ford's press secretary Ron Nessen, embracing the zeitgeist, appeared on the show as a guest host.

The most important cultural catalyst of the seventies was TV producer Norman Lear. His *All in the Family* and *Maude* took sixties civil rights and feminist ideas and popularized them for tens of millions of people who had never attended a teach-in. During most of the seventies, *All in the Family* was the most-watched TV show in the United States, and *Maude* was regularly in the top ten.

Democrats were resurgent in Congress in 1974, winning a huge majority with "Watergate baby" candidates. Although, as Tom Hayden pointed out, these Democrats were for the most part beneficiaries of the feminist, civil rights, environmental, and antiwar movements rather than participants, they were elected in a climate where such movements were part of the Democratic coalition, and a number of antidiscrimination and environmental laws were passed.

In 1976, Jimmy Carter, the governor of Georgia, emerged as a surprise winner in several Democratic primaries, defeating such Washington stalwarts as Hubert Humphrey, Henry "Scoop" Jackson, and George McGovern. Carter shrewdly positioned himself as a political outsider and made conscious efforts to reach out to the counterculture. One of Carter's earliest supporters in the media was Hunter S. Thompson, "gonzo" reporter for *Rolling Stone,* who reported approvingly that Carter's standard stump speech included a Bob Dylan quote: "He not busy being born is busy dying."

Twenty years later, when both Bill Clinton and Al Gore used the same Dylan quote, it had the hollow ring of a well-worn cliché. But in 1976 it was unheard of and exciting to hear a presidential candidate quoting Dylan. Carter corresponded with Thompson and gave him access to his campaign at a time when conventional Democratic campaign managers considered *Rolling Stone* irrelevant compared to "serious" journalism. Carter and his advisors knew the magazine reached a huge audience of younger voters.

Short of money in the early stages of the primaries, Governor Carter turned to the rock and roll business in Georgia, specifically to Phil Walden, owner and president of Capricorn Records, which at the time was riding high with the southern rock of the Allman Brothers and other bands. Walden had been Otis Redding's manager and was passionate about civil rights. He saw Carter as the paradigm of an enlightened southerner. When I managed the Allman Brothers in the late 1980s, they proudly told me of their role in getting Carter to the White House.

I had wondered whether or not the Allmans exaggerated their early value to Carter until the mid-nineties, when, as president of Mercury Records, I made a deal with Phil Walden to distribute his Capricorn label, and he arranged for Jimmy and Rosalynn Carter to have dinner with my wife Rosemary and me.

"I never could have gotten elected if it weren't for Phil Walden," the former president recalled with pride. "The concerts that the Capricorn artists did for us in the early primaries kept us going. Otherwise we would have been completely out of money." Twenty years later Carter's eyes still lit up when he talked about the All-man Brothers, remembering with delight not just their help in raising money and attracting supporters, but their extraordinary southern blues-rock musical chemistry.

The term "yuppie" was coined by the media sometime in the eighties, apparently an acronym of young, upwardly mobile, and professional. The word became a catchall to describe former hippies who rechanneled all their energy into making money and living elegantly hip lives.

Yippie co-founder Jerry Rubin tried to institutionalize the phenomenon by staging "salons" at which ambitious people could "network." Rubin sought me out to participate in music-business salons. I found Rubin a lovable rogue but never could relate to his endeavors, which seemed contrived. I didn't think you had to deny your political beliefs to be able to focus on a career, so while I enjoyed Rubin's occasional company, I stayed away from his events.

The 1983 film *The Big Chill*, written and directed by Lawrence Kasdan, captured (and helped mold) conventional wisdom about so-called yuppies. *The Big Chill* is a very well-written and acted ensemble comedy/drama about seven college friends from the sixties who are reunited fifteen years later for the funeral of a friend who has committed suicide. Symbolically, he is the first of their group to die.

The movie leans heavily on music as shorthand for a sense of community. Motown songs are played repeatedly, and the Kevin Kline character boasts that he only listens to music from the sixties. In a crucial early scene, the JoBeth Williams character plays the Rolling Stones' "You Can't Always Get What You Want" on a church organ, evoking smiles of recognition and sixties camaraderie from the other main characters.

*The Big Chill* became a big hit and helped establish a cartoon version of yuppies with its extremely cynical take on sixties activists. Sam, a former campus radical leader played by Tom Berenger, now made millions as an actor starring in a cheesy TV action show, and most of the other characters had drifted far from the political commitment of their college days.

I actually wish that some radical activists from the sixties had become TV stars, but most of them entered academia and remained committed to causes like civil rights and feminism, in the main out of the glare of publicity. Few of them actually turned into yuppies.

I never fit the yuppie stereotype of caring about the vintage of wine or the provenance of cheese, nor did I change my political views, but I did focus my energy on my career after I began working for Lee Solters. My focus became crystallized when I started representing Led Zeppelin.

They were about to become the biggest rock band in the world, and I eagerly threw myself into their tours, starting in 1973. Led Zeppelin's live shows were the most intense of their time, highlighting lead singer Robert Plant's screeching high vocals, guitar hero Jimmy Page's Hendrix-like pyrotechnics, and virtuoso drummer John Bonham, who did the loudest, longest drum solos in rock and roll, and who became the role model for several generations of hard rock drummers. In their recordings, Led Zeppelin would alternate sexually blatant hard-rock shouts with sensitive, impressionistic, mystical numbers like "Stairway to Heaven," which for twenty years has been the most requested song on rock radio stations around the world.

Like Grand Funk, Zeppelin was disdained by snobbish rock critics for whom all creativity had stopped in 1969. To publicize the band, I followed the Solters formula of finding good stories; for example, issuing press releases that stressed Led Zeppelin's impressive statistical accomplishments—they had even broken some Beatles attendance records. Eschewing *Rolling Stone*, I made sure the band did interviews with the less trendy and thus more receptive music writers from daily newspapers around the country.

In LA, I hooked them up with a fifteen-year-old journalistic prodigy that the *LA Times* had begun using, Cameron Crowe. I was in a suite with Cameron and Zeppelin singer Robert Plant at the Ambassador Hotel in Chicago when Robert said to him, "I am a golden god," which Cameron later ascribed to a character in his wonderful cinematic memoir of the early seventies, *Almost Famous*.

The next year, Zeppelin hired me as vice president of their record label, Swan Song. Peter Grant, Led Zeppelin's manager, was a hulking Cockney 300-pound ex-wrestler, but he was also one of the great geniuses of the music business at that time. Coarse, profane, and physically intimidating, Peter cared only about keeping his clients happy and successful. When Peter started as a manager, concert promoters got 50 percent of the gross profits of a show. Peter invented the concept of the "90/10 deal," with the artist keeping 90 percent. Many of the most successful British managers and performers of the time, including Queen and the Rolling Stones, would ask Peter for advice on how to deal with promoters and record companies.

One evening, Peter Grant took me aside during a Zeppelin stadium concert and excitedly pointed to cars streaming down a freeway, zooming off into the night oblivious to the concert. "In here," said Peter, "fifty thousand people are having the time of their lives, and out there those people in their cars don't have any idea what's going on here." I told that story later to Stephen Davis, who wrote the brilliant and definitive (albeit "unauthorized") Led Zeppelin biography, the best-selling *Hammer of the Gods*. Stephen misinterpreted the story, taking Peter's gesture as a command for me to make Zeppelin famous to all those "straight" people.

In fact, Peter was not separating the world into us and them in any judgmental sense—he was not waving a flag in a culture war—he was marveling at the disparity of cultures coexisting in one geographical spot, dazzled by the diversity of human enthusiasms and the sheer bigness of America. Even 50,000 concert fans were a subculture.

The Swan Song job required me to travel all over the United States. Whereas movies are promoted via massive advertising campaigns and press junkets organized by a central office in Los Angeles, records are promoted in a decentralized manner defined by the radius of a radio station's signal. Zeppelin fans were as intense and plentiful in Salt Lake City or Tampa or Detroit as they were in New York or Los Angeles. Direct experience with so much of the country came in handy years later, when people in Washington accused those of us in the music business of being "elitists." We were quite the opposite, and could demonstrate it.

In addition to the power of artists, I also learned about the power of the public. Our first release on Swan Song was by a Scottish singer named Maggie Bell. At the peak of my PR abilities and with Zeppelin in my back pocket, I got her enormous press coverage, including features in both *Time* and *Newsweek*, unheard of for a new artist. We also got her on the music TV shows of the time, and Atlantic made sure the important radio stations played her music. Peter Grant used his favors in the concert business to showcase her in front of ideal rock audiences. The public didn't buy it.

The next artist we put out, Bad Company, exploded instantly because of their hit song "Can't Get Enough of Your Love." Same business team, same kind of promotion, radically different results. Bad Company's debut album went to number one.

The third group we released was actually Led Zeppelin's favorite, The Pretty Things. Zeppelin personally introduced them to the rock press at several parties, and they too got all the promotional clout of a major label. Their records bombed.

Many of my rock critic friends were experiencing the same sense of limitation. The New York Dolls and MC-5 could not have been more beloved by critics but had limited public appeal. "The Dolls were the best band any of us had ever seen," said Dave Marsh, "and when they didn't conquer the world, it was very confusing."

It wasn't that critics were always wrong. Another press favorite, David Bowie, became a huge phenomenon. But the lesson was clear, and I had to internalize it quickly—the public itself created stars. The music professionals and the artists could lengthen or shorten the odds, but the business was ultimately driven by an elusive connection between artists and their music and millions of people whose names they would never know. It was great to fight for music I loved, but I realized that to be successful meant also respecting the mysteries of the marketplace.

I left Swan Song in 1976. I wanted to be a manager like Peter Grant, but clients were hard to come by, and the one I was most involved with, Mink Deville, was a critical darling but didn't generate much money. I was, however, in demand as a publicist and so I started Danny Goldberg Inc., a PR firm that represented KISS, Electric Light Orchestra (ELO), and Todd Rundgren, among others.

One of my clients was Bearsville Records, owned by Paul Fishkin and my ex-boss Albert Grossman. Albert recommended me as a PR person for a new film Bob Dylan was working on. A few weeks later I entered my idol's house in Malibu and together we watched the full length of his legendary four-and-a-half-hour surreal autobiographical documentary *Renaldo and Clara*. Dylan commented on it as it went by on the editing machine.

Sitting next to Dylan that afternoon, listening to him free-associate about movies, obscure folk singers, the music press, and his own mythology satisfied some deep yearning I'd been harboring since high school. Soon thereafter, Dylan decided he didn't want a press agent for the project after all, but my inner teenager has been forever grateful for the time spent with him.

Of course, an afternoon with Bob Dylan was not the usual run of business. I spent a lot of my time contriving photo-ops, combining clients with other celebrities. For instance, although the Electric Light Orchestra was led by a shy genius named Jeff Lynne who would have been happy with no publicity, ELO's manager Don Arden was of the British tough-guy school, and he coveted the limelight. I satisfied Don by staging a party at the disco Regine's following an ELO concert and got former heavyweight champion Joe Frazier to attend.

When a photo from the Regine's party ran in *Billboard*, I was assured several more months of fees, but I had a sinking feeling that I'd become a schlock cliché. One writer for a New York newspaper who liked to drink more than he liked to write would put just about anything in his column as long as I wrote it out in his style word for word. I was afraid that doing PR was making me a little cynical. Thus I was excited when I was drawn into political activism by one of my clients, John Hall, who had written songs for Janis Joplin and Bonnie Raitt and whose group Orleans had a couple of big hits, "Still the One" and "Dance with Me."

Not long after his first daughter was born, Hall read that a nuclear power plant was going to be constructed near his home in Saugerties, New York. John had been a physics major in college and was worried about the health consequences of the plant. He was convinced that cancer risks were greatly increased by nuclear power and became an antinuclear activist.

John asked me to arrange a press conference with him, Bonnie Raitt, James Taylor, and Carly Simon to announce that a group of musicians were coming out for safe energy. At the time, Carly Simon was the biggest name of the four because of her recent gigantic hit "You're So Vain." Aided by political PR expert David Fenton, we were preparing the musicians for questions before opening the doors to the media when Carly announced that her manager, Arlene Rothberg, didn't want her to participate.

James Taylor, then married to Carly, sat impassively, his gorgeous blue eyes staring into space as if focused a thousand miles away. Bonnie simply got up and walked out of the room. John Hall, the least famous of the group he had assembled, looked at me with panic in his eyes.

I think my activist career began at this exact moment. I had spent a large part of the previous five years ass-kissing artists and managers to get them to trust me as a publicist. Conventional careerism called for me to accept Carly's course reversal and make the best of it. But I had been so energized by John Hall's explanation of the environmental hazards of nuclear power I felt transported back to my high school persona. This was civil rights and Vietnam all over again! I asked Carly for Arlene's phone number.

Arlene told me that Carly had a long-standing policy of not participating in political events. She had turned down several requests from her feminist friends for press conferences. I snapped back that Carly had given permission for her name to be on the media pitch and explained that there were a dozen reporters outside, several of them with camera crews.

"If she doesn't do this," I said, "the story is going to be about Carly pulling out, and that will cause a lot more questions than if she participates." Arlene gruffly threw out an olive branch, agreeing that Carly would answer questions but not make an opening statement.

At the press conference, a member of my staff directed the first question at Carly and she proceeded to describe the cancer-causing dangers of radiation, the questionable safety features of most plants, and the difficulty of safely storing nuclear waste for long periods of time. Overall she gave the most eloquent and coherent statement against nuclear power of the day. Her eloquence provided the sound bite that ran on TV and a key quote for the newspapers.

The next year, after the Three Mile Island nuclear accident, the issue became big news. John and several other artists and activists created Musicians United for Safe Energy (MUSE) and began planning several concerts at Madison Square Garden to benefit antinuclear and environmental groups. John, remembering my passion at the press conference, asked if I wanted to participate, and I suggested making a musical documentary film.

Jackson Browne was first among equals in the MUSE organization. Although I had absolutely no background in making films of any kind, Jackson bought into my notion that only a movie would maximize the audience for the political ideas underlying the MUSE concerts.

Having just released the multi-platinum album *Running on Empty*, Jackson was at his peak in popularity. He had combined his timely and insightful lyrics with the zeitgeist of California rock music. With the cheekbones of a model and what Bonnie Raitt called "rock and roll's most perfect hair," Jackson was a powerful combination of poet and pinup.

I met Jackson for the first time at his Hollywood home and was immediately disarmed by his unpretentiousness. The $500,000 advance we got for recording rights to the upcoming concerts was plowed into the costs of filming the shows. Only Jackson's steadfast endorsement of the movie fended off the anxious concerns of the political activists, who feared their grassroots grants from MUSE might go up in smoke if we didn't get an adequate return on the movie.

Jackson's one major request was that we include Native American leader John Trudell, who was organizing a protest of planned uranium mining in the Black Hills of South Dakota, sacred to Native Americans. With a small documentary crew, I flew to South Dakota for the march the following week. Trudell was indeed a mesmerizing speaker, as was the then-teenage Winona LaDuke—two decades later, she would become Ralph Nader's running mate in the 2000 presidential election.

Jackson joined Trudell on a fifty-mile walk through the Black Hills. I had already turned yellow from a case of hepatitis and begged off. I returned to LA, where I now had a home, to recuperate.

Graham Nash, like John Hall, had developed an intense interest in banning nuclear power because it came close to home. Nuclear waste was slated to be stored on the Farralon Islands near where Graham lived in Northern California, and he had written a song called "Barrels of Pain" about the potential devastation such waste could cause. Graham was and is one of the clearest-thinking, most pragmatic artists I have ever met, and he reunited the fractured Crosby, Stills & Nash for the MUSE concerts.

Bonnie Raitt, who joked that she was the "token woman" on many benefit concerts, was the other artist deeply involved in MUSE's creation and administration. The definitive female blues singer and guitarist of her generation, Bonnie had a bawdy sense of humor, a razor-sharp intellect, and a deep political commitment grounded in her upbringing as a Quaker. Her father, singer John Raitt, had been an important Broadway star in the 1950s and had encouraged his children to support the civil rights and peace movements. Bonnie was integrally involved with every aspect of MUSE.

The most prominent of the activists involved in MUSE was Sam Lovejoy, who had attracted national attention for toppling a tower of a proposed nuclear power site in his native Massachusetts.

Lovejoy represented himself at trial and emerged as a Jimmy Stewart–like hero, pleading self-defense on behalf of his community and using the trial as a platform to lay out the health hazards of radiation from nuclear power plants. He was acquitted.

Also on the MUSE board was Howard Kohn, who had written the *Rolling Stone* articles bringing into full light the struggles of Karen Silkwood to alert her Oklahoma community to safety hazards in the nuclear power plant where she worked. She died in a mysterious car accident. The hit film *Silkwood*, with Meryl Streep in the title role, was based on Kohn's articles.

Tom Hayden showed up at a few meetings but stayed pretty much in the background. Journalist Harvey Wasserman, who over the years has consistently written the most coherent analyses of the nuclear power issue, was on the board, as was Tom Campbell, an ex-union organizer who acted as a trusted liaison between Bonnie and Jackson and various grassroots groups. He helped supervise physical production and twenty years later was still organizing benefits on behalf of those artists and others.

But it was Jackson Browne whose energy drove the events. It is very rare for an established star to take the emotional risks of conflict and rejection that a conventional concert producer regularly deals with. I will never forget watching him on the phone pleading with Joni Mitchell to join the concerts. Jackson had the vision that her song "Shadow and Light" would add a unique, creative layer to the concerts, and spent the better part of an hour vainly trying to persuade her. Jackson was more successful in recruiting the Doobie Brothers to headline the first two evenings, with Bruce Springsteen and Jackson himself headlining the other nights.

In September of 1979, five nights of concerts packed Madison Square Garden, and a post-concert rally in Battery Park, beneath the Twin Towers of the World Trade Center, drew 250,000 people.

Performers included Jackson, Bonnie, John Hall, Crosby, Stills & Nash, Springsteen and the E Street Band, James Taylor, the Doobie Brothers, Jesse Colin Young, Gil Scott-Heron, Peter Tosh, Tom Petty and the Heartbreakers, and many others. Roughly a million dollars was raised.

The activists in MUSE had wanted to make sure that there was a political element to the film, so they had teamed me up with Barbara Kopple. She had won a best documentary Oscar for her 1977 film on coal mine workers, *Harlan County, U.S.A.* Oscar-winning cinematographer Haskell Wexler, best known for *Medium Cool*, a harrowing quasi-documentary about protests at the 1968 Democratic Convention, also joined the team.

At the concerts, Kopple and Wexler shot backstage footage for the documentary. The performances themselves were filmed by a group of camera people assembled by New York writer and filmmaker David Silver. Barbara introduced me to her friend, former Paramount film executive Julian Schlossberg, who agreed to co-produce the film, which was a godsend since Julian brought filmmaking experience and talent that the rest of us lacked.

It soon became clear that Kopple and Wexler, backed by some of the activists, wanted to make a traditional political documentary with a little rock music in the background. To me, this was an echo of the controversy around the be-in in the sixties—culturally tone-deaf political activists were undermining their own cause. The purpose of the movie was to reach people who weren't already activists.

Ironically, Julian Schlossberg ended up siding with me. To us, a rock and roll–driven movie was preferable politically. We could reach a million rock fans who hadn't been able to go to the concerts. And we could create a document that would live on, and might be seen by another million or so on TV. Moreover, a concert film could make back the $500,000 we had invested, and then some. A pure documentary almost certainly would not.

Jackson, Graham, and Bonnie agreed to do the film our way. Barbara Kopple and Haskell Wexler quit. Julian and I became co-directors as well as the co-producers of No Nukes. (We ended up giving Anthony Potenza, the film's editor, a co-director credit as well.)

To sell the movie to a film distributor, we edited together around forty minutes of musical performances. Jackson Browne was famously slow in finishing and delivering his albums, and his producer Greg Ladanyi was appalled when I explained that he only had two days to mix Jackson's songs. Ladanyi looked at Jackson with raised eyebrows, expecting the auteur to explode, but Jackson's political activist persona trumped his inner perfectionist, and he told Ladanyi to meet our deadlines.

But the biggest star in terms of selling the movie was Bruce Springsteen. He was just beginning his long and well-deserved run as a superstar and there existed, at the time, very little film footage of his extraordinarily dynamic stage performances. Bruce came to see our forty-minute presentation, which included two of his songs. A few hours later, Bruce's manager, Jon Landau, called to say that Bruce had some ideas about the movie he wanted to discuss over dinner at Patsy's Italian restaurant.

Although I would find in later encounters with Bruce that he is among the most articulate of men, I had a hard time figuring out what he wanted at first. He was downbeat about what he felt was a prosaic collection of performances, mostly oldies. I think he was trying to be polite and thus he obliquely suggested, "It should be more like the movie Mean Streets."

I nodded earnestly but had no idea what he was talking about. Mean Streets was a drama, this was a documentary. Over the course of the dinner I figured out that he was trying to say that he wanted the "drama" of a potent message, not just a series of well-performed songs. I assured him that after we sold the film it was our intention to make the final product around 20 percent political.

After much pleading on my part, we were permitted to use Bruce's name in the sales pitch to studios with the proviso that he would get to see a final version before he decided which songs we could use. Bruce was particularly worried that his version of the Gary U.S. Bonds rock and roll classic "Quarter to Three," which he liked to use as an audience-rousing encore, was too trivial for a political documentary. From our point of view, the theatrics and physical energy of "Quarter to Three" were the highlight of the movie and we were desperate to keep it.

Armed with this tenuous commitment, Julian shopped the film to various studio heads. Terry Semel at Warner Bros. bought it for $1 million, low even by 1980 standards, but enough to finish the film and to return the $500,000 record advance to MUSE so that the grassroots grants could be given out.

We shot interviews with Jackson Browne and Graham Nash, who were articulate about their reasons for doing the concerts, but the movie still didn't have enough teeth. We added the overtly political songs "We Almost Lost Detroit" by my old high school pal Gil Scott-Heron, Graham's "Barrels of Pain," Hall's antinuclear anthem "Power," and Jackson's prophetic "Before the Deluge."

Julian Schlossberg was friends with Elaine May, a genius whose many talents include the ability to "fix" troubled movies. Usually paid opulent sums by the likes of Warren Beatty for her insights, Elaine worked without pay, as Julian and I and all of the performers had. She created a movie within the movie that included a conversation with nuclear scientist Dr. John Gofman, historical footage from TV networks, and a brief clip of Trudell's speech in South Dakota, fulfilling my early promise to Jackson. We ended with shots of the huge rally in Battery Park, including excerpts of speeches from Ralph Nader, Jane Fonda, and Gray Panther leader Maggie Kuhn, and ended with John Hall's stirring "Power" and Jesse Colin Young's sixties anthem "Get Together."

When Bruce saw the now-politicized version of the movie, he hugged me approvingly and promptly gave his permission to include any of his songs that we wanted. Even though Bruce himself never uttered a political word in the movie, his motivation was to get a message out. Once his stage gymnastics were put in that context, he embraced the film, and his performance was the galvanizing highlight and got the lion's share of attention from the press.

*No Nukes* was released in July 1980, less than ten months after the concerts. It played for only a few weeks in theaters, but it has been shown almost every year since on PBS or VH-1 and has had a long life in home video. Twenty years later, after the September 11 attack on the World Trade Center, some of the issues raised by MUSE, including the safety hazards of nuclear power plants and the value of energy conservation and alternatives to oil, had renewed salience.

In subsequent years, as Springsteen became one of the world's biggest rock stars, he always supported grassroots groups and periodically would align himself with political positions; for example, by recording the Edwin Starr antiwar song "War" in the mid-eighties, when the Reagan administration was making aggressive moves in Central America. His 1995 album *The Ghost of Tom Joad* is filled with romantic political idealism, and in 1999 Springsteen wrote the song "51 Shots" to protest the police killing of Amadou Diallo in New York in 1999.

(In 2002 Springsteen released *The Rising*, which was filled with eloquent references to September 11, but this particular body of work is more about grief, recovery, heroism, compassion, and universal humanity than about any particular political point of view.)

Bonnie, Jackson, John Hall, Crosby, Stills & Nash, Jesse Colin Young, James Taylor, and many of the other MUSE artists have continued to raise money for progressive groups and to hand out literature at their concerts. The MUSE artists have proven over the course of a quarter century that they are indeed the worthy successors to Woody Guthrie, Pete Seeger, and Joan Baez.

Of course, not all rock stars are like Bonnie Raitt and Jackson Browne. In the summer of 1980, I was at a party making small talk with California governor Jerry Brown about No Nukes when Mick Jagger walked up and said, "I think nuclear power is a bullshit issue." "Why?" said Brown, always ready for a tussle. "It's just a bullshit issue, that's all," giggled Jagger, and walked away.

That November, Jimmy Carter lost the presidency to Ronald Reagan. At least some of the blame for his defeat has to fall on the Washington liberal elite, politicians, and pundits who were uncomfortable with Carter's populist tendencies and wrote and spoke of him with ill-disguised scorn.

Carter should have hung on to his egalitarianism. Instead, the candidate who had said he could not have won the Democratic nomination without the Allman Brothers, the president who had invited Willie Nelson to the White House, seems to have blinked under the haughty stares of the Washington snobs. He tried to refashion himself as a traditional Democrat, going so far as to tone down symbolic gestures such as carrying his own garment bag, and wound up with a blurred image. This allowed the media wizard Reagan to masquerade as an outsider, even though his policies were aimed at protecting and reinforcing the wealth and power of the superrich.

As the Reagan era dawned, very few graduates of the sixties movements actually became conservatives, contrary to the popular myth. But in the face of the maddening similarity of messages coming from the two parties, and the virtual disappearance of left-wing ideas from mass media discourse, many simply retreated from politics altogether.

CHAPTER 4

# The Early Eighties

Ronald Reagan
and the New Hollywood Left

B Y 1980, I finally was able to succeed in the music business as something other than a publicist. I formed Modern Records with my friend Paul Fishkin and Fleetwood Mac star Stevie Nicks. Modern's primary purpose was to produce and release Stevie's solo albums.

Although she had little interest in politics, Stevie was very much influenced by hippie culture. She had a very romantic notion of the relationship between her inner voice and her art, and she felt very close to her fans. Many of Stevie's female fans imitated her long, fluffy hairstyle and wore shawls like the ones she twirled around onstage. Backstage, she would spend as much time with fans as she would with the music and media heavies.

Because of Fleetwood Mac's immense popularity (their then-current album *Rumours* was number one for a record thirty-nine weeks), Stevie was exposed to music professionals far more powerful than me. The key to our arrangement was my intense emotional commitment to her as an artist. The entourage around Fleetwood Mac treated her as a "chick singer" rather than as a major talent and a superstar, which is how I saw her. Stevie's first album for us, the quadruple-platinum *Bella Donna*, became the number one seller in the United States in 1981, and her solo career was launched.

I had moved my primary residence and office to Los Angeles when I started working with Stevie Nicks. In the wake of Ronald Reagan's 1980 victory over Jimmy Carter, I started getting calls from liberal politicians and public interest groups asking for help with publicity and raising money. It was as if the amorphous connections between the music, the hippie culture, and politics that were symbolized by the Woodstock Festival finally coalesced for me a decade and a half later.

Entertainment and politics were coming together in a dynamic way in Hollywood in the eighties. Jane Fonda and Tom Hayden had frequent salons in their Santa Monica home, attracting a new generation of entertainers to political activism. Warren Beatty, Barbra Streisand, and Paul Newman supported liberal candidates for office. Songwriter Marilyn Bergman and others, including Barbara Corday, Susan Grode, Pat Lee, film producer Paula Weinstein, Fonda, and Streisand, formed the Hollywood Women's Political Committee.

Stanley Sheinbaum, who was married to movie mogul Harry Warner's daughter Betty, was a major force in the progressive community. Stanley was a member of the University of California Board of Regents and publisher of *New Perspectives Quarterly*. He had been active in the McGovern campaign and frequently collaborated with entertainment figures on liberal causes, playing a significant behind-the-scenes role in virtually every Southern California progressive initiative of the time. He and Betty hosted dozens of American and international intellectual and political leaders in their Brentwood home. Stanley would become my primary mentor in entering the activist world.

As I became more involved with Hollywood liberals and progressives in the 1980s, pundits, left-wing activists, and politicians—perhaps irked by the sharp questions some of us posed—would ask me what on earth show business had to do with the serious, complex issues of politics.

I always invoked Ronald Reagan.

For conservatives, Reagan was a galvanizing force, but his ability to get a large majority of Americans behind him had a lot to do with his ability to speak to nonconservatives who liked his accessibility, even if they disagreed with him about such issues as abortion. Reagan's mass appeal was directly related to his background as an actor, and he enthusiastically used all of the tools of public relations that more conventional politicians resisted. Reagan shaped perceptions and gave them concreteness. Millions of working-class whites might already have been thinking their personal economic problems were somehow related to the civil rights movement, but Reagan legitimized their worst feelings when he talked about mythical "welfare mothers with Cadillacs."

In press conferences, Reagan used humor better than anyone since John F. Kennedy, and unlike any president before or since, Reagan used entertainment-business references to bond with a broad range of Americans. Referring to the Carter administration, Reagan said, "We were being led by a team of people with good intentions and bad ideas, people with all the common sense of Huey, Dewey, and Louie."

Campaigning at the Grand Ole Opry in Nashville, Reagan said, "The other side's promises are a little like Minnie Pearl's hat. They both have big price tags hanging from them." On a college campus, Reagan responded to cheers by saying, "If you ask me, as Robert Palmer has been singing recently, you are simply irresistible." Even on a very serious occasion like his 1986 State of Union address, President Reagan quoted from the film *Back to the Future*: "Where we're going, we don't need roads."

First Lady Nancy Reagan kissed TV star Mr. T on the head at the White House and appeared as herself, preaching against drugs, in an episode of the sitcom *Diff'rent Strokes*. When Ron Reagan Jr., parodying a scene from the film *Risky Business*, danced in his underwear on *Saturday Night Live*, President Reagan said, "Like father, like son."

In 1983, President Reagan posed shirtless and pumping iron for a cover story in *Parade* magazine headlined "Move Over Jane Fonda, Here Comes the Ronald Reagan Workout Plan." Reagan even tried to co-opt the Boss in 1984, saying in a campaign speech, "America's future...rests in a message of hope in the songs of a man so many young Americans admire, New Jersey's own Bruce Springsteen." Springsteen, a progressive Democrat, rebuffed Reagan the next day at a Pittsburgh concert: "The president was mentioning my name the other day and I kinda got to wondering what his favorite album must have been. I don't think it was the *Nebraska* album," referring to his recently released collection of songs about the dark side of the American soul.

Inspired by Reagan's success, many other conservatives, like young Georgia congressman Newt Gingrich, became highly attuned to popular culture and posed as rebels and outsiders. Conservative Republican representative John Kasich went so far as to talk enthusiastically about his love for the Grateful Dead, and he made his anti-tax libertarianism sound like a plan for personal growth instead of a scheme to make the rich richer.

In 1983, I sold my half of Modern to Atlantic Records and created Gold Mountain Entertainment. I was the executive producer of Bette Midler's *No Frills* album and supervised music and soundtrack albums for movies and television, most memorably the film *Dirty Dancing* and the TV series *Miami Vice*. But my primary focus was the management of musical artists. Gold Mountain clients included Belinda Carlisle from the Go-Gos, who had a number one song with "Heaven Is a Place on Earth," Alannah Myles, who had a number one song with "Black Velvet," and Bonnie Raitt.

Bonnie was being dropped by her longtime label, Warner Bros. But my partner, Ron Stone, and I were convinced her best years lay ahead. Happily, for all of us, they did.

With my *No Nukes* partner, Julian Schlossberg, I also started a small label called Gold Castle that made new recordings of some of my early-sixties folk music heroes: Joan Baez, Judy Collins, and Peter, Paul, and Mary. They all had fought long and hard for such causes as civil rights and peace. All later agreed to appear in a series of concerts I organized to raise money to lobby Congress against aiding the right-wing contras in Nicaragua.

Outside of the activist musicians, the two entertainment figures who would have the most impact on me were Norman Lear and Ed Asner.

Norman was at his peak of TV prestige in 1980, having come off the decade as the producer of the hit TV series *All in the Family*, *Maude*, *The Jeffersons*, *One Day at a Time*, *Mary Hartman Mary Hartman*, and so on. These series, unlike anything that had come before, dealt head-on from a liberal perspective with cultural issues such as feminism, gay rights, and race relations.

Following the 1980 election, Norman became fascinated and

appalled by the right-wing Christians who had become part of Reagan's electoral majority. They were building huge followings via cable TV and mass mailings. The most prominent was the Reverend Jerry Falwell, who called his organization the Moral Majority.

Norman recalls, "After a decade of producing TV shows I wanted to do something different and was developing a movie for Robin Williams and Richard Pryor about mail-order ministers. While I was doing research I started watching Falwell and Jimmy Swaggart and Jim Bakker and I was stunned by the hatred and vitriol coming out of them. I actually heard a TV preacher once ask people to pray that a member of the Supreme Court would die. And I was frightened. I was frightened as an American, I was frightened as a Jewish man."

Norman created People for the American Way to counter conservative Christians who were trying to define patriotism solely through their beliefs. Twenty years later, Norman could remember in precise detail his approach: "I wrote the first TV spot, and it set the pattern for all of them. It was a guy not unlike Archie Bunker. He was sitting on a piece of heavy equipment in a factory yard with a hard hat on. And the camera moved in slowly on him as he talked about himself and his wife and his kids, saying that they have various political points of view and they all love each other and they fight all the time about these political points of view.

"'But now [he says] comes this group of ministers on the radio and the television and in the mail, right in my home, telling us we're good Christians or bad Christians depending on our political point of view.' He's saying, 'I would tell you my wife's the best Christian in this family and there's nobody that's going to disagree with that. But somehow these guys think I'm the best and I'm the one that's going to heaven because I agree with them. So we've been thinking, there's got to be something wrong when ministers tell you you're a good Christian or a bad Christian depending on your political point of view.'"

Norman, still burning with quiet, intense indignation after all these years, concludes: "And his last line was, 'That ain't the American way.'"

Through TV specials, mass mailings, countless op-ed submissions, and many TV appearances, People for the American Way launched an alternative vision of patriotism and morality, one that celebrated American traditions but opposed bigotry and narrowmindedness, that saw tolerance and diversity as a part of the American dream, not as a contradiction to it. No political or academic figure affected American perception on this issue as much as Norman Lear.

Norman invited intellectuals, politicians, and other prominent people to his home to meet movie stars and other Hollywood figures. When I moved to Los Angeles, his assistant, Betsy Kenny, made sure I was on the guest list for these fascinating evenings, and I got to know many people I would work with in Hollywood.

In 1981, Ed Asner, a brilliant actor who had starred in two top-rated TV series, *The Mary Tyler Moore Show* and *Lou Grant*, won the presidency of the Screen Actors Guild—the post that had launched Reagan's political career in the 1950s. A committed progressive, the avuncular Asner was a constant force from Hollywood evoking an alternate vision to Reagan's.

Ed got particularly involved in opposing the Reagan administration's unwavering support of the government of El Salvador while right-wing death squads from the Salvadoran military were torturing and killing people. Most notoriously, four American Mary Knoll nuns who worked with the poor were murdered, followed by activist Catholic Archbishop Romero.

Officially, the United States backed the Salvadoran government uncritically because of its supposed strategic value in fighting the spread of communism in Central America. Asner lent his name to opposition groups. When *Lou Grant* was canceled in 1982, pickets appeared at CBS, and Asner himself was among those who blamed right-wing pressure on advertisers and the network for the cancellation.

That same year, Pam Lippe, who had helped organize the No Nukes rally, introduced me to her new boss, Russ Hemenway, executive director of the National Committee for an Effective Congress. The NCEC had been formed by Eleanor Roosevelt and others in the early 1950s to encourage liberals to run for Congress and to support their campaigns.

Along with screenwriter/director Carl Gottlieb, we organized an HBO special called "Night of More Than a Dozen Stars" starring Asner, Robin Williams, Chevy Chase, and others, the proceeds of which went to NCEC. Hemenway, who continues to run NCEC in his late seventies, has a patrician accent reminiscent of the Roosevelts and yet has more populist inclinations than anyone in the current Democratic party establishment.

In 1984, I teamed up with another No Nukes alumnus, stage manager Tim Sexton, to create voter registration spots aimed at young people. We approached MTV, which had started a few years earlier and had quickly become the dominant national voice of pop and rock music.

After a polite reception from the MTV higher-ups, the idea was assigned to Judy McGrath, who at the time was in charge of in-house promotion, including the dazzling MTV network ID spots. Judy, who shared our political passion, embraced the idea and made sure our spots ran frequently. Over the years Judy has been the force for MTV's socially conscious programming even as she's risen in the hierarchy—eventually, she would become president of the network.

With MTV's imprimatur, it was easy to get cooperation from managers and artists. We made spots with a number of top stars of the time, including Huey Lewis, Cyndi Lauper, and KISS. Peter Wolf, who had just left the J. Geils Band, did a spot with Afrika Bambaataa, a pioneer in the then-new genre of rap. I had read that young people felt powerless, so I came up with the slogan "Feel the Power," and in homage to my hippie ideals I got the rights to use an excerpt of Jimi Hendrix's performance of the "Star-Spangled Banner" at Woodstock. These commercials were a precursor to the Rock the Vote campaigns that started several years later.

I was stunned when several local liberals implied that the spots might be counterproductive—Reagan had captured the imagination of many young people, so maybe it was better for Democrats if young people didn't vote. Democratic congressman Tom Harkin of Iowa, who was running for the Senate, didn't feel that way. "If I can't get the votes of young people I don't deserve to win," Harkin told us, his Midwestern twang evoking memories of Jimmy Stewart. Iowa had a particularly high concentration of cable TV homes, and he was glad that MTV had committed to run our spots. Despite the Reagan landslide in 1984, Harkin did win, and he always maintains that the MTV spots helped.

One day, influential Democratic lawyer Mickey Kantor asked Tim Sexton and me to meet with Congressman Al Gore Jr., who was running for his father's old Senate seat in Tennessee. Kantor had been a key advisor to Jerry Brown when he was governor. He was now a partner in the powerful law firm of Manatt, Phelps & Phillips. Kantor's biggest client, oil magnate Armand Hammer, had asked him to set up Hollywood meetings for Gore, an old friend and beneficiary. We met in the bar at the Beverly Hills Hotel.

I asked Gore about the so-called nuclear freeze proposal—basically, no more nuclear weapons would be made by either side. It was a hot issue with many on the left. We were concerned both about the amount of federal money being spent on nuclear weapons and about the danger of a war triggered by the arms race itself.

Gore's face then had the unlined perfection of a TV anchorman's. He earnestly responded, "Not long ago I had a nightmare in which I actually experienced what a nuclear war would be like. I was so shaken by it that when I woke up I promised myself that limiting the nuclear arms race would be the number one priority for the rest of my life." I found it somewhat unlikely that the congressman had actually had such a dream. It just seemed a bit too convenient. My own dreams have never been that literal. But I appreciated the sentiment and didn't want to insult Mickey Kantor, so I gave his campaign $250.

About that time, as Mikhail Gorbachev assumed power in the Soviet Union, opportunities opened up for Americans to communicate with Russians.

No one I know ever had the slightest enthusiasm for the Soviet regime. It is impossible for someone who loves free speech and the other guarantees of the Bill of Rights to identify with totalitarian regimes, and as a Jew I was appalled by the mistreatment of Soviet Jews. But many of us had long and fervently hoped for a break in the Cold War and were nervous about President Reagan's description of the Soviet Union as an "evil empire." And I, for one, was terrified of nuclear war.

I joined in various "person to person" exchanges, where American citizens could meet with Russians. I also went to meetings organized by 20th Century Fox production executive Claire Townsend with people from the media, as well as film stars like Sally Field, to discuss ways of lowering the temperature on the arms race. One memorable visitor was Dr. Helen Caldicott, the Australian who had organized Physicians for Social Responsibility, a group of thousands of doctors who opposed nuclear testing and proliferation.

In 1985, Bonnie Raitt asked me to accompany her to Russia. Raitt, Carlos Santana, James Taylor, and the Doobie Brothers had been invited to perform in Moscow near the end of the Cold War. The Berlin Wall hadn't come down yet, but Mikhail Gorbachev had begun his "glasnost" program in the Soviet Union. American rock promoter Bill Graham had organized the first visit to Russia of American rock artists in many years.

The day before the show, we were given a tour of Red Square by a nervous Soviet guide. James Taylor asked to see the house that Leo Tolstoy had lived in, and we basked in the glow of the perfectly preserved nineteenth-century home of the literary and political genius. *San Francisco Chronicle* music critic Joel Selvin and I broke away from the group and found a small synagogue, where we prayed with a group of beleaguered Soviet Jews, most of whom probably left the country a few years later when Gorbachev opened up Jewish emigration.

The concert the next afternoon featured several government-sanctioned Soviet rock bands, and concert tickets had been distributed by the Communist Party. The venue for the event was a sports stadium that could have held 40,000 spectators. Soviet officials, however, limited the crowd to 10,000. They filled most of the grassy field, leaving the stands virtually empty.

We stood onstage in amazement as about 500 Soviet soldiers ran out onto the field to "protect" the stage from the audience, creating a vast space as a kind of no-man's-land. Graham had one of his famous temper tantrums and threatened to cancel the show. After an hour of fevered negotiations, the soldiers split the difference and let the audience come closer.

The day-long concert, middle-of-the-road rock even by eighties standards, went on under the watchful eyes of hundreds of armed Soviet soldiers. The paranoid Soviets had long banned the Beatles, KISS, and other Western rock musicians from polluting the minds of Soviet youth. Now they were acting as if James Taylor and the Doobie Brothers could spark another revolution. What, we kept asking one another, were they so afraid of?

Later that same year, I was invited to Central America on a trip that was organized by Margery Tabankin, who had run VISTA for President Carter and was executive director of the Washington-based Arca Foundation. Arca lobbies for liberal and progressive causes.

Many people I respected had become convinced that Reagan's policy in Central America was wrong-headed, supporting repressive elements in El Salvador and opposing a fledgling democracy in Nicaragua without considering the wishes and rights of the people of those regions. The Reagan administration had a knee-jerk bias in favor of any faction that was anti-Communist or opposed to Cuba.

Marge, an astute political analyst who was a true Washington insider without being trapped in Washington groupthink, decided that the only way to change the policy was to change public opinion, because Democrats in Congress were not likely to oppose the Reagan administration unless the issue meant something to voters.

"You can't just rely on investigative reports and a few liberal congressmen," she explained. "You need other megaphones when you're up against an administration in power."

A number of groups were already organized on the issue. Some of them had a naïve sympathy for the Communist forces in the region, but most were veterans of the antiwar movement who saw eerie similarities between our Central American policy and our support years earlier for an unpopular, brutal anti-Communist regime in Vietnam.

A key to Marge's strategy of arousing public interest in the issue was getting celebrities and opinion makers, including political moderates, to visit El Salvador and Nicaragua. The group I was invited to join included several freshmen Democratic Congressmen: Bart Gordon, who had taken over Gore's district in Tennessee, Jim Traficant of Ohio, and Albert Bustamante of Texas. Also with us were writers Rose Styron and Galway Kinnell, Carter administration State Department official John Holum, actors Mandy Patinkin and Peter Horton, and Robert Kennedy's oldest child, Kathleen Kennedy Townsend, who would later be elected lieutenant governor of Maryland.

At a meeting with El Salvadoran president Duarte, we kept asking questions about the murderers of the Mary Knoll nuns. I asked the president why he didn't arrest the military men strongly rumored to have been involved.

"Everything has to go at its own speed," Duarte said in perfect English. "It's like records. Some go around at seventy-eight, some at forty-five and some more slowly at thirty-three." Several members of our group started giggling. "Forgive me, Mr. President," said Kathleen Townsend, "but the member of our delegation you are talking to is in the music business."

"Oh," replied Duarte, extending his arms toward me expansively, "then you know exactly what I am talking about," as if his nonsensical answer had responded to my question.

In Nicaragua, we met up with another American delegation that included Jackson Browne and his girlfriend at the time, actress Daryl Hannah, and Senators Harkin and John F. Kerry. Most of us from both groups were disappointed in the authoritarian attitude of the Sandinista officials. They were the sullen, humorless military leaders of a successful revolution who seemed to have little regard for freedom of speech and dissent and other rights associated with liberty and democracy.

Kathleen Townsend was very moved by a private meeting with Violetta Chamorro, the widow of a slain leader of the opposition.

But we saw no justification for American intervention to over-throw the Sandinista government. The poor population, still reel-ing from the earthquake in Managua of several years earlier, seemed relieved to be out from under the yoke of the longtime dic-tator Somoza. An aggressive American presence could have led to a Vietnam-like nightmare, with the United States supporting unpopular anti-Communist puppets.

Another issue that captured the imagination of many in the entertainment world was South African apartheid. Bruce Spring-steen's guitarist Steve Van Zandt returned from a visit to South Africa in 1984 and organized a benefit recording and music video of his angry anti-apartheid anthem "Sun City." My clients Peter Wolf and Bonnie Raitt joined Bruce Springsteen and dozens of others in the 1985 recording.

Six years later, black leader Nelson Mandela was released from prison in South Africa after twenty-seven years. I accompanied Bon-nie Raitt on a trip to London for a concert with Peter Gabriel, U2, and many others in support of Mandela's African National Con-gress, which would become the country's ruling party. Mandela came backstage before the show and eloquently thanked the creative community for its long support of his cause.

While some on the left were using mass communications to advance causes, others had gone into academia and developed a kind of intolerance that soon became easily caricatured by the right as "political correctness." Some feminists spent their moral capital attacking what they defined as pornography in bizarre coali-tions with right-wing Christians, who detested every other feminist agenda. Many campuses adopted codes of conduct banning so-called hate speech, and student groups booed and drowned out cam-pus speakers whose positions they didn't agree with.

"There was a moment in the eighties when people on the left

could have themselves opposed [these] undemocratic excesses," says former Berkeley radical Michael Lerner, who emerged from the Vietnam protest years as an academic, a rabbi, and the editor of the progressive Jewish periodical *Tikkun*. "Instead we all stayed silent and the right was able to coin the phrase and define so-called political correctness, which then became a tool for attacking legitimate concerns about prejudice and inequality."

On the national political stage, Democrats who had a feel for populist communication fell away one by one. Mario Cuomo chose not to run for president. Jesse Jackson could not overcome the resistance of Democratic insiders. And former California governor Jerry Brown, who had run for president in 1976 and 1980, was handily defeated in his 1984 run for the Senate by San Diego mayor Pete Wilson. Brown left the national stage for several years.

Jerry Brown had strong personal connections with pop culture. He dated Linda Ronstadt, and musical stars like the Eagles helped him raise money. Possessed of a contrarian mind and a deep intellectual curiosity about subjects ranging from metaphysics to pest control, Brown, during his two terms as governor, brought many bright and innovative people into state government who wouldn't otherwise have been there.

Ultimately, however, Brown seemed to overintellectualize politics to a degree that turned off many voters who might otherwise have supported him. And he tended to resist the simplification of issues (he would probably call it "oversimplification") required to lead and govern.

The one candidate in the best position to take on Reaganism in 1984—and the one most tuned to pop as well as political culture— was Gary Hart, Democratic senator from Colorado and the former head of George McGovern's presidential campaign. Years later, Hart described his 1984 rationale to me as follows:

"Those of us who were newer members of Congress or newer elected officials in the seventies and early eighties were trying to come up with a set of beliefs, or a set of principles, ideals, policies, and programs, that were true to our liberal heritage but were new in approach and method. Find new ways to redistribute wealth and take care of those at the bottom. And that's what the so-called Campaign of New Ideas was really all about."

Hart sees himself as a forerunner of Bill Clinton, but he also was a forerunner of nontraditional candidates like Ross Perot, Ralph Nader, and John McCain in the sense that he had an enormous impact very quickly because he was perceived as authentic by a mass audience.

Hart recalls, "If I had any talent at all in those days, I think it was not to talk down to people, not to simplify, but to talk up to them. I always found in Colorado and then across the country that the more you engage people in a serious dialogue and debate about the issues of the day, the more they respond to that. The more you treated them as adults—and I mean, here I'm talking about seventeen- and eighteen-year-olds as well as fifty-five-year-olds—the more they responded to that, because most politicians talk down to them."

Hart utilized the services of pollster/consultant Pat Cadell, who helped shape a campaign whose images included high-tech lettering in the graphics on his ads and photo-ops that conveyed youth and energy. The most famous one was of Hart throwing a large axe after winning the New Hampshire primary.

Because of his association with McGovern, Hart had a ready-made group of Hollywood supporters that included Warren Beatty, Shirley MacLaine, Robert Redford, and Jack Nicholson. Hart explains, "[They were] just emerging as the takeover generation in Hollywood in the mid-seventies in the same way my generation was doing it in politics. So I think there was very much a generational component." Musicians such as Carole King and Jimmy Buffett also supported Hart and helped give him a strong identity.

Unfortunately for Hart's media-savvy advisors, their candidate was, if anything, too sincere, too earnest, too reluctant to practice the kind of media manipulation that came so easily to Reagan and later to Clinton. "I think I was different from most politicians," he says. "I did read books. I was interested in a lot of other things; literature, history. I read a lot. The reason the press didn't get it was because I didn't fit their idea of what a politician should be...the key on the typewriter in those days was 'cool and aloof.' But it was [my] basic shyness, really. I just never enjoyed the backslapping and the working-the-room the way a Clinton did."

Hart had no strategy at all to deal with Mondale's "Where's the beef?" attack on his campaign. "He knew I couldn't put [my] new ideas on a bumper strip. And since politics was increasingly in that bumper-strip mode, people like me had difficulty."

The Democratic establishment's media allies chipped away at Hart's personal integrity, labeling him "weird" because he'd shortened his name from Hartpence and listed his birthday a year later than it actually was. (Four years later, of course, it was Hart's personal life that destroyed him as a national candidate.)

Despite Hart's liabilities, he won almost half of the primaries and only lost at the convention because of Mondale's lock on the political insiders.

In retrospect, Hart now says he was wrong to have underestimated the power of the stripped-down political communications strategy of which Ronald Reagan was a master. "I bought the liberal line that Reagan was too dumb to be president. He was able to reduce an entire political philosophy to four or five sentences. 'I'm going to cut your taxes, strengthen the military, stand up to the

Soviets, reduce the size of government.' And those were principles that people could understand. And they were ready for it."

While all this was going on in party politics, the mid-eighties brought an explosion of activism from the music business. In England, Bob Geldof saw a news report on the famine in Ethiopia and quickly organized British musicians to do a benefit recording of his song "Do They Know It's Christmas?" featuring members of U2 and Duran Duran. Michael Jackson and Lionel Richie followed with the massive "We Are the World" benefit, which featured Bruce Springsteen, Cyndi Lauper, and other stars. The next year came the Live Aid concerts, which raised tens of millions of dollars for famine victims.

Willie Nelson and John Mellencamp, moved by the plight of the American family farmer, organized Farm Aid. (Bonnie Raitt participated.) Shortly thereafter, Sting and U2 did a concert tour to raise money for Amnesty International. Popular culture was making enormous contributions to liberal and progressive causes, which were gaining increasing support across the country.

Meanwhile, the Democratic party was backpedaling to the right. The party had no defining leader, and it was divided about the use of military force in what turned out to be the latter stages of the Cold War.

Al Gore was elected to the U.S. Senate in 1984, as Reagan won the presidency over Mondale in a landslide. Despite the "nightmare" of nuclear war he had told me about in Beverly Hills, Gore's campaign speeches in Tennessee proclaimed that America needed to learn the "right" lessons from Vietnam and be willing to intervene militarily when the situation called for it. In early 1985, Gore and a few other Democrats broke with the party's leadership and helped the Republicans gain a majority vote to fund the MX missile, a new nuclear weapons system. So much for Gore's "nightmare."

A few months later, Tipper Gore launched an organization called the Parents Music Resource Center. The PMRC, it seemed to me, threatened almost everything I had worked for and cared about.

**CHAPTER 5**

# 1985

## The Parents Music Resource Center

I N AUGUST OF 1985, an opinion piece condemning "offensive" rock lyrics appeared in the *Newsweek* column "My Way." The authors were Susan Baker, wife of Treasury Secretary James Baker, and Tipper Gore, wife of the recently elected junior senator from Tennessee.

Shortly thereafter, Tipper Gore and Susan Baker went on the *Phil Donahue Show* to unveil an organization they called the Parents Music Resource Center (PMRC), whose board included numerous other wives of prominent politicians. *People* magazine responded with a cover story asking, "Has Rock Gone Too Far?"

The PMRC disclaimed any desire for legislation or government censorship but called on the record industry to create its own panel that would assign ratings similar to those the film industry had established in the 1960s. Popular columnists like Mike Royko and Ann Landers applauded the PMRC, and the group was backed by the National PTA and the American Medical Association. Supporters cited a National Council of Churches study that purportedly showed a "direct causal relationship between violence in the media and aggressive behavior in society."

As far as I can tell, there have never been any studies of the effects of popular music on behavior, so I have to assume that these well-intentioned watchdogs were referring to studies of viewing television, a totally different experience.

The PMRC advocated a lyrics ratings system with categories of X for sexual explicitness, V for violence, D/A for drug or alcohol references, and O for occult references.

There was nothing new about conservatives going after rock music. Indeed, such attacks went back to the very early fifties, even before rock and roll was a well-defined genre. As Eric Nuzum's *Parental Advisory: Music Censorship in America* chronicles, radio stations, prompted by the FCC, banned Dottie O'Brien's "Four or Five Times" and Dean Martin's "Wham Bam, Thank You Ma'am," for being too sexually suggestive in 1951. In 1953, country singer Webb Pierce's "There Stands the Glass" was banned from radio because of supposedly pro-drinking lyrics. About the same time, the Boston Catholic Youth Organization began campaigning to stop airplay of "obscene" songs, and Congresswoman Ruth Thompson, a Republican from Michigan, introduced a bill to ban mailing of "pornographic records."

In 1955, Pat Boone began his career covering and sanitizing R&B hits, changing "drinkin' wine" to "drinkin' Coca-Cola" in T-Bone Walker's blues classic "Stormy Monday," and replacing "Boys don't you know what she do to me?" in Little Richard's "Tutti-Frutti" with "Pretty little Susie is the girl for me." The Juvenile Delinquency and

Crime Commission of Houston, Texas, banned thirty songs—almost all by black artists. The CBS network canceled *Alan Freed's Rock 'n' Roll Dance Party* after R&B singer Frankie Lyman danced with a white girl on the television show.

In 1956, ABC Radio banned Billie Holiday's version of Cole Porter's "Love for Sale" because of its allusions to prostitution. Most famously, in 1957 the top-rated *Ed Sullivan Show* insisted that Elvis Presley be televised above the waist so that America's teens could not see him swiveling his hips.

The attacks continued in the sixties. In one of the silliest antirock campaigns, Indiana governor Matthew Welsh vitriolically attacked the Kingsmen's classic party rocker "Louie Louie" for supposedly conveying obscene messages. A campaign was launched to ban the song. After a long study, including an investigation by the FBI, the FCC concluded that the words were unintelligible and thus not obscene.

In 1967, Doors singer Jim Morrison was arrested for lewd remarks in New Haven. In 1969, police in New York seized 30,000 copies of the John Lennon/Yoko Ono album *Two Virgins*, which had a nude photograph of them on the cover. Later that year the Catholic Diocese of Seattle ran an ad calling for prosecution of rock musicians and for bans of "rock festivals and their drug-sex-rock squalor culture."

In 1970, Vice President Spiro Agnew made his notorious attacks on supposed drug references in the Beatles' "Lucy in the Sky with Diamonds" and "A Little Help from My Friends." Over the next couple of years, prompted by Agnew, the FCC threatened to pull the licenses of stations that played songs that "glorify drugs," without supplying any criteria. In language that would be adopted by liberal politicians in the decades to come, conservative

Republican senator James Buckley wrote a report linking rock to drug use and called for record companies to establish "self-regulation before government takes action."

In 1982, with MTV only a year old, Ronald Reagan's surgeon general, C. Everett Koop, said fans of rock video would probably have trouble "having satisfying relationships with the opposite sex" because they had been "raised with rock music that uses both pornography and violence."

So for thirty years, successive generations of young rock fans understood that conservatives were against them.

But the floodgates of liberal baby-boom resentment over the younger generation's culture were opened by Mrs. Albert Gore. In 1985, Tipper Gore was in her late thirties and was raising four children ranging in age from three to twelve. The wife of a Democratic senator, Tipper legitimized to many liberal baby boomers the snobbish, indeed arrogant, notion that their children were being exposed to music far less moral than the songs they'd grown up with.

The PMRC's list of songs with "offensive" lyrics included Madonna's "Like a Virgin," Prince's "Darling Nikki," which included the line about a girl "masturbating with a magazine," and Cyndi Lauper's "She Bop," with its sly double entendre references to masturbation. The group also attacked heavy metal groups such as Motley Crüe and the rightfully obscure Wasp, whose single "Fuck Like a Beast" had a sleeve that showed a chainsaw between a man's legs. (I couldn't stand the Wasp record myself, and I often gave it as an example of a record I wouldn't want to be involved with but that should be strictly a personal decision in a free society.)

The summer of 1985 had been a slow time for my business. The Gold Mountain management company was just starting. Belinda Carlisle hadn't had her big hit yet. Bonnie Raitt was in between record deals. Nirvana would not come into my life for several years. Gold Mountain Records was struggling along with a brilliant but only moderately successful record from Bruce Cockburn called *Stealing Fire.*

I was thirty-five, and in a bit of a funk. The publicity about the PMRC pushed some button in me. The PMRC seemed to me to be attempting, at the height of Reagan's popularity, to repress popular culture, a culture that reflected an America very different from the one that ruled in Washington. The fact that it was a prominent Democrat's wife who was leading the charge of a bipartisan group made it even more dangerous.

For years, I had argued with friends outside of the music business who persisted in belittling each successive wave of teenage music. Given the incredible opportunities we baby boomers had been given to express ourselves culturally and politically, I was disturbed that so many people my age had so little empathy for younger generations.

To me, songs like Johnny Cash's sixties classic "Folsom Prison Blues," with its famous lyric "I shot a man in Reno just to watch him die," dramatized the absurdity of a rating system for lyrics. So did the violence and the intense sexuality of many classical operas. What criteria could be used?

Washington pressure on entertainers also had echoes of the dark side of the 1950s. Among my parents' best friends when I was growing up was the actor Howard Da Silva, who had been in more than forty movies before 1950. Blacklisted for alleged Communist affiliations—among his accusers, according to FBI files made public in 2002, was Ronald Reagan—he wasn't permitted to work in films again until the late sixties. Da Silva had a philosophical attitude about the blacklist and found ways to earn a living in theater. But he and my parents talked about dozens of talented people who were never able to regain their footing after having been deprived of work because of their political beliefs. Some committed suicide. Others turned on their old friends and "named names" to curry favor with Congressional committees. Any left-wing activity was deemed sympathetic to communism. In truth, there was never any security threat to the United States from anyone in the entertainment business, and by the late 1960s the blacklist was abandoned and discredited, but hundreds of careers had been ruined. I never forgot Da Silva and the blacklisting tragedy.

One of the biggest weapons the PMRC held was the popularity of the film rating system. Film ratings, although criticized by many directors, had, at least, some objective criteria: nudity, sex, violence, gore, and obscene language. Song lyrics, which are often poetic and symbolic, have always been interpreted differently by different people. Many of the most popular lyrics are filled with sarcasm, irony, metaphor, and words used for their sound more than their literal meaning.

I opposed ratings for lyrics for the same reason that publishers would have fiercely resisted any attempt to "rate" their books, newspapers, or magazines. Besides, even for linear uses of language, the only concrete criterion for "rating" words that has ever been developed were the "seven dirty words" that the FCC for a while banned from broadcast. The majority of supposedly objectionable lyrics didn't even contain these words.

The record companies, then as now, were represented in Washington, D.C., by the Record Industry Association of America (RIAA). This was long before the era of the Internet and before extensive pirating of records put the RIAA in the spotlight. It was a sleepy organization that mainly addressed copyright legislation when it came up in Congress and was run by a retired record executive named Stan Gortikov, a sweet, affable man who was clearly blindsided by the attacks on lyrics from senators' wives. I and most people I knew in the business felt Gortikov's early responses were far too conciliatory.

The one voice opposing the Washington Wives, as they were quickly dubbed, was Frank Zappa, legendary rock singer, composer, producer, and cultural icon. Zappa was quotable but in a quirky way, calling the PMRC "a group of bored housewives" who wanted to "housebreak all composers and performers because of the lyrics of a few." While smart and gutsy, Zappa did not frame the issue in mainstream terms.

It seemed to me that this was an issue on which most Americans would disagree with the pundits and politicians. Attacks on art and entertainment reflected on the personal choices of millions of Americans. The real energy behind the attacks focused not on the themes or the lyrics but on the songs' supposedly lowbrow aesthetics. Critics were objecting to four-letter words, to coarse expression, to bad taste. But America was the home of "bad taste": Las Vegas, Burt Reynolds movies, soap operas, Evel Knievel, Liberace, and rock and roll (rap was not to emerge as mass culture for another year or two). The PMRC wasn't going after avant-garde poetry and art, they were going after the heart and soul of Middle America.

As I saw it, the whole culture that I was a part of was at risk. In my mind, there could be no Bruce Springsteen if heavy metal lyrics were repressed. And once censorship began, where would it end? You never knew when cheap shoot-'em-up western movies would evolve into the majestic works of John Ford; the same musical genre that had inspired "Louie Louie" and "Splish Splash" had nourished the works of Bob Dylan and John Lennon. As it turned out, most of the artists who joined me in fighting back, like Don Henley of the Eagles, were not themselves under attack but felt the same way I did. It was as if the creative oxygen of every artist were intermixed, and any intimidation of one artist would narrow the field of "acceptable" content for all artists.

Marge Tabankin arranged for me to meet with Ira Glasser, executive director of the American Civil Liberties Union. He had taken over the post in 1978 and revitalized the ACLU during a time when many other progressive organizations declined in membership and influence, building it up to 300,000 members with affiliates in all fifty states.

A native of Brooklyn who still mourned the departure of the Dodgers, Glasser, then in his early fifties, was robust, dynamic, and well-muscled from regular playground basketball games. Unlike most ACLU staffers, Glasser himself is not a lawyer. He has a down-to-earth manner and can translate complex legal ideas into ordinary language. He turned out to be the perfect partner for me in the upcoming battles, and our first meeting led to a long friendship and working relationship.

I told him I wanted to create a committee called the Musical Majority, a takeoff on Falwell's Moral Majority. The name struck a spark with Glasser, as did the implication that most Americans didn't want regulation of popular music. He agreed on the spot that I could claim an affiliation with the ACLU.

I flew back to Los Angeles and starting making phone calls. Within a few days I had a list of supporters—personal managers, artists, radio programmers, and PR people, among others, including the leading music PR guys Mitchell Schneider and Howard Bloom.

Artists involved directly or indirectly via their representatives included Tina Turner, Cyndi Lauper, Don Johnson, Don Henley, Chicago, Prince, Lionel Ritchie, Dolly Parton, The Pointer Sisters, John Cougar Mellencamp, and members of the rock bands Duran Duran and Kiss.

In the press release announcing our formation, I announced

myself as Chairman of the newly formed group and I gave the following portentous quotes: "With all due respect to the RIAA, I've talked to a cross section of some of the leading figures in our business and we're sick and tired of every extremist that wants to get their name in the papers using rock as a whipping boy. American music is one of the best goodwill ambassadors our country has. Anywhere you go in the world, people love American music. We empathize with parents who want their children to grow up in a better world and are concerned about outside influences. Labeling or rating records, however, will do nothing to remedy this problem but will cause greater problems, imposing an atmosphere of censorship on the creative community. It will interfere with a free marketplace. It will erode the First Amendment. It will damage two of the most wonderful American traditions: freedom of expression and music."

No record company executives would or could add their names because the companies were all divisions of bigger entities with strict corporate policies limiting executives' freedom to comment on controversial matters.

On September 13, 1985, a front-page story in *Variety* read:

MUSICAL MAJORITY FORMED TO COUNTER ATTEMPTS
AT IMPOSING DISK WARNINGS
A major counter-offensive to attempts to impose "obscenity" ratings on recorded musical product has been launched, with the formation of the Musical Majority, a committee of artists, managers, publishers, publicists, and other industry figures.

Formation of the group comes in the wake of concessions by the Recording Industry Association of America representing all the major labels to demands made by the Parents Resource Center for detailed labeling/warnings on records and tapes.

"By marshalling the music community, Musical Majority hopes to reach out to the generations under 40 years of age which have grown up with rock music and thereby demonstrate that we define the majority in a positive way," Goldberg told *Daily Variety*.

The story, to my amazement, included all my quotes from the press releases and concluded with five paragraphs listing artists, programmers, agents, managers, PR people and others in the music business who supported us. Either it was a slow news day or someone at *Variety* agreed with us.

The next day, I got calls from several TV shows and wire services. I had become a source for sound bites. I quickly developed a new interest—in being quoted and being seen on TV. I had a whole new identity that made me more interesting to journalists, politicos, and artists. Publicity is an intoxicating drug, and based on my own experience, I never analyze the motivations of an advocate without taking into consideration the sheer attachment to visibility that coexists with political conviction in even the purest heart.

On September 19, the Senate Commerce, Science and Transportation Committee, of which Al Gore was a member, held a hearing on rock lyrics. In my new role as a spokesman for free speech, I attended with Barry Lynn, then executive director of the Washington, D.C., ACLU.

The vast, stately hearing room, which had been used for some of the Watergate testimony, was intimidating. It was packed with several hundred spectators, most of them with press badges. In front was a long row of TV cameras, their bright lights darting off the massive crystal chandeliers, signaling a full-fledged media event.

I had hurriedly run off several hundred copies of our press release denouncing the hearings. Ira Glasser had given us a quote with the appropriate civil liberties gravitas:

"It is highly improper, and we think unconstitutional, for the Congress to be making an inquiry into the content of published material with a view toward classifying it or regulating that content by legislation, and legislation is the only reason to hold a hearing. What they are doing is using the threat of legislation to force voluntary compliance."

Anticipating the constitutional problems, Senator John Danforth, the Republican committee chairman, quickly made it clear that he contemplated no legislation. Instead, he said, the hearings were "providing a forum to air what is a real problem."

The primary spokesman for the PMRC was the Reverend Jeff Ling, who identified himself as a former rock musician. Ling quoted lines out of context from the songs of various metal bands. When he got to AC/DC, he reminded the committee that "one of their fans" was accused serial murderer Richard Ramirez.

But the TV cameras were there for the rock stars. After Frank Zappa called the proposed ratings system "the equivalent of treating dandruff by decapitation," Senator James Exon, a Nebraska Democrat, questioned why there should be a hearing in the first place since no legislation was likely. I grunted encouragingly, but Barry Lynn cautioned that Exon was mercurial. A few minutes later, Exon barked at the music people there, "Clean up your act."

We did not know why John Denver was called, and I was dreading that he might side with the PMRC. Instead, the earnest, apple-cheeked, middle-of-the-road balladeer became the most powerful witness against a ratings system.

Denver told the senators that his early-seventies song "Rocky Mountain High," a clearly inoffensive paean to nature and clean living, had been irrationally banned by several radio stations whose management had decided the song was about getting high on drugs. A few years later, several newspapers had refused to carry advertising for Denver's equally inoffensive film comedy Oh God because they thought it was blasphemous. Even the most innocuous entertainment can be misinterpreted, Denver said. That's why he did not want any organization, created by the record industry or anyone else, to have the power to interpret and label artistic work.

Senator Gore told Denver that he admired his music. He had said much the same thing to Zappa. Then he was confronted by Dee Snider, lead singer of Twisted Sister. Snider, with his frizzed-out hair and black tank top, looked like many parents' rock and roll nightmare, but he quickly identified himself as a father and a Christian who didn't smoke, drink, or do drugs.

As Gore began questioning Snider, the heavy metal rocker slyly interjected a question of his own. Was Gore going to say he admired Twisted Sister's music as well?

"No, I'm not," Gore replied sternly and then asked Snider for the name of the group's fan club.

"SMF Friends of Twisted Sister," rasped Snider in his tough-sounding New York accent. Eyes gleaming with prosecutorial zeal, Gore asked Snider what the letters SMF stood for, and nodded self-righteously when Snider answered, with appropriate rock and roll panache, "Sick Mother Fucking." Looking satisfied at having unmasked a sinner, Gore sarcastically asked, "Is that a Christian group?" But Snider had the last word, snapping back, "Christianity has nothing to do with profanity."

Later, when the video of Twisted Sister's "We're Not Gonna Take It Anymore" was played as an example of the horrors teenagers were subjected to, I applauded, along with several musicians in the room. Danforth solemnly insisted that the audience maintain its decorum.

The song is a classic antiauthority anthem, and the video was the fantasy of a young teenage boy berated by a domineering father. The kid finally "can't take it anymore" and wreaks havoc. Demonizing such an inoffensive piece of teen kitsch (the music video contained no spillage of blood, no guns, no nudity, and no profanity) was the kind of overreaching that consistently hurt the PMRC.

Stan Gortikov did the best he could fielding questions from senators on behalf of the major record companies, but he seemed pretty ineffectual and almost apologetic in debate. The job of the Musical Majority, as I saw it, was keeping pressure on the record companies not to cave.

A week or so later, a PMRC staffer remarked in an interview that Bruce Springsteen's song "I'm on Fire" was too sexually suggestive to be appropriate for young children. "Even Bruce isn't clean," she said. We immediately placed the quote in our press kit. It was a lot easier to defend Bruce Springsteen than Motley Crüe.

Although no members of Congress were interested in opposing the PMRC, Los Angeles mayor Tom Bradley on September 30 held a press conference with me and a few other Musical Majority members. Bradley, who was in his second term as the first African American mayor of Los Angeles, had begun his long career in city government as a police officer. Well over six feet tall, with broad shoulders and an affable if somewhat impenetrable personality, Bradley seemed to me like a local antidote to President Reagan. He heartily welcomed us and made us feel that people in the music business had a defender. I did not realize at the time how rare such political support for the music business and for free speech would be.

Mayor Bradley spoke about what a good time he'd had at a Springsteen concert at the LA Forum a few nights earlier, and then asked, "What do Elvis Presley and Bruce Springsteen have in common? Both have been targets of a small group of people who want to impose their standards on all American families. Fortunately, would-be censors have lost nearly every round against popular music.

"The people who have joined me today represent a multibillion-dollar industry that has been quick to respond to those in need," Bradley said, referring to the recent Live Aid and Farm Aid concerts. "Now they need our help to stop this crazy notion that by rating records we can somehow protect our children from the evils of the world."

Bradley emphasized, "We can and must protect children, but that is a role best filled by concerned parents, not by government. Parents must regulate what their children see, hear, and read, whether it is a movie, a record, or a book. If a small group of people are allowed to dictate what we can hear, how about what we read? If tens of thousands of records should be rated each year, why not a similar standard on books? The very idea is repugnant."

The speech delighted the small group of supporters I had brought to the press conference, including Kim Carnes, who was coming off a huge number one record, "Bette Davis Eyes," Duran Duran's Andy Taylor, and most significant, Irving Azoff, then-president and CEO of MCA Music, a dominant company in the recording business. Azoff announced that MCA would not participate in any record-ratings scheme, effectively dooming any system that would include movie-style rankings.

One evening, Jimmy Iovine, who had produced the Stevie Nicks albums, invited me to one of his recording sessions for Bob Seger. I was a huge Seger fan and was thrilled to be there and hear the Detroit superstar deliver his trademark, scratchy-throated, soulful vocals. A few weeks later, Seger asked if he could come play me his new album.

Seger has "delivery anxiety," not uncommon among recording artists, and likes to play his records for sympathetic ears before giving them to the record company. The friendly, bearded Michigan rock pillar arrived at my rented Laurel Canyon house the next afternoon and played me *Like a Rock*, the title song of which would have a second life in innumerable TV commercials for Chevrolet trucks.

I particularly liked "American Storm," one of those rare rock songs with a direct message, in this case a scathing indictment of the cocaine abuse that had ravaged Seger's generation of rock musicians. "That's the best antidrug song I ever heard," I enthused. Seger looked at me sadly and said, "I don't think I'm gonna put it on the album. You know it's an antidrug song and I know it's an antidrug song, but what if the people who want to sticker records don't know it's an antidrug song, and then I won't be able to get my album into most of the stores."

Not long before, the equally commercial Midwestern rock band Styx had been attacked by a religious group, who wrongly thought that an anti-cocaine song called "Snow Blind" encouraged drug use. I assured Bob that the attacks were not remotely likely to affect him. Seger, with his romantic, bittersweet references to "old-time rock and roll," was exactly the kind of rock star the Tipper Gores of the world were likely to embrace. Seger left the song on the album, and as I predicted, it created no controversy. However the fact that a multimillionaire mainstream rocker like Seger would feel threatened by record labeling struck me as exactly the kind of hidden damage that could come from the attacks on rock music. If Bob Seger felt uncertain and inhibited and contemplated censoring himself, how would a powerless, broke, unsigned artist feel?

About that time, I was invited to debate Susan Baker on the Washington talk show *Panorama*. In the Washington TV studio I found my adversary intimidatingly well dressed, with impeccably coiffed hair, tasteful make-up, and breathtaking southern charm.

I did not want to fit the rock and roll stereotype. Wearing a conservative pinstripe suit and couching my arguments in terms of preserving cherished American traditions, I empathized with all parents concerned about raising their kids but stressed the Musical Majority's main points:

1. Entertainment is not like soup. The ingredients can't be listed and judged in an objective fashion. Different people and different families have different views of appropriate language.
2. Parents in the fifties were worried about the exact same issues as parents in the eighties. Everyone knew that Elvis Presley wanted to be more to a girl than merely her Teddy Bear. The distinction between the songs of the two eras was cosmetic, on the surface, not substantive.
3. Even though many who were concerned about popular music in the eighties were moderates, it was inevitable that the politicization of culture would empower right-wing culture critics. This was already evident in the call for an "O" rating for occult lyrics, which seemed inspired by specific conservative Christian groups.

The fun of this argument for a longtime lefty like myself was that, for a change, we were defending the status quo instead of attacking it.

*People* magazine's "Has Rock Gone Too Far?" story, with its pro-PMRC slant, had generated 2,035 letters—the most in the twelve-year history of the magazine. In its November 4 issue, *People* noted that 90 percent of the mail had been critical of the magazine for seeming to support censorship. And Ann Landers, the Middle American icon of sensible adult advice, had gotten 20,000 letters opposing the linkage in her column of popular music with drug abuse and teen suicide.

*People* referred to the Musical Majority as "the most prominent counter-offensive" to the PMRC and ran a full-page photo of me and the seven supporters I was able to round up one Tuesday after-

noon to rush over to my office. They included Alan Arkush, director of many of the *Fame* episodes, singer Michael Des Barres, R&B
producer Ollie Brown, and Donny Osmond. Like John Denver,
Osmond had extra value because of the inoffensive mass appeal of
his oeuvre.

I thanked Osmond, who I assumed had run over merely at the
direction of his voluble PR guy, Norman Winter, but it turned out
that the singer was quite focused in his opposition to ratings.
"We're Mormons," he said of his family, "and we were always
under attack from one Christian group or another. I would never
want people like that to have any say over what I do."

The "consensus" that was so clear in Washington truly didn't
exist in the rest of the country. For me, the best part of the *People*
magazine article was a quote from AC/DC's Angus Young, who to
this day I've never met. He said, "People who want to strangle
other people's rights are possessed by one of the worst devils
around, the Satan in their souls, which is called intolerance. Rock
and roll is about one simple thing, freedom. When someone tries
to murder freedom, we're against it."

In November, San Antonio passed a law banning unaccompa-
nied children under the age of fourteen from concerts or other
theatrical presentations that "constitute obscene performances."
The ordinance included a number of specific topics that were
defined as "obscene to a child," ranging from "bestial sexual relations" to "vulgar or indecent reference to sexual intercourse,
excretory functions of the body, or male or female genitals." The
law was championed and signed by the mayor of San Antonio,
Henry Cisneros, a rising star in the Democratic party.

The law presumed that the Supreme Court standard for
obscenity did not apply to minors. Kids under the age of fourteen
were permitted at so-called obscene concerts if they were accom-

panied by a parent or legal guardian, but the prospect of young teens having to drag a parent to a hard rock show, and of parents having to document their relationship with their kids at the door, significantly dampened attendance at concerts by KISS, Motley Crüe, and AC/DC.

The leading promoter in San Antonio, Jack Orbin, enlisted the Texas ACLU to fight the law, which was eventually overturned. But the San Antonio law demonstrated the slippery slope laid down by the PMRC. Even though the group insisted that it opposed federal legislation, its stigmatizing of lyrics had led to local legislation. And San Antonio was the first of dozens of jurisdictions around the country that tried to throw legal roadblocks between teen entertainment and its fans.

The first week of November, the PMRC and the RIAA announced a compromise. There would be no ratings system, but each record company would place "parental advisory" stickers on albums it thought warranted them. I decided to declare victory while holding my nose. None of the artists who'd supported the Musical Majority wanted to fight against all of the big record companies, and neither, at that point, did I.

"On one hand, the PMRC backed down considerably from their original position," I told the LA Times. "On the other hand, I think it's a terrible mistake to have compromised with these people at all. It's like compromising with terrorists. These people are cultural terrorists and I'm worried that the industry will live to regret any agreement which lends credence to right-wing pressure elements operating in the guise of a parents' organization."

Irving Azoff of MCA also tried to have it both ways: "I have no problems as long as judging what is explicit is left up to each record company," he said, and added slyly: "Then it would be fair to assume that any label which cares about the First Amendment could honor this agreement and not find any lyrics that were objectionable, couldn't they?" (As a practical matter, MCA would do the same thing as the other record companies—put stickers on albums with dirty words.)

Bob Merlis of Warner Bros. put his finger on the eternal issue of interpretation: "What we might view as oblique, the PMRC may see as explicit. They've put Madonna's current hit 'Dress You Up' on their Top Offenders list. Now, we can't figure out what evil thoughts they see here. I guess you can say that filth is in the ear of the beholder."

The week after the settlement, Frank Zappa released an album called *Frank Zappa versus the Mothers of Prevention*. It included the song "Porn Wars," which featured excerpts of comments by Gore and other senators at the ratings hearings. A couple of weeks later, somewhat anticlimactically, I finally met Tipper Gore in person in San Francisco on a local TV talk show. Since the PMRC no longer had any demands, and was supposedly happy with the RIAA compromise, all we could do was rehash the arguments we had previously made. I once again cautioned that demonizing rock lyrics could be used to promote conservative agendas.

During a commercial break, Mrs. Gore turned to me with what seemed like genuine bewilderment. "Why do you keep saying we're conservative?" she asked. "My husband and I are liberal Democrats." That led to a remarkably frank and interesting discussion of Democratic politics and of what I saw as the abandonment of a progressive agenda. I didn't back away from my position, but I found her very likable, surprisingly open, and vulnerable. It also became obvious that Tipper Gore loved being on TV as much as I did.

This was six years before her husband was elected Vice President of the United States. She was just one of hundreds of congressional wives. Rock lyrics had gotten Tipper on TV, and Tipper had gotten me on TV. Now that the compromise had been made, I assumed that Tipper would soon be out of my life, and that the controversy would quickly wither away. It didn't turn out that way.

CHAPTER 6

# The Late Eighties

GOLD MOUNTAIN finally came into its own as a management company in 1987, when Bonnie Raitt won four Grammys, including the award for Album of the Year, for *Nick of Time*. That album eventually sold more than 4 million copies, and her next album, *Luck of the Draw*, sold more than 5 million, so Bonnie's so-called comeback was far more successful than her first time around. Unlike some artists of her generation, she never backed away from her strong political beliefs—indeed, her high political visibility and clearly sincere commitment to ideals shared by millions probably made her a bigger star.

Around the same time, two other Gold Mountain artists had significant success. Belinda Carlisle had a number one hit with "Heaven Is a Place on Earth," and Alannah Myles went to number one with "Black Velvet." We also got the opportunity to manage a couple of musical legends: the great rock and roll tenor Roy Orbison, who had not made a record in nineteen years, and the reunited Allman Brothers Band.

The Allman Brothers Band, with its deep and vital southern roots and its instrumental virtuosity, gave me some of the best evenings of music I have ever had. Dickie Betts's guitar improvisations merged blues, rock and roll, and jazz in a way no one else has ever done, and Gregg Allman's husky voice is a virtually perfect vehicle for the blues. The members of the band had a spiritual and intuitive connection with one another that came through passionately in their music, like the Grateful Dead at their best.

Gold Mountain also picked up Pat Benatar, with whom I worked closely, and I began managing record producer David Foster. Our first project together was Natalie Cole's *Unforgettable, With Love*, which went on to win multiple Grammys.

Many of the artists I worked with in the mid- and late eighties were recovering alcoholics and drug addicts. California attorney general John Van De Kamp approached me to produce antidrug public service TV spots with musical stars and provided a $25,000 grant, which Pepsi-Cola matched. With directors and most crews donating their services, we were able to produce around a dozen spots.

MTV agreed to broadcast the spots, as it had aired the voter registration spots several years earlier. Gene Simmons of KISS did a spot with monster makeup that later won a prestigious advertising award. Bon Jovi, then America's biggest rock band, let us shoot on the set of its music video for "Living on a Prayer," where we did a commercial that included the ambiguous line "Drugs are not a part of my everyday life."

Michael Des Barres, my longtime client and friend, suggested calling the campaign Rock Against Drugs. Comedian Sam Kinison later took a shot at the name, cracking that it was like calling an organization "Christians Against Christ," but the vast majority of teens at MTV focus groups were comfortable with the spots, which were less preachy and more accessible than conventional antidrug commercials.

Politically, I became involved in early 1987 with Senator Gary Hart's campaign for the 1988 Democratic presidential nomination. Mike Medavoy, president of Orion Pictures, had been one of Hart's key campaign officials in 1984. In anticipation of the 1988 campaign, his wife, Patricia, put together numerous events at their Beverly Hills home to introduce Hollywood people to Hart.

A stunning blonde beauty even by Hollywood standards, Patricia was an accessible and skillful organizer and schmoozer with a solid political background—she had previously worked in Washington as an aide to Senator Chris Dodd. Hart was delighted by the help, not only because of the funds raised but also because of the visibility the entertainment business could give him both nationally and locally—Los Angeles was the biggest population center in the key primary state of California.

One afternoon I sat at lunch with Barbra Streisand, director Paul Mazursky, and others from Hollywood and listened to Senator Hart hold forth on an array of domestic and international issues. I was inspired by Hart's courage in criticizing defense policy and in envisioning an end to the Cold War—attacking the defense establishment and the nuclear status quo had for some time been considered political suicide for national candidates. Hart had met with Soviet leader Mikhail Gorbachev and was convinced that a major de-escalation in the arms race could come soon. The senator articulated well-reasoned proposals for the reallocation of money the United States was spending on arms to domestic priorities.

It didn't hurt with our group that Hart also seemed extremely interested in art and entertainment. He talked to Mazursky about the role of movies in creating political mythology. "If you were ever portrayed in a film, who would you envision playing you? Clint Eastwood?" asked Mazursky.

Without a moment's pause, Hart shook his head and said, "Sam Shepard." For better or for worse, this was a subject to which Hart had clearly given some thought.

Streisand seemed particularly impressed by his views on foreign policy and agreed to support Hart, as did I. Almost immediately, I found myself in meetings with Hart's campaign staff, and for a few months I had the heady pleasure of contributing ideas and energy to a campaign for someone we all thought would be the next president.

The illusion came crashing down in May of 1987 when Hart was caught with a young woman named Donna Rice. (As it happened, I had met Donna Rice several months earlier in Miami when Don Johnson was recording his first album and she was hanging around the studio, looking available.)

I found Hart to be very intelligent, thoughtful, and a great listener; he also had a sharp wit. Once in Denver, when I was in a group helping him prepare for a televised debate, one of his young aides asked him, "What do you say if Al Gore asks you if there's ever been a time when you disagreed with a position taken by the AFL-CIO?"

Hart stared into space for a moment and then said, "How about if I just say, 'Al—I don't like your smug face'?"

Years later, when I interviewed Hart for this book I asked him about his relationship with Warren Beatty, who I heard him refer to as "the pro." Campaign staff had said that Hart sought Beatty's advice before television appearances. "I learned a lot from Warren about things like staging and public relations," Hart recalled. "But the most significant thing I'd say about Warren is that he is a real friend. When people think you might be president, everyone wants to be your friend, but over the years I have found that Warren has been completely consistent in a way, frankly, that most of my Washington friends have not."

I still feel that were it not for the Donna Rice scandal, Hart could have fashioned a Democratic victory over George Bush in 1988. He had some of the same notions about recasting the party's image as Bill Clinton four years later. Hart was a more committed progressive than Clinton, although, alas, he obviously was not as resourceful a politician. He has a piercing intellect that has never settled for conventional wisdom, and his departure from the national scene was a great loss. After the terrible acts of September 11, 2001, it was recalled that less than a year earlier, Hart and former Republican senator Warren Rudman had warned after a lengthy bipartisan study that America was perilously vulnerable to a major terrorist attack.

After Hart left the race, Patricia Medavoy helped create Show Coalition to keep people in the entertainment business informed about politics. I and many other Hart supporters joined, and we quickly arranged meetings with other Democratic candidates. But I was tiring of receptions where politicians traded their canned remarks for money and visibility. I didn't see what difference I could make this way.

I was rescued by my mentor Stanley Sheinbaum. Stanley was then in his late sixties, with a long gray beard that gave him the affect of an Old Testament patriarch. A well-established member of the Hollywood liberal elite, he had been appointed to the Board of Regents of the University of California by Governor Jerry Brown and was an influential critic of the university's nuclear research program. Stanley also published the *New Perspective Quarterly*, a well-respected political journal, and had intellectual and political contacts all over the world.

In the early 1970s, Stanley had become the principal fund-raiser for the defense of Daniel Ellsberg in his trials for releasing the secret Pentagon Papers, which damned government policy in Vietnam. The experience left him with a lasting commitment to due process. Stanley then became chair of the American Civil Liberties Union Foundation of Southern California, whose significant supporters included such Hollywood luminaries as Burt Lancaster (one of Stanley's predecessors as chair), Sidney Poitier, Gregory Peck, and Barbra Streisand. With Executive Director Ramona Ripston and others in Stanley's orbit, they had helped transform a nearly bankrupt ACLU affiliate into the best funded and staffed in the nation.

I was surprised and delighted when Stanley suggested I become the new Southern California ACLU Foundation chair: "If you're serious about doing things, there's nothing like it. You have a constituency of twenty-five thousand members and it gets you into most of the issues you care about." He paused and peered at me shrewdly through his thick spectacles before he hooked me with, "Of course, it means that you're always gonna be a bit outside the political mainstream, but at least you'll stand for something."

Rosemary Carroll, my fiancée at the time, had a dim view of Hollywood meetings with politicians but was very enthusiastic about the ACLU, reinforcing my own instincts. I hastily accepted. My only bona fides, other than my battles with Tipper Gore, were Stanley's and Ramona Ripston's belief in me. But the board had absolute belief in them, so in 1987, I became chair of the ACLU Foundation of Southern California.

Among the most committed ACLU board members were Alan and Marilyn Bergman, who had written many songs recorded by Barbra Streisand, including "The Way We Were." Marilyn was one of Barbra's most trusted advisors on political matters and had helped form the Hollywood Women's Political Committee a few years earlier. Alan and Marilyn were steeped in traditional song-writing—indeed, they are acknowledged to be the masters of the form, having won many Oscars, Grammys, and other songwriting awards. They detested rock and roll and found rap barely deserving of being called music, but they never wavered in the ACLU's defense of free speech in those genres, any more than they wavered when the organization defended the rights of Nazis to march.

Much of the work of the Southern California ACLU involved the treatment of minorities and the powerless. The organization had successfully sued to get an Orange County schoolteacher's job back after he'd been fired for having AIDS. It helped monitor conditions in local jails and children's facilities and handled more appeals of the death penalty than any other California organization.

The ACLU represented racial minorities who had grievances with the local police, hardly an insignificant matter in Los Angeles at that time. Police Chief Daryl Gates had a particularly bad relationship with the African American community. After more than a dozen black men (and no white ones) had been killed by LA policemen using chokeholds, Gates denied that there was any racial prejudice in the application of the choke hold but speculated that the neck arteries of blacks were more sensitive to pressure than those of whites. The ACLU fought Gates and his increasingly notorious department through much of the eighties and early nineties.

After Gary Hart dropped out of the presidential race, Senator Al Gore started making overtures to Hollywood about his own recently announced candidacy for president, and one day I got a call from Mike Medavoy asking me to meet Gore at his house. "You're both friends of mine," said the avuncular Medavoy, "and you should be friends with each other."

We met in Medavoy's home on Coldwater Canyon Drive, a relatively modest place by mogul standards, but a sunny, comfortable

Beverly Hills home with plenty of rooms to get lost in. After making us comfortable and offering drinks, Mike retreated to his study. If things went well, he'd get the credit; if they didn't, he didn't want either of us mad at him. Accompanying Gore was Peter Knight, then Gore's chief of staff and later the campaign chairman for the Clinton-Gore reelection effort in 1996. Mrs. Gore did not attend.

The senator looked uncomfortable. Elected officials do a lot of ass-kissing to get where they are, but it must have been particularly galling for him to be meeting with a mid-level rock manager to deal with his wife's "issue." Presumably, he'd been convinced that meeting with me would make him look like a mensch in the eyes of other possible Hollywood supporters. The strain of the effort showed.

"One thing I wanted to bring up, before we get into the other issues," he began, "is that you had said in an interview that I wasn't really for arms control because I voted for the MX missile." Gore was referring to a remark I made in the *Village Voice* in an article about Tipper. "There was a nuance there that you don't understand," he said in that stiff, professorial voice that years later would be fodder for late-night television comedians. "This was a bargaining chip to prevent an even bigger weapons system."

Gore spoke in a pained tone that suggested there were subtleties in government that mere mortals couldn't understand. I shrugged my shoulders. I was certainly not going to start arguing with him about nuclear weapons. Why he would care what a rock manager said about the subject in the *Village Voice* was beyond me.

Gore then addressed the "Tipper" issue. "She's very sincere about this," he said, "but she's not on some kind of crusade." Gore said he regretted the Senate hearing two years before and stressed that he envisioned no future hearings. "The point was to create awareness," he said.

We talked for about a half an hour, exchanging platitudes, and Gore said he had to go to the airport. He and Knight took me up on my offer to drive them there, and once we were in the car, and the awkwardness of the "meeting" was over, the conversation became more animated. "Come on," I said, "don't you remember being a teenager and laughing at Spiro Agnew when he said the Beatles were causing people to take drugs?" Gore answered, "What about 'I get high with a little help from my friends'?" He drew out the word "high."

I told him that I'd taken a lot of drugs in the sixties, but I also thought of "A Little Help from My Friends" as a song about friendship. Gore laughed skeptically, but I was being serious. I launched into a monologue about the positive value of music and the mysteries of the subconscious as it related to music.

"I believe deeply in God," I said, about to connect the Beatles song with a positive spirituality.

"You do?" interrupted Gore, sounding amazed. I felt that it was Gore's single unguarded moment with me that afternoon, one that revealed the unvarnished truth of his assumptions about me and my world. It was as if he thought that someone in rock and roll, someone who would oppose his wife's noble efforts, couldn't possibly believe in the same God he did. His words hung in the air while we both realized that his revelation of genuine surprise was just too real for a friendly ride to the airport, and we resumed our light banter, staying away from the subject of Tipper Gore.

But Tipper remained a presence in my life and in the news.

Her *Raising PG Kids in an X-rated World* would soon be published. I was mentioned in it inoffensively a couple of times, but I had serious problems with many other parts of the book. She repeated the PMRC habit of lumping mainstream artists with more extreme ones. I was particularly disturbed by an attack on pop singer Sheena Easton, whom I was co-managing at the time. The book also regurgitated propaganda linking rock with the occult that obviously had come from right-wing Christians like the Reverend Jeff Ling. I was surprised that the rhetoric wasn't more muted, coming from a senator's wife who hoped someday soon to be the First Lady.

In the back of *Raising PG Kids*, an appendix listed sympathetic organizations parents could contact. The list included Back in Control, an Orange County organization run by ex-parole officer Gregg Bodenhamer who claimed to "de-program" teenagers from the evils of heavy metal music. I had debated Bodenhamer on *CBS Morning News* when he first started his organization and found him to be as hostile and humorless off-camera as on.

In a piece about the Tipper book for the *B'nai B'rith Messenger*, a long-established and respected LA Jewish weekly, journalist Phyllis Pollack revealed that Back in Control published a handbook listing the Jewish star as an "occult symbol." The piece, headlined "Presidential Candidate's Strange Ties," had this devastating lead: "Tipper Gore, wife of recently announced Democratic candidate Sen. Albert Gore of Tennessee, has ties with a Southern California group that claims the Star of David is a symbol of the devil."

Tipper Gore and the fruits of her campaign against rock and roll seemed to pop up everywhere in my life in those days. Our ACLU chapter was defending the punk rock group the Dead Kennedys in LA against obscenity charges—their album *Frankenchrist* included a poster by H. R. Giger that depicted penises. Our lawyers eventually beat the charge, but the group spent so much time and money on the case that they and their independent record label, Alternative Tentacles, never really recovered. (The prosecutor in the Dead Kennedys case, incidentally, was City Attorney James Hahn, another Democrat and a future mayor of Los Angeles.)

For a story that appeared in *Musician Magazine*, writer Charles M. Young asked Mrs. Gore about the case, in light of her repeated statements that she was opposed to government censorship. "I'm not going to defend or attack the Dead Kennedys," Tipper replied.

Like me, Young "found Tipper difficult to dislike on a personal level," but added, "there is something eerie about her as there is with almost everyone connected with the national government...she might as well have been on Mars during the sixties." Bizarrely, she told Young that the sixties was a time when there was more music that "parents and children could enjoy together." Young got no response when he pointed out that the most influential album of the 1967 "Summer of Love," *Sergeant Pepper*, included a song about a girl running away from her parents, and the next most important album, *The Doors*, featured "The End," a twelve-minute song about a son killing his father.

In late October 1987, I joined other entertainment executives to meet with Al and Tipper Gore over lunch at Universal Studios. Included in the group were Norman Lear; Irving Azoff of MCA, a key figure in the record-labeling compromise; Michael Mann, a film director who also was the executive producer of *Miami Vice*, which was at the peak of its popularity; and several lawyers from Manatt, Phelps & Phillips, including Gore's friend Mickey Kantor. The only musician in attendance was singer/songwriter Don Henley of the Eagles.

Tipper Gore quickly adapted a conciliatory tone, calling the 1985 Commerce Committee hearing "a mistake that sent the wrong message."

She said, "We sent the message that there's going to be censorship and that's clearly not the case. I am not for government intervention. I am not for legislation." Her husband elaborated, saying that as a humble minority-party freshman senator he had been in no position to stop the proceedings. "I did not ask for the hearing," he said. "I was not in favor of the hearing." He suggested, much as he had a few months earlier in defending his vote for the MX missile, that he had helped neutralize the Republicans, who would have done something far more drastic if left to their own devices.

He then defended his wife's crusade.

Even I, who detested the crusade, could feel some sympathy for a husband defending his wife. I could see clearly, as I had when we met privately, that he cared deeply for her—one of his most attractive qualities. My sympathy ended, however, as he recycled the notion that parents were "outraged about trends in popular culture." How could he imagine that he could speak for all parents?

I reiterated my belief that opposing legal censorship, as the Gores said they did, didn't deal with the chilling effect that came down when public officials (and their wives) jawboned the entertainment industry. And I objected to a typical catchall passage from Tipper's book in which she listed Sheena Easton with artists who sang about such subjects as "masturbation, intercourse, and sexual sadism." I indignantly asked why the sexually suggestive "Sugar Walls" was linked with sadism. I was not just defending my client but attacking the strong tendency of the book and the PMRC to make sweeping and generalized attacks that lumped eroticism with sadism and did not differentiate between pop romantics and the most in-your-face heavy metal acts.

Henley agreed. "'Sugar Walls' is the highest form of innuendo," he said. "Sometimes I write songs that have three or four different meanings. Who is qualified to interpret those lyrics? Who on a panel is going to say 'this is what you meant'? And what if they're wrong?"

When the topic turned to television, Michael Mann made what I thought was the most interesting observation of the day. "It seems to me that there are three types of TV violence," he said. "There's cartoon violence, which is what we all grew up with where you see a bad guy getting killed very neatly with no blood. There are realistic depictions of violence, which is what we try to do on *Miami Vice*. And there's the kind of psychic violence of something like the *Cosby Show*, in which the audience is made to feel that every American family has a big nice house and a Cuisinart. What about the alienation that poor people feel [because] no one who looks like them or lives like them is ever on TV?"

Tipper Gore avoided the premise of the question, but did say she was sometimes disturbed by *Miami Vice* and gave a general exhortation for less TV violence.

Newspaper reports of the meeting mentioned Gore's attempts to distance himself from the Commerce Committee record-industry hearing. A staffer for Senator John Danforth, the Republican chairman of the committee, was outraged. He directed a reporter at *Daily Variety* to passages from the *Congressional Record* transcript of the hearing that showed Gore had been one of its primary advocates. The resulting detailed story was headlined "Records Show Gore Backed Hearing."

The meeting at Universal is mentioned in several biographies of Al Gore as an example of the senator's waffling, of the apparent ease with which he shifted his principles to curry favor with financially useful show business executives. Actually, I wish that Al and Tipper Gore had changed their position, but they didn't back off from their criticism of popular music in any meaningful way.

Three months later, in January of 1988, I debated Tipper Gore on the CNN show *Crossfire*. She and the show's co-hosts, Tom Braden and Robert Novak, were in Washington, and I was televised remote from CNN's Hollywood studio. When asked by Novak if she and Senator Gore had "agreed to back off" attacks on "the record moguls," Tipper tried to have it both ways. She had not backed off from her concern about offensive lyrics, she said, but had wanted to meet with entertainment executives to set the record straight because "inaccurate press reports" had described her as "representing censorship," which she always had opposed.

Novak turned to me and barked, with his trademark sneer, "Mr. Goldberg, you've been hounding Mrs. Gore for months."

I interrupted irately, "It's my business that has been hounded. I felt used as part of a presidential campaign."

"Let's face it, Mr. Novak," I continued, "the Gore strategy is the southern primaries. In the South there are a lot of fundamentalists. Fundamentalists often like people who attack rock music, and this was an opportunity to show those people that Mr. Gore may be attractive to people with those so-called moral beliefs."

In retrospect, I now see that I was wrong to identify Mrs. Gore's positions only with conservatives. She represented an elite Washington consensus that included many politicians and pundits who thought of themselves as liberals. But she was wrong to think that elite spoke for most Americans.

One of the musicians who was the most informed, focused, and committed on this issue was Don Henley, who as a member of the Eagles and as a solo artist has been one of the most successful rock musicians of all time. A graduate of the University of North Texas, Henley was viewed as an unofficial guru by many Southern California rock musicians. One night I had dinner with Stevie Nicks and Jackson Browne, and Stevie, typically passionate, blurted out, "You know, when I write my songs I'm really trying to please Don." Jackson, more self-contained, looked at her with understanding and quietly replied, "So am I."

In the years before he got married, Henley palled around with Warren Beatty and Jack Nicholson, and earned a reputation as a party animal second to none. In the recording studio, however, he was known as an exacting perfectionist who insisted that other musicians and colleagues live up to his high standards.

In the political realm, Henley was known for reading every piece of mail addressed to him and for writing voluminous memos and letters to those with whom he disagreed. I once sent him a note asking for help on an ACLU project. Henley returned the note with the grammar corrected, accompanied by a stern reminder that our political effectiveness would be undermined if we came across as less than literate. But Don Henley does not hesitate to step up to help a cause he believes in.

A week or two after the Gore luncheon, Henley and I confronted one of Gore's opponents for the nomination, Illinois senator Paul Simon, at a Show Coalition political event. Simon was running for the Democratic presidential nomination as an "old-fashioned liberal," while his wife, Jeanne, was listed as a member of the PMRC. We cornered Senator Simon and told him how offensive we thought the PMRC was, and how intimidating the attacks were to entertainment corporations. We were upset that his wife, using the prestige of his position, was adding to our woes. Simon, nattily dressed in a suit and his trademark bowtie, peered over his owlish glasses and listened with the trained politeness of a professional pol. His already pink face got a bit pinker as he denied any knowledge of the PMRC and recited his First Amendment bona fides. Henley smiled and asked, "So talk to the missus for us, will you?"

The next day, Jeanne Simon called me. "Paul was very upset with me," she said, and proceeded to explain how she had only the vaguest relationship with the PMRC and never participated in any of their planning. She had no idea that creative people were so upset and would resign forthwith. (If she did, she did it very quietly.)

Neither Gore nor Simon got far in the Democratic primaries,

and Massachusetts governor Michael Dukakis went into the Democratic Convention in August with enough delegates to win the nomination. I attended the Democratic Convention in Atlanta as part of a Hollywood contingent put together by California assemblyman Tom Hayden, who was then married to Jane Fonda. The group included Sarah Jessica Parker, Daphne Zuniga, Ally Sheedy, Alec Baldwin, Ed Asner, and Rob Lowe, among others.

The convention nominated Dukakis and Texas senator Lloyd Bentsen. The vice presidential nomination of the conservative southerner Bentsen had blindsided the Reverend Jesse Jackson, who had hoped Dukakis would name him, or at least someone more to his political liking. Asked by a news reporter if he was angry at not having been told before the news was made public, Jackson said, "No. I am too controlled, too clear, too mature to be angry." The highlight of the final session was Jackson's eloquent and gracious speech, calling for the party to unite on "common ground" to defeat the Republicans.

After the last session, there was a party for our group at our hotel, the Hyatt, in an open area on the floor where all of our rooms were. John F. Kennedy Jr. and some of his cousins had joined us. Inspired by Jackson, we looked ahead with hope to the fall.

As we were watching some TV postmortems, a law student who had helped organize a young Hollywood group rushed over to me and said excitedly, "Danny, you've got to come upstairs. The Gore party is one flight up and Tipper is drunk and coming on to Rob Lowe."

I protested that it would be rude for me to crash the Gore party. I had made disparaging comments about him to political writers throughout his presidential campaign. But the young man was insistent, so I agreed. It was a night of common ground, of celebration, and everyone was in a good mood. And I just had to see this.

We walked one flight upstairs to a suite that held around fifty people, most of whom seemed to be from Tennessee. Tipper was cheerfully chatting with Lowe, although certainly not coming on to him. (A few weeks later the tabloids would gleefully reveal that later that night Lowe slept with two underage girls who happened to have a video camera with them.)

After a few minutes, I was about to slip out when Tipper spotted me and shouted across the room, "Al, look, it's Danny Goldberg!"

The senator glanced at me quizzically. As people stared, nonplussed, Tipper zoomed over and kissed me on the cheek. "We're a little drunk," she giggled, "but what the heck. I told the kids, every once in awhile you have to have a blowout."

I asked Tipper if it was really OK that I was here at the Tennessee party. "Of course," she said, echoing Jesse Jackson's speech that night. "We have common ground." Then with a sarcasm I didn't know she had, she said, "Anyway, I'm too mature to be angry."

She looked at me and said, this time in a tone of high school boastfulness, "You know, Bea Bentsen is on the PMRC advisory board," referring to the wife of Dukakis's running mate.

"Will you stop with this stuff?" I berated her good-naturedly, but with a serious intent. "It doesn't do you any good. All you do with the PMRC is alienate natural supporters."

She turned serious for a moment. "Tonight is not the time to talk about it," she said, "but call me when you're coming to Washington." She proceeded to write out her home telephone number.

After several minutes of banter, an older woman tapped me on the shoulder and asked, with a ladylike southern drawl, "Mr. Goldberg, can I speak to you for a moment?"

It was Tipper's Tennessee aide-de-camp. She drew me aside and said, "Tipper would really like to go to your party downstairs, and she feels she might not be welcome there, and I wonder if you would take her." I readily agreed. A few minutes later, Tom Hayden rolled his eyes at me and said, "Now I've seen everything!" as I escorted Tipper into the Hollywood party.

Minutes later, Al Gore appeared, tieless and cheerful. He had left the Tennessee delegation to themselves and was down among the Hollywood folk as well, volubly schmoozing. For the moment, the Gores had joined the party.

Over the next few months I entered a period my wife refers to as "sucking up to Tipper." Shortly after the convention, with Mickey Kantor and other LA politicos pressing me to give the Gores a break, I wrote her that "many of my friends got a kick out of tales that you and I found 'common ground.'" I suggested that she withdraw from the PMRC quietly, without ever criticizing it. Without that roadblock, I suggested, it would be easier for me and others in the music business to work with her on issues such as homelessness, which she had talked about with so much passion at the convention.

Tipper sent me a handwritten note saying, "It was fun to be with you in Atlanta," and then described her homeless project in detail. She had organized meetings of congressional wives to discuss the issue and invited knowledgeable people to speak. Homeless advocate Mitch Snyder had spoken so powerfully, she said, "that he had several people sobbing."

She ended with, "Thank you for your kindness, your suggestions. I'll think about them."

Michael Dukakis ran a dreadful campaign, one typified by a line from his convention speech: "This election is not about ideology, it's about competence." Democrats would never win that argument. The party's entire rationale is ideological, to use government to stand up for ordinary and underprivileged people against injustice, the inequities of the marketplace, or just plain bad luck. And Reagan had been quite competent at serving the interests of his supporters.

I watched the first Dukakis-Bush debate at the Medavoys' house with a crowd that included Gary Hart. At one point, the Massachusetts governor was asked by CNN's Bernie Shaw whether he would still be against the death penalty if his wife, Kitty, were murdered. Dukakis answered that he would be, in his pedantic, seemingly emotionless singsong voice. "I don't think the death penalty is a deterrent," he explained.

I had long opposed the death penalty, both personally and through my work with the ACLU, but I was distraught at the political ineptness of the answer. I had heard Mario Cuomo and others answer questions like that with feeling, beginning by saying they fully understood and empathized with the pain and the rage of the families of victims of crime.

I got up from Mike and Patricia's soft sofa and paced into an adjoining room, where I encountered Gary Hart. His face seemed to be a mask of self-directed rage. I rolled my eyes in the direction of the TV set and Hart shook his head and quietly muttered, with bitter irony, "Unfortunately, Dukakis is right, the election *is* going to be about competence."

In that same debate, Bush noted that he was a proud member of the National Rifle Association. Dukakis, on the other hand, he said, was a "card-carrying member of the ACLU." His prosecutorial tone made it sound tantamount to being a member of the Communist party. In the days that followed, Dukakis's membership in the ACLU was listed by the political media as part of his out-of-touch "liberal" pattern, along with his opposition to the death penalty and his support for a Massachusetts furlough program that spawned the infamous "Willie Horton" TV ad.

Dukakis's response to such attacks was to claim imperiously

that they were diversions from the real issues. He never once explained why he was a member of the ACLU and why there was nothing wrong with that.

We at the ACLU had mixed feelings. The immediate result of the attack was a huge increase in ACLU memberships, as thousands of Americans who'd harbored vague feelings of support toward the organization formally became members. National director Ira Glasser quipped that if Bush lost the election he could find a job at the ACLU as membership director.

On the other hand, ACLU affiliates in small states in the South and Midwest, with staffs of two or three people, felt nervous and vulnerable after being, in effect, blacklisted by the vice president of the United States. In any event, it was in our nature to respond to attacks. I hastily contacted several celebrities and television directors to craft some public service announcements, on the theory that if we moved quickly enough we could make the news shows, even if we couldn't get stations to run them for free or raise the money to buy time.

It turned out that the national ACLU office in New York also wanted to create TV spots, and I was asked to fly to New York to see if we could have a unified campaign. Although there were hardly any specific policy or ideological differences between the national organization and that of Southern California, the geographical distance and freewheeling style of Los Angeles leaders had caused tension over the years. Ira Glasser and his staff produced some advertising types from the Chiat Day agency who informed me that celebrities were irrelevant on this issue.

Despite the fact that I admired Ira enormously, I was extremely irked by this patronizing and naïve position. The organization didn't have millions of dollars to buy time, and celebrities were the only way of getting a message out quickly.

Ramona Ripston and I decided to do our own spots in LA anyway. Michael Tucker and Jill Eikenberry, a husband-and-wife team who both appeared on the TV series *LA Law*, quickly put one together. For another, Barbra Streisand gave us a recording of her singing "America the Beautiful," which we played over a beautiful montage of patriotic images filmed by Louis Schwartzberg.

The spot that got most of the attention featured Burt Lancaster, the great actor who Ed Asner says showed everybody in Hollywood "how to be a liberal with balls." The Los Angeles ACLU staff had written copy for several different possible versions of the commercial, including quotes about the ACLU from ex-Presidents Eisenhower and Kennedy. Lancaster, well into his seventies, was still a commanding presence, with a husky weight lifter's frame, a full head of white hair, and a booming, immediately recognizable voice.

As staffers tried to explain the versions to him, Lancaster called me over and said in an agitated voice, "I don't like any of these. I want to say, 'I'm a card-carrying member of the ACLU.' That's what I came here to say and after that, within the thirty seconds I'll say some of the rest of this stuff." I quickly nodded in agreement, and Lancaster's instincts turned out to be absolutely right. He expanded the line to "I have a confession to make. I'm a card-carrying member of the ACLU." Those forthright sentences from this famous man were prominent on the evening news. The spot was also broadcast on the *Today* show, and ACLU affiliates around the country asked to use it and our other celebrity spots for local fund-raising.

The national ACLU ads made by the "experts" were never broadcast anywhere.

The Reagan administration's policies in Central America remained a contentious political issue in the late eighties, and one of great concern to many of us who had lived through the Vietnam era. A number of leading Democrats opposed aid to the Nicaraguan

Contras. The administration's support for these killers was unappealing to a majority of voters, particularly after the Iran/Contra scandal came to light near the end of Reagan's second term.

Nonetheless, the presidency had enormous power, and the political influence of anti-Castro Cuban Americans deterred Democrats in Florida and a few other locales from opposing Contra aid. Marge Tabankin at the Arca Foundation had formed a group called Countdown '87. Its purpose was to put pressure on several dozen congressional swing votes on the issue of Contra aid.

Tabankin, whose self-deprecating, informal style masks a steel-trap mind for political tactics and a fierce unwavering commitment to progressive ideals, wanted to make Contra aid what pollsters called "a push issue." That means, she said, "a priority to voters that would affect their electoral decision instead of an issue way down on the list." This would be accomplished with TV commercials in the targeted districts. My role was to help raise money to pay for the fight. I organized benefit concerts in Washington, New York, and Los Angeles with performances by Don Henley, Bonnie Raitt, Judy Collins, Joan Baez, and Peter, Paul, and Mary.

Contra aid was banned by a narrow vote in Congress.

Shortly after Bush won the election, I visited Washington. To my surprise, Tipper Gore not only took my phone call but invited me to her house for lunch. Having asked my office about my preference in food, Tipper cooked me some mixed vegetables and we ate and chatted in the Gore home in a woodsy suburb of Washington. The kids must have been in school, and as far as I could tell there were no servants.

Tipper had a piece of artwork from a Guns N' Roses album that flaunted a lurid drawing of a robot who seemingly had just attacked a scantily clad woman. "Do you really think this is okay?" she asked.

I replied, "I'm not really a big fan of comic book art, and I'm not a teenage boy...but if you're asking me whether or not I think this is dangerous in any way—no, I don't."

We proceeded to have a relaxed and friendly rehash of our previous discussions. I felt the warm glow of Washington-insider schmoozing, and understood a little better the force that made ideological opposites move closer together. I told her again I thought she should quit the PMRC and focus her energies elsewhere. I said that no discussion, no matter how friendly and cordial, would change my strong feelings about art and free speech, nor the deep opposition most people in my business and millions of fans felt toward attacks on popular culture.

A few weeks later, another article by Tipper Gore attacking the current deplorable state of popular music appeared in the op-ed section of the *Washington Post*. The piece singled out the Guns N' Roses album—which was already stickered with the exact kind of label she had advocated.

**CHAPTER 7**

# Who Ruined the Democratic Party?

The Late-Eighties Version

I N THE WAKE OF THE 1988 ELECTION, Democrats and progressives argued fiercely about how Michael Dukakis, once well ahead in the polls, had managed to snatch defeat from the jaws of victory. In my mind, and apparently in the minds of a majority of voters, Dukakis was a dry, emotionless candidate, steeped in policy jargon and academics, and he had a snobbish contempt for mass communication. He and his advisors ran a clumsy campaign and managed to convey the notion that this ambition-driven son of Greek immigrants was a typical Harvard East Coast elitist, a liberal snob.

The patrician Bush, a Yale graduate and former head of the ultra-Establishment CIA, was ably advised by his campaign manager, Lee Atwater, to cloak himself in populist symbols—this wealthy son and grandson of northeastern privilege posed as a regular guy who loved nothing more than chewing pork rinds while listening to country music. And the Bush campaign invoked patriotism through such well-conceived media events as a visit to a flag factory, whereas Dukakis managed to look stupid standing up in a tank.

Some progressive Democrats decided it had been a mistake for the left to identify with social issues instead of the traditional class-oriented economic ones. These New Deal fundamentalists were forever trying to recreate the coalition that, according to legend, had been coalescing around Robert Kennedy at the time of his assassination in 1968.

I was at a late-eighties conference on the future of the American left when fierce debate broke out on this topic. Richard Goodwin, whose illustrious career as a speechwriter and policy advisor included Kennedy's 1968 campaign, and Pat Cadell, Jimmy Carter's former pollster, both strongly advised us to avoid being "distracted" by divisive social issues such as freedom of choice.

Marge Tabankin, who had moved from Washington to Los Angeles to become the executive director of the Hollywood Women's Political Committee (HWPC), was stunned. She interjected in a quiet, barely controlled voice, "To most women that I know in politics, choice on abortion is the emotional equivalent of the civil rights movement. If you want a movement that includes women, you really can't exclude this issue."

I hastily agreed and said that a broad progressive agenda, if it was going to inspire millions of people, needed to include issues like women's and minority rights. Cadell, a large and striking figure with a salt-and-pepper goatee and one wandering eye, rose like a Biblical prophet, face flushed and finger waving, and shouted at me, "It's people like you, Danny, who have ruined the Democratic party."

Goodwin emphatically agreed. Marge and I shook our heads in disbelief. We thought it was obvious that one reason President Reagan had so much credibility in knocking government programs was that people like Dukakis, Goodwin, and Cadell had failed to explain to working people why those programs were in their interest, relying instead on an arrogant sense of entitlement—their great intellects alone should be sufficient to secure the trust of the great unwashed. We felt that the left needed to develop a common touch, stay linked to popular social movements, and learn to use popular culture and the mass media to get its ideas across.

For instance, many members of Marge's HWPC were disturbed by attacks on the Catholic Church and banners calling for "Abortion on Demand" at demonstrations in Washington. Marge's influence among progressive groups extended well beyond her own organization. She met with feminist leaders, and it was decided to emphasize "choice" instead of abortion. NARAL, the national abortion rights organization, recruited actress Holly Hunter as one of their spokespersons.

"We succeeded in changing the way the issue was framed, which made a lot of difference politically," Marge recalled. "A lot more people, especially women, are comfortable with the concept of choice, which is the legal reality of the policy debate. [Abortion] is just one of the possible choices."

Also, in protesting Vietnam and Watergate, the left had created a strong antigovernment style and had been unable to shift to *advocating* government programs that helped average Americans. Democrats would have lost by far greater majorities if it weren't for the so-called cultural issues. Large majorities supported stricter environmental regulation and opposed the religious right's crusade to make abortion illegal, two of the issues that economic leftists found trivial. Instead of blaming cultural forces on the left, I told the group, the economic left should embrace them.

A few months later I was asked to be part of an all-day conference on "discarded children" convened by Democratic congressmen John Lewis of Georgia, Tom Downey of New York, and George Miller of California.

George Miller and John Lewis are two of the people I admire most in politics. Lewis is a former leader of the seminal civil rights group SNCC, and he was brutally beaten in the course of fighting segregation. As a congressman he has been unusually passionate, guileless, and consistent. Miller, similarly, has won a reputation for uncompromising progressive beliefs, straight talk, and personal integrity. Over the course of several hours, they and several staff people spoke in eloquent and heart-wrenching detail about the many crises facing children in poverty.

Finally Downey addressed the "communications people" and said to us, "We need you to get this issue on the cover of *Time* magazine. We can't get the attention of the public ourselves in a way that can make it a political priority. That's why we asked you here. That's what we need."

I chatted briefly with the other media advisors, who included Henry Hampton, producer of the brilliant PBS series on the civil rights movement, *Eyes on the Prize*, and the well-known political and media consultant Mandy Grunwald. We all had the same reaction.

I told the congressmen that the speakers had framed not one but numerous related issues. We had heard, among other things, about lack of full funding for Head Start, failure of public schools to teach poor kids to read, woefully inadequate education on nutrition for pregnant mothers, profound flaws in the foster care system, and the low quality of public day care programs. Each needed to be explained separately.

You can get the public to focus on one of these issues, but not on all of them at once. Which one, I asked, do you want on the cover of *Time?*

This is PR 101. Focus and repetition are the only ways to make an impact. Blurred, multiple messages cancel each other out and don't stick in people's minds.

The congressmen and the policy analysts were horrified. It was as if we were offering them a version of *Sophie's Choice.* How could they kill any of their babies? The meeting dwindled away into an unfocused muddle of frustration and resentment. Nothing came of it.

During the late eighties, I got to know Ron Brownstein, a political writer for the *Los Angeles Times.* Then in his mid-twenties, Ron was a journalistic prodigy, much younger than other writers covering politics, and he had an affable, disarming style and an incisive mind, both reminiscent of the young Cameron Crowe. Ron made the beat of Hollywood and politics his own. In 1990, he published his definitive book on the Washington–Los Angeles axis, *The Power and the Glitter.*

The early chapters of *The Power and the Glitter* contain the best work I have seen on the political activity of early film moguls like Louis B. Mayer and more recent ones like Lew Wasserman. The last third of the book covers the late 1980s, and Ron is particularly generous to me in his analysis.

But despite his affinity for Hollywood, and a well-balanced presentation of various points of view, Ron's personal take on the entertainment business and politics post-Dukakis reflects the jaundiced attitude of the Washington media and political establishment. For example, he mentions that in the 1986 elections, two Democratic candidates for the Senate, Harriett Woods in Missouri and Tom Daschle in South Dakota, were each attacked by Republican opponents for a connection to Jane Fonda. Fonda had made a donation to Woods and testified before a congressional subcommittee chaired by Daschle.

When Barbra Streisand hosted a Hollywood Women's Political Committee fund-raiser at her home in Malibu, Woods decided to stay away and to distance herself from Hollywood, while Daschle chose to attend. Woods made a point of criticizing Fonda's long-ago decision to travel to Hanoi during the Vietnam War and offered to donate Fonda's $2,000 contribution to a veterans' charity. Daschle ran ads mocking his opponent for attacking him on such a flimsy basis.

Daschle was elected. Woods was defeated. She complained that the Fonda attacks "helped to keep me from mainstreaming myself," and Brownstein concludes that Woods lost because of an overidentification with Hollywood.

My conclusion is the opposite. Woods was defeated because she acted like the kind of politician who easily caves in to pressure, whereas Daschle, running in a politically more conservative state, was victorious because he came across as consistent, gutsy, and comfortable with himself.

Publications of the political elite enjoyed ridiculing show business activists. The *Washington Post*'s Jonathan Yardley wrote a diatribe belittling Barbra Streisand, and the *New Republic* referred to Barbra and other celebrity activists as "bubbleheads."

Hollywood certainly has its share of flaky dilettantes, but I have found Streisand, among others, to be extremely well read and thoughtful on the various issues we've discussed over the years. Her intensity can be overwhelming, but her intelligence and commitment cannot be reasonably questioned.

Similarly, Robert Redford is an effective, self-effacing, and tenacious environmentalist. Warren Beatty is intelligent and thoughtful and knowledgeable about the issues. Paul Newman has, quietly, been one of the biggest financial donors to the progressive *Nation*, and millions of dollars of profits from Newman's Own line of foods have been donated to grassroots organizations working for progressive causes. To dismiss all politically active celebrities with glib or condescending phrases is neither intellectually serious nor politically effective.

In 1989, I married music business attorney Rosemary Carroll. Our wedding reception was held on Stanley Sheinbaum's front lawn. My management business, Gold Mountain, was continuing to thrive, but Rosemary was continually prodding me to get involved with the next generation of rock and roll, which at the time was called "alternative rock."

My opportunity came when the groundbreaking New York band Sonic Youth had a falling out with their manager just as they were delivering to Geffen Records their first major-label album, *Goo*. My colleague John Silva and I shepherded them through the system with no artistic compromises and a doubling of their sales.

Sonic Youth liked to introduce exciting new alternative bands as opening acts. Lead guitarist Thurston Moore raved to me about one, Nirvana, which had released an indie album on the Seattle label Sub-Pop. We flew the band to Los Angeles and quickly signed them. Silva had already seen Nirvana open for Sonic Youth in Europe. I had heard their record but did not actually see them until a couple of weeks after they had become clients, when they opened for Dinosaur Jr. at the Hollywood Palace. I drove home afterward in a state of euphoria, knowing that I had seen one of the best bands ever. I negotiated a record deal with Geffen. Nirvana became the most important rock group of the 1990s.

Kurt Cobain, Nirvana's lead singer and songwriter, was one of the few real geniuses I have ever known. Kurt always identified with progressive causes, and his emotional connection with politics came through the so-called social issues. As Nirvana's *Never-mind* was being released, soon to be the number one selling album in the world, the band played a benefit for the abortion rights group Rock for Choice. It was one of their first LA shows.

I have taken liberties with one of Kurt's most famous images by using the phrase "teen spirit" as a metaphor for the political energy of new generations. This is quite different from the way he originally used it in Nirvana's biggest song "Smells Like Teen Spirit," which regularly shows up in rock magazine polls as the most popular song of the 1990s. Kurt originally used the phrase "teen spirit" because it was the name of a deodorant. The song itself uses the phrase sarcastically in a cynical comment about assorted hypocrisies, including the shallowness of most teen entertainment.

Although he never wanted to flaunt it, Kurt had strong political feelings about certain issues. In 1992, he and Courtney Love contributed to Jerry Brown's presidential campaign after hearing him on the radio.

Kurt's lyrics are rich in metaphor and symbolism and laced with irony. *Nevermind* includes "Polly," an anti-rape song that Kurt delivers in the voice of an obviously repulsive misogynist. Virtually every reviewer and listener understood the song's harsh indictment of abusive men, but one mentally disturbed fan in Colorado sang "Polly" while committing a rape. Kurt was devastated and sent financial help to the victim's family.

At the next MTV Awards, Kurt wanted to preview his new song "Rape Me," another strong, irony-laced feminist statement. MTV staffers got nervous and insisted that the band do a more familiar song. MTV president Judy McGrath later said one of her greatest regrets has been that she did not intervene and let the band do "Rape Me."

The biggest American band before Nirvana was Guns N' Roses, whose lead singer, Axl Rose, seemed to personify exactly the kind of macho rock and roll that Kurt was rebelling against. The week that *Nevermind* came out, Axl came backstage at a Nirvana concert. Kurt asked me to walk out of the dressing room close to him to help him avoid meeting Axl.

The next year, backstage at the MTV Awards, Kurt came over to Rosemary and me shaking his head in disgust after an unpleasant confrontation with Axl. Kurt's wife, Courtney Love, had been teasing Axl about his habit of dating models. Flanked by two burly security guards, Rose looked menacingly down at the slight five foot six inch Kurt Cobain and yelled, "If you don't shut your woman up, I'm gonna slam you to the pavement."

A week later, at the request of film director Gus Van Sant, whom Kurt greatly admired, Nirvana played at a benefit to help defeat an Oregon ballot proposition that essentially would have legalized discrimination against gays and lesbians. Kurt, who usually didn't talk much to audiences during concerts, told the Axl story. He said that prejudice against gays and contempt for women were part of the same sickness, and that the kind of rock culture he stood for had no room for it. Suddenly, a fan jumped up on the stage. Sensing that he was in no danger, Kurt waved away the security guards and let the kid take the microphone.

"Kurt," the teenager said, "I love you and I love Axl. Why do I have to choose? I just want to rock." I watched Kurt take in the boy's comments with the compassion that made him so special. Nonetheless, after giving the fan his say, Kurt reiterated his message. He didn't want fans who were bigots. To this day, I'm torn between sympathy for Kurt's point of view and the fan's.

On the next Nirvana album, an anthology of early works called *Incesticide*, Kurt wrote into his liner notes a message to his listeners that said he didn't want any fans who were antiwomen or anti-gay, to my knowledge the only time an artist discouraged anyone from being a fan.

Kurt was a unique and inspiring person and a brilliant artist. His suicide haunts me every day.

In the aftermath of the disastrous 1988 election, I and many of my friends in LA focused on issues rather than candidates, although we discovered it was sometimes hard to separate the two.

The Southern California affiliate of the ACLU was growing, thanks to Ramona Ripston, and I stayed busy. We had an annual budget and case load greater than any other ACLU affiliate in the country. We put on two dinners a year honoring people we admired who supported us and our ideals. The numerous honorees included Sarah Jessica Parker, Jane Fonda, Barbra Streisand, Martin Scorsese, Joan Baez, Kirk Douglas, Congresswoman Maxine Waters, and former mayor Tom Bradley. Performers such as Bonnie Raitt, Elvis Costello, Billy Crystal, Warren Beatty, Tracy Chapman, and Jackson Browne appeared at the dinners. Meegan Ochs, daughter of Phil Ochs, did, and continues to do, a brilliant job of organizing these fundraisers.

Many in Hollywood focused on the environment. Norman Lear and his wife, Lyn, put together the Environmental Media Association of entertainment executives. EMA educated many TV and film producers about environmental hazards. Numerous shows adapted minor plot lines in which protagonists were earth-friendly, such as the TV character Murphy Brown, who was shown recycling trash and joining a car pool. Former Ted Kennedy aide Bonnie Reiss created the Earth Communications Office to organize celebrities around the environment. Barbra Streisand and Belinda Carlisle, among others, promoted environmental causes on their albums, and at Earth Day rallies in 1990, celebrities were ubiquitous.

The music business had its own environmental issue, the so-called long box, which had been created by record companies to placate music retailers when compact disc sales rapidly began replacing vinyl and cassettes over the course of the 1980s. The retailers didn't want to build new display cases and requested packages that fit the ones created for 12 x 12 vinyl albums. Gary Stewart, an executive at Rhino Records, then a small compilation label, become obsessed with the waste of paper that these boxes entailed. Like the situation we had with the Musical Majority, Gary had to create a coalition that didn't include major-label executives, since they were all bound by corporate policies. While still at Gold Mountain I became a member of his committee, and Don Henley and I did a press conference urging passage of a California bill that would restrict wasteful packaging on various consumer products, including the long box. Shortly thereafter the major labels capitulated and eliminated the long box, and music retail rapidly adjusted.

The spring of 1989, a Hollywood forum on the environment was assembled by the Hollywood Women's Political Committee and Show Coalition, the Patricia Medavoy political organization I had been involved with from the beginning. The featured speakers were to be two of the most environmentally active members of the U.S. Senate, Tim Wirth of Colorado and Albert Gore of Tennessee.

Our group really didn't have anything to do with putting the program together. It flashed through my mind that it was weird for Hollywood to legitimize Gore, given his and his wife's attacks on the music business. But Gore was a genuine environmentalist, so I bit my tongue. I joined in the unanimous vote to co-sponsor the forum. We agreed to mail invitations to all of our members on our official stationery, which featured my name prominently—for no particular reason, I was at the top of a long list of founders.

Don Henley responded by firing off an irate letter castigating us for hosting Gore. I loved Henley and understood his point of view, but shrugged it off. However, the letter got around.

The event was held at a fabled Beverly Hills mansion owned by Interscope founder Ted Field, which had been built by silent screen comedian Harold Lloyd. Several hundred people attended. They had to pay close attention to the program after the public address system broke down.

On one of those perfect, clear, and balmy Southern California afternoons, Gore was particularly impressive. In the absence of amplification, Gore switched from his pedantic professorial voice to an old-fashioned stump shout, and his heartfelt passion for the environment came through with eloquence and authenticity.

After the speech, I walked over to Gore in one of the many foyers of the mansion and told him I thought he had been great and that it was obvious he had genuine passion for the issue. Gore turned and frowned at me and said, angrily, "I know what you did—how you tried to embarrass me."

Surprised, I snapped back, "Just because Don Henley was complaining about you doesn't mean I had anything to do with that. Everybody in the music business doesn't agree about everything all the time."

"That's bullshit!" Gore screamed at the top of his lungs. "You and your fucking group sent out that letter. You and your fucking group tried to embarrass me."

As Bob Burkett, Ted Field's political advisor, watched in horror, I yelled back, "You don't know what the fuck you're talking about—look at the stationery." I waved a sheet of Show Coalition stationery with my name on top. "I'm one of the people who was attacked by Henley for having you speak." He looked startled by this information, but nonetheless walked away in a huff. I would have preferred that Gore acknowledge his misconception of where the objection to him came from, but I think he was still furious at anyone who had criticized him in the past, and I actually appreciated the emotional honesty of his anger, which was a welcome contrast to the insincere affability of most politicians.

On August 3, 1990, our first child, Katie, was born. As Rosemary and I watched the TV news from her hospital room, we saw President Bush threatening war against Iraq, which had invaded Kuwait a few days earlier. At the time, although I understood the rationale of the war, I was opposed to it. As with Vietnam, my opposition was to the war, not to the Americans who were sent overseas by their government to fight. Gold Mountain clients would soon put out the preeminent antiwar song (and video) of the time, Lenny Kravitz's reworking of "Give Peace a Chance," and the best-known song supporting our troops, David Foster's "Voices That Care."

Kravitz, a management client, called me in mid-August extremely worried about the possibility of the conflict spreading into a world war, and I suggested that he call Yoko Ono and Sean Lennon about doing an updated version of John Lennon's Vietnam-era "Give Peace a Chance." A couple of days later, Lenny reported excitedly that Sean and he had written new lyrics and the project was happening.

Miles Mogelescu of Propaganda Films, one of the leading music video producers, shared the same political passion and agreed to produce a music video for cost. And Danny Shechter, who'd directed an antiapartheid "Sun City" video with Steve Van Zandt, agreed to do a "making of" documentary that would be sold on home video.

Lenny, Miles, and I called everyone we knew to join in the recording session. About a dozen stars agreed, including Bonnie Raitt. Our big score was rapper M. C. Hammer, who at the time had the highest-selling record of the year with "Can't Touch This." Hammer had been in the navy and went to great lengths to explain that he supported servicemen but opposed sending them to the Gulf to fight.

After the recording Lenny asked me to take him to Washington to learn more about the issue so he could speak knowledgeably in interviews. I was able to arrange time for us with Senators Bill Bradley and Ted Kennedy and with Jesse Jackson's foreign policy advisor, Bob Borosage.

MTV played the video in heavy rotation for a week, and Lenny and friends did a spirited version of "Give Peace a Chance" on the *Arsenio Hall Show*. Lenny became uncharacteristically tongue-tied when Hall asked him about his reasons for recording it. Happily, Tony Bennett was also a guest on the show, and he picked up the ball. Bennett turned out to be extremely knowledgeable, passionate about peace, and eloquent.

The next week, when the troops had finally been assembled in the desert and the war against Iraq actually started, the media pulled behind the war effort and the song pretty much died.

The song for the troops, "Voices That Care," was written by David Foster and his wife, Linda Thompson. Its main thrust was support for the young men and women risking their lives overseas for American foreign policy. I admired the song but had trouble with a line that championed the policy as well as the soldiers. I told Linda, the lyricist, that she could reach more people if the focus stayed on the troops. "Quincy Jones told me the same thing," said Linda, who proceeded to make the change.

David Foster had grown up in Canada and was an icon there. He had developed a close social friendship with Canadian prime minister Brian Mulroney, said to be one of President Bush's closest friends among world leaders. I asked David to get Mulroney's perspective on why Bush had launched the Gulf War. David reported back that the prime minister had "confidentially" told him, "George is really pissed off at Saddam Hussein."

David enlisted movie and television celebrities for a "Voices That Care" TV special, which was hosted by actor James Woods. A few months later, I sat with David at a USO luncheon honoring the people involved with "Voices That Care." The speakers were Colin Powell, chairman of the joint chiefs of staff, Secretary of Defense Richard Cheney, and President George Bush. To my knowledge, Lenny Kravitz was never acknowledged in any way by members of the peace movement. This contrast is typical of a pattern I have observed repeatedly. Conservatives cherish their supporters from the world of entertainment and progressives often take theirs for granted, ignore them, or condescend to them.

In 1991, Oliver Stone's film *JFK* was released. Popular with the public and widely admired among film critics and the creative community in the film business, *JFK* was universally reviled by the political press, left and right. As a result of the barrage of criticism, the conventional wisdom about the film in Washington was that it was a woolly-headed collection of absurd conspiracy theories. To my mind the film is clearly a cinematic, impressionistic work about a major historical event, the facts of which are unlikely ever to be known. The contrast in the reaction of the public and that of liberal snobs in Washington to *JFK*, is another milestone in the widening of the gap between the punditocracy and the tens of millions of ordinary people who were inspired by the film. Not being in the film business, I never worked professionally with Oliver. In the world of progressive politics he has been one of the most generous and unpretentious contributors, always a soft touch for a good cause. He has been particularly supportive of the ACLU.

As a Jew, I have been unable to ignore the terrible decades-long conflict in the Middle East, and emotionally I have a great love for Israel. In 1987, I was asked by the CRB Foundation (set up by philanthropist Charles R. Bronfman) to try to put together a concert in the Negev Desert for the upcoming fortieth anniversary of the nation. The concert, which was to have both Israeli and Egyptian participation, was heavily supported by the Israeli left. Foreign Minister Shimon Peres and leaders of the Israeli group Peace Now came to Los Angeles to promote the concert, and I made several preparatory trips to Israel that only strengthened my emotional ties to the nation. Sadly, the beginning of the first intifada ended the plans for the concert.

Two years later, the actor Richard Dreyfuss asked me to accompany him on his first trip to Israel. We had become friends through the ACLU, and Richard had developed a passion for the cause of peace in the Middle East.

As the star of Spielberg's immensely popular *Jaws* and *Close Encounters of the Third Kind*, and an Oscar winner for *The Goodbye Girl*, Richard was one of the most famous Jewish actors in the world, and he was able to meet with leaders on the highest level in every major faction of Israelis and Palestinians. We dined in the Knesset with Defense Minister Moshe Arens, met with influential rabbis, visited military facilities, and sat in the homes of Israeli peace activists as well as militant West Bank settlers. We also visited Palestinian refugee camps and spoke with several Palestinian leaders. Palestinian journalist Daoud Kuttab asked Richard when he thought Hollywood would depict a Palestinian as a hero. Richard tried to explain how such decisions are made at movie studios, which usually focus on offending the least number of people. Kuttab listened as Dreyfuss explained to him that only on rare occasions were Hollywood characters identified as Jewish despite the large number of Jews behind the scenes in the business, the orthodox theory being that ethnicity of any kind limits mass appeal. It was obvious from his mournful expression that Kuttab mistakenly thought Dreyfus was being disingenuous. I was reminded once again of how much the Hollywood stamp of approval means to people around the world. With all of the efforts being made to convince the Muslim world that the United States respects them, some Muslim heroes in Hollywood films might create more goodwill than some of the more heavy-handed government-sponsored efforts have done.

I know there are no easy answers to this tragic and seemingly intractable conflict. I continue to identify with the so-called Israeli left and have been a member of the board of Americans for Peace Now for many years, but I part company from my friends on the American left when they uncritically glamorize the PLO or trivialize Israel's vulnerability.

I can offer at least a partial explanation for why some on the left feel the way they do, in terms of the theme of this book. In the early years of the nation, bonds between Israel and American progressives and young people were strengthened through popular culture, through books and movies like *Exodus,* and through support for the young nation by famous American entertainers. As Israel grew older, the American entertainers who vocally supported it grew older too, and moved from prime-time television to the veterans' wing of the dais at Friars' Club roasts.

At the same time, established American Jewish organizations grew more and more conservative, working up far more passion for attacking off-the-cuff remarks by the Reverend Jesse Jackson than for identifying with America's poor. And starting in the Reagan era, Israeli leaders bonded with American defense hawks and Christian conservatives and ignored the progressive political world. I don't see how it helps Israel that many younger American progressives perceive support of Israel as a right-wing cause. This need not have happened, and need not be.

Attacks on free speech continued to come from both the left and the right. Because of my ACLU position, Allen Ginsberg contacted me in 1990 to help with a lawsuit he and Boston civil liberties attorney Harvey Silverglate had filed against the FCC, a continuation of his decades-long battle against censorship of his poem "Howl."

Under Reagan, the FCC had created new limits on free speech for broadcasters. Radio stations previously had broad latitude on what they aired very late at night—a "safe harbor" when young children were extremely unlikely to be listening. The new doctrine prohibited "indecency" from being broadcast at any time. Indecency was not defined.

Pacifica noncommercial radio stations, like WBAI in New York and KPKF in Los Angeles, would air "Howl" once a year as a statement of free speech as well as artistic admiration. They stopped lest they be subject to crippling fines or possible loss of license.

I jumped at the chance to meet with Allen Ginsberg. Over croissants and coffee at a Santa Monica bistro, Allen reviewed in precise detail the long battle he had waged for artistic freedom and stressed how important it was for people to hear his poems, not just read them.

"My work is enhanced by hearing it," he said. "It takes on a different life as an oral work and not merely written."

We discussed a pending court case in which parents of a kid who committed suicide were suing the rock band Judas Priest, claiming that the band's lyrics "caused" the tragic act. I was deriding social scientists and prosecutors who said that music caused violent behavior.

Allen interrupted. "Don't ever say art has no effect," he said in a firm voice. "We spent a lot of effort on the idea that art *does* have an effect."

When Allen said "we," I felt a thrill. He was speaking for generations of visionary artists, for Walt Whitman and William Blake, for all-night impassioned brainstorming sessions with Jack Kerouac and William Burroughs, for the world in which Allen had been a pivotal influence since the 1950s. I quickly explained that I merely meant that art couldn't be held accountable for crime. Allen agreed. But the exchange underscored the subtlety of the underlying issues, as did his statement "It's much better to fight these battles over art than over porn, you know." But Allen was no snob. Then in his mid-sixties, Allen was as up to date on rock and roll as any teenager.

In the FCC case, thirty years after the landmark court decision in favor of "Howl," Ginsberg and his allies were unsuccessful in using his most famous poem to further pry open the doors of government censorship.

Another free-speech battle over popular culture was triggered in 1989 when the rapper Professor Griff, a member of Public Enemy, made anti-Semitic remarks similar to some of Louis Farrakhan's. Under the leadership of the remarkable Chuck D., Public Enemy was the most politically conscious, thoughtful group that popular music had produced in many years. Chuck D. immediately denounced the remarks and asked Professor Griff to leave the group.

Bill Adler, a Jewish publicist for the group, arranged for Chuck D. to meet with Rabbi Abe Cooper of LA's Wiesenthal Center, which had created the "Museum of Tolerance" to educate the public about the Holocaust and the terrible costs of ethnic bigotry.

Adler did not realize that despite the moral power of the museum, the organization behind it was culturally quite conservative, even by the centrist standards of the organized Jewish community.

Thus, even though Chuck D. had not made the offensive statement and had gotten rid of the man who had, he was prepared to apologize on behalf of the group. Instead of accepting his apology, Rabbi Cooper insisted on more mea culpas and publicly chastised the rapper.

Later that year, Public Enemy released an album called *Welcome to the Terrordome* that featured Chuck D. rapping "I asked the Rab to get off the rag." The Wiesenthal Center and the Anti-Defamation League promptly branded the new song as anti-Semitic. I was nauseated by these attacks. Chuck D. clearly was criticizing a specific rabbi for refusing to accept a sincerely offered apology, not all rabbis or all Jews. I said so in an *LA Times* op-ed piece, which was the beginning of a long friendship with Chuck D. and Bill Adler.

On January 8, 1990, Tipper Gore weighed in with her own op-ed piece in the *Washington Post*. Headlined "Hate, Rape and Rap," it echoed Rabbi Cooper's criticisms of Public Enemy and also condemned the use of the words "bitch" and "nigger" by rapper Ice T. "We must raise our voices in protest and put pressure on those who not only reflect this hatred but also package, polish, promote and market it," Mrs. Gore wrote. To me, this glib and mindless dismissal of Public Enemy showed that Tipper Gore was as snobbish and closed-minded as ever.

Such attacks inspired legislators across the country to try to limit access by minors to records and performances. In Missouri, Republican Jeanne Dixon introduced a bill requiring mandatory labeling of "offensive" records and limiting attendance to concerts to those over eighteen if "offensive" subjects were raised. Similar bills were introduced in Pennsylvania, Oklahoma, Arizona, Delaware, Florida, Alaska, Rhode Island, and Tennessee.

I revived the Musical Majority. In April of 1990, with the help of radio programming consultant Jeff Pollack and the ACLU of eastern Missouri, we organized a rally in St. Louis opposing the Dixon bill. The big local rock station, KSHE, co-sponsored and broadcast the rally, which featured Alannah Miles and the indefatigable Don Henley. Defeated Senate candidate Harriett Woods, who evidently had gotten over her aversion to the entertainment business, spoke at the rally. So did Missouri lieutenant governor Mel Carnahan, who thus became, to my knowledge, the first elected official since Los Angeles mayor Bradley to stand up for free speech in the music business.

Shortly afterward, the Missouri bill was killed in committee. By the end of April, most of the other bills were either defeated or withdrawn.

Later that year, the rapper Luke Skyywalker of 2 Live Crew was arrested after an adults-only performance in Broward County, Florida, that featured songs from the group's controversial new album, *As Nasty as They Wanna Be*. Republican libertarians responded to the arrest with more sensitivity to the First Amendment than did Democrats.

"These are adults," said Republican congressman Dana Rohrabacher of California. "This is a First Amendment question and the government should not be involved."

And Republican senator Connie Mack of Florida said, "Freedom is a precious and sometimes delicate issue. I'm sure many people find the lyrics reprehensible. And I agree. But words are words. Our Constitution protects our right to say what we feel . . . Once we begin selectively defining which words are acceptable, we enter a slippery slope where freedom is compromised. Sometimes the price of freedom is high. But no price is as high as the loss of freedom."

By contrast, the Democratic senator from Florida, Bob Graham, avoided the point by generalizing, "No freedom is unlimited. All freedom occurs in the context of freedom for others." He said he had not heard the record nor read its lyrics.

The actual arrest of a musician galvanized the music community. Bruce Springsteen gave Luke Skyywalker the rights to his song "Born in the USA" for a rap version called "Banned in the USA." Skyywalker was acquitted, with the help of the Florida ACLU.

In any event, 2 Live Crew was never considered a significant rap group, and, deprived of controversy, their records quickly declined in sales.

In July, the Judas Priest trial took place in Reno, Nevada. The rock group had been sued by the parents of Raymond Belknap, an eighteen-year-old who killed himself with a sawed-off shotgun while listening to the heavy metal group's album *Stained Class*. Lawyers for the family claimed there were subliminal messages in several songs that were "causative factors" in the suicide.

At the trial, it was revealed that Belknap had been an abused child, had a history of heavy drug and alcohol use, and had been intoxicated when he shot himself. The lawsuit was dismissed.

Amidst all the attacks on rock and rap music, Jeff Ayeroff and Jordan Harris of Virgin Records formed an organization called Rock the Vote to encourage young people to make their voices heard in politics. I was happy to support them.

Ayeroff was filled with zeal. He pounded the phones to get support from hundreds of music executives. He commissioned a spectacular poster called "Censorship Is Un-American" that showed a young black man with a restraining hand over his mouth.

Former California governor Jerry Brown, who had recently become the chairman of the state Democratic party, agreed to be the main speaker at Rock the Vote's inaugural event.

Although I had met him only a few times, I was apparently the only person in the holding area before the event who Brown knew at all. He motioned me over to him and asked in a whisper what was going on and what I suggested he say to the crowd. I explained to Jerry that the people in the audience made a good living and could be not only Democratic voters but also significant contributors.

Most of them had families, I told him, and had been in the music business for all of their adult life. Most of them were liberals who had been busy with their careers for the last decade and hadn't been politically active since the end of the Vietnam War. They were proud of what they did for a living and deeply resented being called pornographers by politicians.

"All you need to do," I said, "is include a couple of sentences saying that you respect the music business and are against censorship in general terms and you've got them for life."

Brown peered at me with his intense, intelligent brown eyes. "I got it," he said. He then proceeded to give a brilliant but rambling and impressionistic speech about the failures of the Reagan and Bush administrations in dealing with poverty, international suffering, and the drug war. Brown spoke for about forty-five minutes and never mentioned free speech, censorship, popular music, or entertainment of any kind.

Ronald Reagan, undoubtedly influenced by his background as an actor, had an honest fascination with popular culture that would have helped humanize many policy-wonk Democrats. His wife, Nancy, shared some of his qualities. I met the former president and First Lady at an event to mark the release of an album to benefit the Pediatric AIDS Foundation, of which the Reagans were honorary co-chairs. I accompanied one of my clients, Pat Benatar, who had donated a song, as had Bruce Springsteen, Michael Jackson, and others.

I was introduced to the Reagans shortly before they were to appear at a press conference. Nancy Reagan, diminutive and intense, immediately grabbed my hands and said, "I know you." It turned out that she'd seen me as a guest on her son Ron's syndicated late-night TV talk show.

"We're changing the show," she told me, never losing eye contact. "The producers have him doing too much serious stuff. People want more humor and entertainment." I nodded silently and agreed wholeheartedly when she said how wonderful her son was. In truth, Ron Reagan was a gracious, self-effacing, and very funny guy.

Only a year or two out of office, President Reagan, though eighty years old, looked extraordinary. With his cheeks as pink as apples, a full head of hair, and a muscular build, he could have easily passed for a man twenty-five years younger.

He raved to his wife about the buffet table, which served Mrs. Fields chocolate chip cookies.

"They're my favorite cookies in the world," Reagan said to me, evidently having decided that if I warranted his wife's attention, I should get some of his, too.

"When we were in the White House, I was very excited when they told me Mrs. Fields herself was going to visit. I imagined a matronly older woman, but Mrs. Fields is only in her forties and has young children. Can you believe it? Can you believe that Mrs. Fields is a young woman?" Mrs. Reagan interrupted his reveries and grabbed him by the elbow and snapped, "Come on, Ronnie, let's do the press conference." Once behind a microphone, Reagan spoke eloquently about AIDS, a subject he'd largely ignored as president.

In January of 1992, I was hired by Atlantic Records CEO Doug

Morris to be the label's senior vice president on the West Coast. My first job at Atlantic was to help bring in some rock bands that would appeal to the now huge alternative rock audience. During my time at Atlantic, I was instrumental in signing Stone Temple Pilots, Hootie and the Blowfish, and Jewel. I also brought in the Matador label, which released the critical faves Pavement and Liz Phair.

As the 1992 election loomed, actor Ron Silver formed a New York–based group called the Creative Coalition. Silver visited Los Angeles to recruit support and was widely critical of the left-wing slant of some of the existing Hollywood organizations. Patrick Lippert, executive director of Rock the Vote, showed Silver a TV spot featuring a scantily clad Madonna urging people to vote. It remains one of the best-known public service announcements ever created. But Silver lectured us on how inappropriate it was. "It's like fighting fire with fire," he said, indicating that his New York actors would do something much classier.

Patrick had spent hundreds of hours launching Rock the Vote, first convincing MTV to get on board, then convincing celebrated artists to make the commercials, and finally getting the TV spots actually produced. The crowning jewel of a year's effort for Patrick, his staff, and Rock the Vote's board was the Madonna spot, which had gotten more media attention than any voter registration spot in memory. I exploded at Silver for his rudeness, which I felt was laden with exactly the sort of elitism that undermined numerous progressive causes.

The Southern California ACLU was extremely busy in that period as Los Angeles seethed with racial tension and anger, much of it directed at the Los Angeles Police Department. In April of 1991, the brutal beating of Rodney King by four LA policemen horrified millions of Americans when an amateur videotape was shown repeatedly on national TV news. For almost a decade, civil rights groups in Los Angeles and the ACLU had been complaining about the LAPD and in particular about Chief Daryl Gates. Long before the term "racial profiling" entered common usage, activists in Los Angeles charged that people of color were far more likely to be stopped or searched by the LAPD than whites. Several black athletes successfully sued the city of Los Angeles for inappropriate and unwarranted stops, apparently based solely on the color of their skin.

Still, Chief Gates retained the support of the vast majority of the Los Angeles elite. In part, he still benefited from the afterglow of the relatively crime-free 1984 LA Olympics.

The Rodney King tape changed the political reality, with the kind of effect on majority opinion that Bull Connor's police dogs attacking nonviolent civil rights demonstrators had generated a quarter of a century earlier. Years of pent-up resentment of Chief Gates came exploding forth.

Ramona Ripston and the ACLU legal staff had been documenting police abuses for more than a decade, and the ACLU played a pivotal role in the ensuing fight against Gates and abusive cops. Ramona put together a campaign and, within a few weeks, got more than 20,000 signatures on a petition calling for Gates's resignation—"more than we got for Nixon's," she told me. A few weeks after the King beating, actor Wesley Snipes was stopped and detained by the police for no reason while driving through Beverly Hills, and he called Ramona fuming with indignation. We organized a press conference for Snipes, Blair Underwood, and several other black actors who had had the same experience.

Not long afterward we had a public forum at which actor Ed Asner played the role of Daryl Gates, reading actual quotes of the embattled chief, including his notorious statement, "In some blacks, when the choke hold is applied, the veins or arteries do not open up like in normal people."

Mayor Bradley, a former police chief, had refrained from criticizing Gates publicly despite many years of pressure from civil rights groups. Now, Bradley too said it was time for the chief to go, and he appointed Stanley Sheinbaum president of the police commission, the five-member body to which the chief officially reported.

Bradley also asked Warren Christopher, the eminent Los Angeles attorney who later would be named Bill Clinton's secretary of state, to create a bipartisan commission to investigate police practices. The Christopher Commission concluded that the vast majority of the 7,000 Los Angeles police officers were excellent, law-abiding officials, but that there was a group of 200 to 300 who were regularly "racist and brutal," and that these officers were responsible for creating a breakdown of trust between the police department and the black community.

It was not until May of 1992, when the streets of Los Angeles exploded in a riot after the policemen charged with beating King were acquitted, that Gates finally was pushed out of office. More painful changes in the Los Angeles Police Department were to come over the next decade, as the full extent of the brutality and corruption of a small but powerful group in the department was revealed.

A year before the Rodney King beating set all the changes in motion, the LA group NWA released an album called *Straight Outta Compton*. It is considered the first gangsta rap album. *Straight Outta Compton* sold 2 million copies despite getting virtually no play on radio or MTV.

Public Enemy star Chuck D. had called rap music "the CNN of the ghetto." If the Los Angeles establishment had been tuning in, they might have wondered why an album with so little marketing clout behind it would have sold so extraordinarily well when its best-known song was called "Fuck the Police."

# CHAPTER 8

# Mend It,
# Don't End It

IN THE EARLY PRIMARIES for the 1992 Democratic presidential nomination, I raised a little money for Senator Tom Harkin, who seemed to be the most progressive viable candidate. But Harkin never created excitement anywhere. By the beginning of May, Arkansas governor Bill Clinton had the nomination all but locked up. After three losses in a row, many Democrats saw a winner in the telegenic moderate southerner, and Clinton had an intellectual depth on issues that attracted many progressives as well. I was very busy at Atlantic and with the ACLU, and I watched from the sidelines.

In May, Vice President Dan Quayle tried to energize the lethargic

*When I first was involved with the music business, the record companies were run by real gangsters. Now the records are rapping about gangsters. From where I sit, this is progress.*

—Rev. Al Sharpton urging Time Warner record labels not to give in to pressure to remove gangsta rap from their rosters.

Bush reelection campaign by launching an attack against the morals of a woman who did not exist. In a campaign speech, Quayle criticized Murphy Brown because the sitcom character played by liberal Democrat Candice Bergen had a baby out of wedlock.

The Murphy Brown jab was not one of Quayle's famous gaffes, but had been carefully planned. It almost certainly came from Quayle's advisor, William Kristol, who was considered one of the bright lights of intellectual conservatism. ("Dan Quayle has one of the best minds in Washington," was the running joke in the nation's capital, "and it belongs to William Kristol.")

Quayle's point was that kids of unmarried mothers, especially poor mothers, are more likely than other kids to have unhappy or destructive lives. Few people of any political philosophy disagreed with the overall statistics he cited, despite the many successful and happy people who have been raised by single parents.

A TV portrayal of a happy, prosperous mom who chose to have an out-of-wedlock birth, Quayle argued, encouraged such behavior among poor teenage girls. His supporters noted that environmental lobbying groups seemed to think recycling could be "taught" by a fictional TV series. So why didn't single pregnancy fall into the same category? This echoed the argument of the Parents Music Resource Center: If corporations spend hundreds of millions of dollars on TV commercials, they must know that TV influences behavior.

From a commonsense point of view, I've always felt viewers may decide to wear a different brand of T-shirt or to recycle trash after watching TV. But that doesn't mean they make profound life decisions, such as whether or not to kill someone, or to have a baby and raise it as a single parent, because of feature films or TV sitcoms or song lyrics. These are forms of storytelling that are understood to be layered with comedy, romanticism, sentimentality, irony, hyperbole, and all the other devices of fiction. People understand that

Murphy Brown is a made-up character in a made-up story, not a real woman living alone in a house that needs a lot of work.

"If Dan Quayle wants to assure that Murphy Brown doesn't have any more children out of wedlock," said the show's executive producer, Diane English, "he should work to assure her that she will be able to have safe, legal abortions." Dazzled by the political adroitness of Diane's riposte to the antichoice Quayle, Ramona Ripston and I suggested that she join the honorees for an upcoming ACLU dinner. Diane promptly agreed and supplied us with a montage of scenes from the show she felt were appropriate for the ACLU. We all felt particularly pleased that she would be part of our program, which also was honoring Mayor Tom Bradley.

At the last minute, we were derailed by the kind of self-destructive freak-out that is so common on the political left. English's production company was feuding with TV unions over procedures on another series. One of the unions threatened to picket the ACLU dinner unless we withdrew the award to English.

LA activist Paul Schrade, who saw himself as the staunchest labor advocate on the ACLU board, hounded Ramona and me to give in to the union. I pointed out to Schrade that the award to English had nothing to do with the TV show he was objecting to, and that to set up a picket line around a dinner for the ACLU, which had absolutely nothing to do with TV production of any kind, was a secondary boycott that was both illegal and a violation of ACLU policy. "Of course you feel that way," Schrade snapped. "You're management."

To my dismay, Ramona felt she had to compromise with the union to avoid the embarrassment of a picket line. She came up with the idea of asking English to allow us to show the montage without coming to the dinner herself.

We sent English the award privately the next day. It was immediately returned. English understandably felt betrayed by the ACLU for caving in and has never spoken to me since. For the only time, I considered resigning from the ACLU, but I didn't want to negate the many good things I felt about the organization because of this one disagreement.

Less than a month later, in mid-June, Bill Clinton launched his own attack against popular culture in one of the defining moments of his campaign. Speaking to Rev. Jesse Jackson's Rainbow Coalition, he harshly criticized Jackson for including on a panel at the group's annual conference an obscure rapper named Sister Souljah.

Sister Souljah had suggested it would have been more rational for blacks to attack white neighborhoods instead of their own in the LA riots. Her statement was clearly ironic—if anything, it could be interpreted as a black critique of the senselessness of the riot.

But Clinton saw it as an opportunity to differentiate himself from Jackson and from previous Democratic nominees. Focus groups of swing voters in Michigan had revealed that many white working-class Democratic voters had switched to Reagan and Bush because they felt that the Democratic party was too deferential toward blacks, as evidenced by the visibility at the 1988 convention of the Reverend Jesse Jackson.

In July, Clinton named Al Gore as his running mate. On the slow news day before the Democratic Convention started, CNN asked me for a comment. I said that I'd rather have Gore a heartbeat away from the White House than Dan Quayle. The morning the sound bite aired, I ran into John Dukakis, Michael Dukakis's son, in a Hollywood dry cleaner's. John was the business manager for Boyz II Men and other musical acts. Usually diffident and soft-spoken, he gave me a hug and enthused, "I'm glad you played it that way, we need to stick together right now." Many of my friends in the music business felt differently. Music journalist Dave Marsh and others, including my wife, accused me of selling out.

Not long afterward, the 1992 campaign bumped up against the music business in a controversy about a song by Ice-T called "Cop Killer." It had been on an album released by Warner Bros. the year before, and had neither sold well nor garnered much critical acclaim. When several police associations found out about the song, in which an aggrieved black man fantasizes about killing a police officer, they made it a cause célèbre.

Time Warner chairman Jerry Levin initially defended the album as a valid artistic work in a *Wall Street Journal* op-ed piece. President George Bush, Bill Clinton, Al Gore, and especially Dan Quayle, the four major candidates in the upcoming national election, weighed in with opposition to the song, each trying to outdo the other in terms of pro-police rhetoric. Police groups and their allies, including National Rifle Association president Charlton Heston, decided to make an issue of "Cop Killer" at the 1992 Time Warner stockholders meeting.

I was then working for Atlantic Records, which was, like Warner Bros., a division of the Warner Music Group. Although relations between Atlantic and Warner Bros. were usually chilly with corporate sibling rivalry, Warner Bros. chairman Mo Ostin asked me to brainstorm with his staff. Mo was a staunch defender of artistic freedom.

"I'd put out an anti-Semitic record if my A&R people told me the music was valid," said Ostin, who is Jewish. It seemed to us that the lyrics had to be considered in the context of the humiliation and frustration many Los Angeles–area African Americans had been feeling about the LAPD under Daryl Gates. Lyrics to songs were typically filled with symbolism and exaggeration. Most important, we did not believe that people decided to become violent because of song lyrics.

I sat quietly in the disruptive shareholders meeting as Charlton Heston urged Time Warner to get rid of the no-longer obscure "Cop Killer." Impassioned police officers spoke in outraged tones about being wounded in the line of duty. No one attempted to make any connection between those tragic assaults and a song, but the sheer existence of "Cop Killer" was considered an affront to many police.

The next week, the Time Warner board of directors called for a retreat. Opera diva Beverly Sills was said to have been particularly hard on Mo Ostin. Articles outlining the violent and perverse plot lines of numerous classic operas did nothing to assuage her.

Under intense corporate pressure, Ostin reluctantly negotiated the return of the album to Ice-T and dropped him as a Warner Bros. artist. Howie Klein, the Warner executive closest to Ice-T, recalls, "Before the controversy, the album had sold a disappointing two hundred thousand copies. Afterward, because of all the publicity, it sold one million. I made up a 'platinum' plaque to present to Dan Quayle to thank him for selling so many more records, but Mo didn't want me to actually give it to him."

Having established his credibility with swing white voters by going after Sister Souljah and Ice-T, Clinton showed the political skills that made him a legend. He tacked back toward black and popular culture by playing the saxophone on the *Arsenio Hall Show* and by cooperating with MTV correspondent Tabitha Soren in the network's "Choose or Lose" voter registration campaign, done in partnership with Rock the Vote.

President Bush avoided MTV until the end of the campaign. When he finally consented to be interviewed by Tabitha, he did so while drinking a cup of coffee, exuding body language of discomfort and even contempt. By comparison, Clinton looked like the hippest of hepcats.

The 1992 election was the first since 1972, when eighteen-year-olds became able to vote, in which the voting rate among young people increased, and Clinton won that demographic by twelve points.

Shortly after Clinton was elected, I met his younger brother, Roger, who was looking for a record deal. A week later, I went to a TV show produced by Clinton friend and media advisor Harry Thomason where Roger performed as a warm-up act with a pop/R&B band he called Politics.

Thomason, white-haired, gregarious, and friendly, speaking with a slight stutter, assured us that the president-elect cared deeply about his brother, Roger, and wanted him to be able to emerge as a performer. Roger, it turned out, had a decent rock/R&B voice, which he used to sing a few oldies and a few forgettable new songs. He clearly was talented enough to get gigs as a singer in a bar band, and clearly not unique or special enough to warrant major-label attention were it not for his last name. He was, however, an extremely likable, earnest guy whose brother was going to be president.

Caught up in the moment, we recorded a single song, a cover of Sam Cooke's "A Change Is Gonna Come," backed by the popular R&B group En Vogue. We later gave the rights to the recording to Roger, who included it on an album he released on Pyramid Records.

Late the afternoon of Inauguration Day there was a reception at the offices of the *New Republic*. Al and Tipper Gore attended. As I passed them on my way out, I made eye contact with Tipper and, over the din of the party, mouthed the word "Congratulations." To the astonishment of my friends, she reached over and gave me a big hug.

That evening, the celebrity-laden MTV Ball attracted an extremely high turnout from members of the new Clinton administration. The new president came and thanked Rock the Vote and MTV for their role in his election, but when Roger Clinton emerged to do his version of "A Change Is Gonna Come," the president was nowhere to be found. I later heard he was angry at Roger for some indiscretion.

MTV's Judy McGrath was still aglow from attending a long meeting with Bill Clinton. With her had been Rock the Vote's executive director, Patrick Lippert, a longtime activist for progressive causes, who was thin and drawn from AIDS. Judy recalled, "Clinton looked at Patrick and then at me, and in one instant I could see that he knew the condition Patrick was in, and he gave Patrick this giant long hug and thanked him for everything he had done. We were all crying."

The Clinton years brought many Democrats and some progressives to the halls of power. I was not a so-called Friend of Bill's, but many of my friends and colleagues found themselves in a relationship with the president of the United States for the first time. People who'd been shunned by the White House for more than a decade suddenly had the opportunity to sleep in the Lincoln bedroom. David Geffen and Barbra Streisand each had raised seven-figure sums for the Democrats, were at the apex of accomplishment, and were compelling, charismatic figures. Stories of their visits to the White House and their conversations with the president quickly made the rounds.

Stanley Sheinbaum, who was more doggedly left wing than most Clinton friends, and less significant as a fund-raiser, also had access to the president. When Clinton had first become governor of Arkansas, Stanley and his wife, Betty, had often let the Clintons stay at their Brentwood home. Stanley's primary concern, once he left the LA police commission, was the conflict in the Middle East, and he frequently peppered Clinton with a far more evenhanded perspective than that which came from the official emissaries of the Jewish community.

But no matter who was in the White House, political attacks on popular culture never went away. Booth Gardner, the newly elected Democratic governor of Washington, proudly identified his state as the home of Nirvana in a 1993 address to the legislature. By then, Nirvana had become the most successful and influential rock band in the world. A few months later, the state legislature passed a bill making it illegal for kids under eighteen to attend rock shows that included profanity, even when there was no liquor present.

I called the governor to ask him to veto the bill, which would effectively end rock concerts in the state of Washington and also signal a terrible disrespect to the music scene in Seattle that he seemingly took pride in.

Gardner replied, "I'm going to sign it, but it's unconstitutional, so it will never be enacted."

I asked why he was going to sign it if he knew it was unconstitutional.

"I think it sends a message," he responded.

I asked just what the message was, the message that he wanted me to give Nirvana.

"It sends a message that needs to be sent. I think the message speaks for itself," the governor concluded, before hastily hanging up.

Rap came under heavy fire as the music became bigger than ever. The most successful label was Death Row out of LA. Its artists included Dr. Dre, Snoop Dogg, and Tupac Shakur.

Death Row was affiliated with Interscope Records, which in turn was affiliated with Atlantic Records. One of my responsibilities at Atlantic was to act as a liaison with Interscope, and I talked to Interscope president Jimmy Iovine every day as the attacks on his artists mounted.

At one point, I set up a meeting between Congresswoman Maxine Waters, Snoop Dogg, and Death Row's controversial owner, Suge Knight. Snoop Dogg was under investigation because his bodyguard had killed someone who supposedly intended to attack Snoop. (Snoop was later acquitted of all charges.) At the meeting, the tall, extremely thin, gangly rap star was soft-spoken, and as polite as the choirboy he had been in his younger years.

After Snoop left the meeting, Suge told Maxine that he intended to build some playgrounds in the poor neighborhoods of her district. Maxine stared at him and said, "I'm not here to talk about playgrounds. You know I speak up for you and that I respect what you do. And as far as I'm concerned, anything you want to put onto your albums is fine. It's your art form. But you have to make sure that there isn't any more violence around you or the people in your business. There are enough people who want to stop you. Don't give them the chance to shut you down."

Maxine talked with emotion about the promising young people she had known who were now in prison. Suge was polite and appeared to listen thoughtfully to everything she said. Subsequent violent events, which led to Suge Knight spending five years in prison, indicated that her message didn't have much impact.

The profanity and aggressiveness of rap music strained generational lines as no music had since the political rock of the sixties. Some middle-aged rock artists who had once been attacked for their music found themselves in strange positions. When Luke Skyywalker was arrested in Florida in 1990, I'd asked Allman Brothers drummer Butch Trucks, a Floridian who supported progressive causes, to make a statement opposing the arrest. Butch demurred. "I hate it when my son listens to that rap shit," he said. "I'd feel like a hypocrite defending it."

Some black intellectuals, like Henry Louis Gates of Harvard, defended hip-hop as an authentic art form. And some older African American musicians saw rap as an exciting new vanguard of creative expression. At a Time Warner forum during which Maya Angelou questioned the morality of some rap artists, arranger/composer Quincy Jones, well into his sixties, got up and said, "I'm with the rappers."

But many African Americans who had lived through the civil rights struggle were embarrassed by the anti-intellectual and, at times, seemingly illiterate persona of rap music.

One night, I was at a dinner party at the home of journalist Jack Newfield with former governor Mario Cuomo, his wife, Matilda, and Stanley Crouch. Prompted by Cuomo, I was describing the tensions between the teen and political cultures when Crouch, who is a great authority on jazz, interrupted and began berating me for defending rap music. I told Crouch that I wasn't comparing rap tracks to the virtuosity and brilliance of Duke Ellington, but was defending the need of each generation to express its rebellion and uniqueness through its own culture.

Crouch snarled that the whole idea of teenage rebellion was a creation of the media and added that he had recently explained to his nineteen-year-old daughter that she was too young to have valuable opinions about anything.

Newfield, who shares my feelings about pop culture and generational snobbery, and who has stood on the front lines of political and cultural battles for decades, stared into his soup, hoping this unexpected moment of tension between two of his friends would go away. Cuomo turned to me and asked, "Do boys and girls still dance?" I nodded that they did. Cuomo responded with a theatrical hand flourish and replied, "As long as they still dance, it's okay."

And the tension left the room.

Not long after being elected, President Clinton answered questions on MTV. When a teenage girl asked whether he wore "boxers or briefs," Clinton laughed and answered, "briefs." The Washington political establishment condemned him, arguing that answering the question demeaned the presidency. Clinton advisor Paul Begala told me later that he thought the answer had been a serious mistake.

I disagreed. American political culture desperately needs connective tissue with young people. However, Clinton was highly sensitive to elite criticism, and he backed away from "lowbrow" media and popular culture early in his first term.

One afternoon in 1993, I was invited, along with a few hundred others in the entertainment business, to hear President Clinton speak at the offices of Creative Artists Agency (CAA). Mike Ovitz, president of CAA at the time, was one of the most powerful men in the entertainment business. As Ovitz and the president walked down to the lobby, Tom Epstein, whom I'd met on the Hart campaign and who was now an assistant to the president, beamed with adulation. He whispered to me, "I think Clinton has something really interesting to say today."

After enthusing about American entertainment, Clinton advanced a theory about the effects of violent entertainment on poor children with disengaged parents. People from conventional backgrounds, such as those listening to him that afternoon, could easily distinguish between reality and fantasy, he said. But poor, neglected kids treat the media as a parent and emulate the media the way normal kids emulate their parents.

Those of us responsible for the content of films, TV, and recordings, the president said, needed to imagine the effect of each work on kids who supposedly view the media as their "third parent."

I would hear this theory repeated many times over the years. I think it is complete nonsense.

According to Justice Department studies, the biggest predictor of violent behavior in individuals is whether or not they have been abused as kids. Compared to the trauma of abuse, the influence of a rap song or horror movie is virtually nil. It bordered on obscene to substitute clichés about entertainment for action on the problems that Congressman George Miller and his colleagues had described to us several years earlier: terrible nutrition, bad education, flawed foster care programs, lack of mentors, physical and mental abuse, and the other soul-destroying effects of poverty and neglect.

Many authorities do not agree that children tend to imitate evil deeds depicted in fiction. Renowned child psychiatrist Bruno Bettelheim discusses this point in his classic book *The Uses of Enchantment: The Meaning and Importance of Fairy Tales*. According to Bettelheim, the violence and villainy of classic fairy tales help kids work out their anxieties and forge their identity.

There is no era or culture with a modicum of freedom whose art and entertainment doesn't include the darkest human impulses as themes. Many artists I've worked with who've written lyrics about alienation and violence get emotional letters from fans thanking them for making them feel less alone.

At an ACLU dinner, music manager Jeff Kwatinetz noted that a high school in Michigan had suspended a student for wearing a T-shirt with the logo of the hard rock band Korn, his client.

"Sure," he said, "Korn's music has not always been free of profanity, but their use of language is always reflective of intense emotions and true, visceral feeling."

He said the band received thousands of letters saying essentially the same thing: "I thought I was all alone, but after hearing your music, now that I know I'm not, I can go on with my life and look forward to better times in the future."

In any event, it would be crippling for artists to limit their work based on the possible reaction of the most emotionally damaged members of their audience. Should the Beatles have tried to imagine the effect "Helter Skelter" would have on the psychopathic mind of Charles Manson and tailored the song accordingly?

Just prior to the 1994 midterm election, I got a call from MTV's Judy McGrath, who had been so excited at the inauguration less than two years earlier. "As far as our viewers go," Judy said to me in disgust, "this election is going to be a disaster for the Democrats. Again and again in focus groups we keep hearing young people say, 'I thought Clinton was one of us and it turns out he was one of them.'"

Republicans won the House of Representatives for the first time in forty years.

By then, Rosemary and I had moved back to New York with our three-year-old daughter, Katie, and our new baby son, Max. My boss, Doug Morris, had named me president of Atlantic Records. I stepped down as chair of the ACLU Foundation of Southern California and accepted the more ceremonial role of foundation president, a title I still hold.

After we got settled in New York, Henry Siegman, the executive director of the American Jewish Congress, suggested that I get involved with that organization.

In the 1960s, the New York–based American Jewish Congress had played a leading role in the civil rights movement. I felt that in recent years the organization had focused more on defending Jewish interests than on fighting for minorities and the poor, which I and many Jewish liberals historically viewed as core Jewish values. My father, Victor Goldberg, felt very strongly that to be a good Jew, one must actively care about the most disadvantaged people. He was retired from the textile business and was interested in becoming involved in promoting those beliefs.

After meeting with the board of the American Jewish Congress, I accepted the post of executive vice president, with the understanding that my father and I would create an institute for intergroup relations that would focus initially on repairing black-Jewish relations.

Unfortunately, Henry Siegman chose this time to leave the AJ Congress, and the board named his deputy, Phil Baum, as an interim executive director.

I became nervous almost immediately when Baum began criticizing Siegman for having been too far "left" on Middle East issues, which meant that Siegman had favored dialogue with the PLO. Shortly afterward, Baum issued a statement criticizing the Reverend Jesse Jackson for "trivializing the Holocaust" in a speech at a New York synagogue. Jackson's speech was primarily a plea for intergroup tolerance. In referring to the intolerance of Pat Robertson's right-wing Christian Coalition, Jackson said that Nazi Germany had had groups like that as well.

I thought Baum's attack on Jackson, who was clearly reaching out to the Jewish community, was incredibly inappropriate. I did not want to be accountable for Baum's behavior so I publicly resigned, citing the attack on Jackson.

Jackson called appreciatively, and he visited me at Atlantic several times. From time to time, Reverend Jackson has hectored entertainment companies about content in a way that seems overreaching to me, such as in the eighties when he criticized the Rolling Stones for their lyrics, and more recently the film *Barbershop*. But because of his experiences in the civil rights movement, he sees music and other forms of entertainment as a valuable tool in political organizing. His daughter Santita is an R&B and gospel singer. The longtime civil rights leader also had a long history with Steve Ross, the recently deceased CEO of Time Warner, who had financially supported many of Jackson's projects.

In my experiences at major corporations, I found Jackson to be very different from the cartoon version that conservative critics have drawn. While he would seek donations from time to time, there was never any sense that his friendship was conditional on them. On the contrary, with Steve Ross's death, Time Warner decreased its support of Jackson, and I was in no position to do much about it. Over the years, he's done much more for me than I have for him. When Jesse includes me among those to whom he delivers his monologues about current events, I am always dazzled by his brilliance. His observations are more penetrating than those of 99 percent of elected officials, academics, and pundits.

Early in 1994, Marge Tabankin accepted a fellowship at the Kennedy School of Government at Harvard. We had long ago become close friends as we fought for common causes, and she invited me to come up to Boston and take part in a forum on entertainment and politics. At a dinner afterward, I sat next to Marvin Kalb, the venerable newscaster, author, and professor, a pillar of the intellectual media establishment.

Kalb asked me about what kinds of records sold well and I told him that sales were dominated by the tastes of teenagers, who bought more albums per person than anyone else, resulting in big sales for rock and roll, pop, and rap music. Kalb looked mournful and asked me, "What percentage of total sales are original cast recordings of classic Broadway shows?"

I told him far less than 1 percent. He shook his head sorrowfully. I asked him when the last time was that he had bought a cast recording, and he said he couldn't remember. Then he said that it reflected very badly on the culture that such "classics" didn't sell.

The implication of Kalb's disapproval was that popular culture and the culture of younger generations was illegitimate, even though he himself had limited passion for the culture of the past. It was a classic paternalistic posture of "do as I say, not as I do."

That same year, a corporate drama began unfolding that would dramatically bring together politics and culture, my professional life, and my activist persona.

Atlantic, where I worked, was one of three record companies in the Warner Music Group, a division of Time Warner. The other two were Elektra and Warner Bros. Records.

Since the mid-1960s, Warner Bros. Records had been run by Mo Ostin, one of the most talented and effective music executives of all time. From a tiny, virtually invisible label, Mo had created the number one record company in the world, with a roster that included Madonna, Rod Stewart, Prince, REM, Van Halen, the Red Hot Chili Peppers, Neil Young, and Green Day.

Following Steve Ross's death in 1994, an internal battle began. Mo Ostin was forced out by Warner Music chairman Robert Morgado. Following more corporate machinations, I was asked to leave Atlantic and become the new chairman of Warner Bros. Records.

A few months later, as I struggled to get acquainted with the vast artist roster and executive team at my new company, Morgado was replaced with HBO chairman Michael Fuchs. The chemistry between Fuchs and my boss, Doug Morris, at that point chairman of Warner Music for the United States, was dreadful from the beginning, so I knew my own situation was precarious.

In the spring of 1995, while we were going through these gut-wrenching corporate changes, Senate majority leader Robert Dole, the front-runner for the Republican presidential nomination in the 1996 election, made a scathing speech about an entertainment culture that he said was rife with "nightmares of depravity." According to *The Choice*, Bob Woodward's book about the election, Dole was urged by political advisor Bill Lacy to gain political ground by an "attack [on] Hollywood directly on the grounds of sex and violence in movies and popular music."

The speech, written by Mari Will (wife of conservative columnist George Will), excoriated "a culture business that makes money from 'music' extolling the pleasures of raping, killing, torturing and mutilating women—from 'songs' about killing policemen and rejecting law."

"The mainstreaming of deviancy must come to an end," Dole proclaimed. "We will name their names and shame them as they deserve to be shamed. One of the companies on the leading edge of coarseness and violence is Time Warner.

"I would ask executives at Time Warner a question," he continued. "Is this what you intended to accomplish with your careers? Must you debase our nation and threaten our children for the sake of corporate profits?"

Dole specifically attacked the films *Natural Born Killers* and *True Romance* and named heavy metal act Cannibal Corpse and rappers Geto Boys and 2 Live Crew, but the most intense criticism was of Atlantic's joint venture with Interscope and its Death Row roster of gangsta rappers.

When reporters asked Dole for more detail about the films and records he'd attacked, he sheepishly admitted that he hadn't watched or heard any of them and had based his comments on what others had told him. He admitted he hadn't seen *True Lies* either, although he had bizarrely cited the gory R-rated action film starring Arnold Schwarzenegger as a family-friendly film. *True Lies* was as violent as the movies he condemned, but Schwarzenegger was one of the few big movie stars who regularly campaigned for Republicans.

Notwithstanding the incoherence and hearsay underlying Dole's position, his speech made front pages around the country and was widely praised by media pundits and politicians of both parties.

I asked Clint Eastwood, a Republican, what he thought of Dole's speech. Eastwood is one of America's great patrons of jazz, and I had set up Malpaso Records at Warner Bros. for jazz artists he wanted to support. "You know politicians," Eastwood grumbled in his gravelly voice. "They'll say anything to get their name in the paper."

The Dole speech triggered intense pressure on Doug Morris to "do something" about Interscope, either to sell Time Warner's half ownership of the label or get it to tone down the Death Row rappers. Jimmy Iovine and Ted Field, who owned the other half of Interscope, had no intention of asking rappers to change music that their fans obviously loved. Dr. Dre's recent album had sold 5 million copies and Snoop Dogg's had sold 6 million, putting them among the most popular recordings of the year.

A press conference to attack rap music and Interscope was called by C. Delores Tucker, a former civil rights activist who had become the most outspoken African American opponent of rap; William Bennett, the former drug czar in the Bush administration; and Democratic senator Joseph Lieberman of Connecticut. The triumvirate got a meeting with top Warner executives Jerry

Levin and Doug Morris, where Bennett challenged Levin to read Dr. Dre's lyrics out loud. Raps, like other lyrics, are obviously not written to be recited by businessmen without accompaniment, but this gimmick would become a staple of confrontations between cultural reactionaries and entertainment executives.

Carla Hills, who had been the U.S. trade representative in the George Bush administration, was a member of the Time Warner board and was said to have been mortified when Dole teased her about the company's rap records at a Republican fundraiser.

Shortly thereafter, the Reverend Al Sharpton asked to meet with us. I joined Doug Morris, Elektra Records chairman Sylvia Rhone, and Ken Sunshine, who had recently been hired by Warner Music as a corporate PR expert, in the Time Warner conference room, where Sharpton urged us not to get rid of rap music.

From his days as a child preacher, the New York civil rights leader had been friends with James Brown. He had later worked with the Jackson family. He had a vivid memory of the fifties and early sixties, when R&B music was banned from pop radio playlists and shunned by many major labels for supposedly moral reasons. Afterward he told a battery of news crews he had urged us not to give in to conservative pressure, which he viewed as racist.

Rev. Jesse Jackson, Representative Maxine Waters, Professor Michael Eric Dyson of the University of North Carolina, and Professor Henry Louis Gates, director of African American Studies at Harvard, were among the black leaders who subsequently echoed Sharpton's sentiments.

Clinton campaign advisors James Carville and Paul Begala called Sunshine and me and gave us a private pep talk, helping us brainstorm about how to spin the issue, but there was no interest elsewhere in the white political or pundit world in refuting the attacks. To the best of my knowledge, no white Democratic officeholder has ever publicly disagreed with the damning of pop culture by Dole and Lieberman.

On a short corporate leash, I did make one public comment criticizing the critics. Asked by the *Washington Post* if I would've signed Nine Inch Nails, one of the Interscope artists who had been attacked, I replied:

"Nine Inch Nails is a Grammy Award–winning, critically acclaimed artist who millions of people love. Why should a corporation listen to a bunch of middle-aged people who don't like the music and don't listen to it and ignore the people who do love it and who do buy it?"

Doug Morris had encouraged me to respond to the attacks on Interscope, but now his boss Fuchs insisted I stop, so I canceled a scheduled appearance on *Face the Nation*. Guest William Bennett gloated at my absence: "I'm not surprised that Warner wouldn't want Mr. Goldberg to represent them. He's with the extreme left of the ACLU."

And Robert Bork would soon slam me for the *Washington Post* quote in his best-seller *Slouching Toward Gomorrah*: "The reason the corporation should listen to those middle-aged people is that they are attempting to uphold some standard of decency, for the protection, among others, of those who love and buy the filth."

Having been too young to make Nixon's enemies list, I figured that being attacked by Bork and Bennett is the closest I can come. As all this was going on, Interscope's Jimmy Iovine called me, laughing, and said, "It's your curse to defend what makes me rich."

In July, Doug Morris was fired by Fuchs. I was out in August, and by the end of the year Fuchs himself had been fired by Time Warner chairman Levin. Early the next year, Time Warner sold its half of Interscope to Universal for $200 million.

In January 1996 I accepted a job as president of Mercury Records, a New York–based label that was a division of Polygram. My predecessor, Ed Eckstine, son of jazz legend Bill Eckstine, had discovered and signed several important R&B artists, including Vanessa Williams, Brian McKnight, and Toni Tone Tony. Bon Jovi and John Cougar Mellencamp had been on the roster since the seventies.

A creative soul whose best work came in the recording studio, Ed was burned out on executive life, but he had left Mercury with two hits, a platinum album (1 million copies sold) by the so-called hippie band Rusted Root, and a brilliant Joan Osborne album called *Relish* that would sell over 4 million. As I arrived, "One of Us," a single from *Relish*, was becoming a huge hit around the world.

"One of Us," written by Eric Bazilian, was one of those very rare songs that was both instantly catchy and genuinely meaningful. The lyrics imagined God physically walking the earth and even taking a bus.

Rather than rejoice that a piece of pop culture was dealing with spirituality on a very human level, William Donahue of the Catholic League attacked the song as "anti-Catholic" because of the supposedly irreverent reference to the Pope. Joan, who was raised as a Catholic, was disgusted.

The furor reminded me of my management days, when one of my clients, the Christian heavy metal band Stryper, was attacked by televangelist Jimmy Swaggart. Regardless of the lyrics, Swaggart maintained, rock and roll was inherently evil because of the sensual rhythm and music. The members of Stryper and their families had been great admirers of Swaggart and ended their concerts by throwing Bibles into the audience. They were devastated by his irrational attack on them.

This kind of wrongheaded, stubbornly narrow interpretation of religious orthodoxy, a kind of spiritual version of political correctness, was not restricted to Christian leaders in the late nineties. Both of my kids were fans of the Nickelodeon TV show *Rugrats*, and one of the things I particularly liked about the show was that it depicted the Pickles family as unambiguously Jewish. *Rugrats* even created Hanukkah and Passover specials. I cannot think of any other TV show, animated or otherwise, in which Jewish traditions were so clearly expressed in the context of a mass appeal entertainment.

Rather than celebrate this remarkable development, the Anti-Defamation League attacked *Rugrats*, followed by the *Washington Post* editorial page. Supposedly, the drawings of the Pickle grandparents resembled anti-Semitic drawings from the 1930s in a Nazi newspaper. Albie Hecht, the Jewish president of Nickelodeon, was flabbergasted by the absurdity of this accusation.

At the same time, Jenette Kahn, the Jewish president of DC Comics, directed that an issue of *Superman* be devoted to the superhero traveling back in time to the days of the Holocaust. Rather than congratulating DC Comics for dramatizing the murder of millions of Jews for a younger generation, the ADL's Abe Foxman criticized the comic because the victims were not explicitly identified as Jewish—despite the fact that they all had Jewish names and spoke Yiddish.

Meanwhile, in Washington a new technology called the V-chip was being eagerly endorsed by many pundits and politicos. The V-chip is designed to let parents program their television sets to block children from watching shows with adult themes.

Dr. Rosalyn Weinman, who was an NBC executive at the time, recalls, "The V-chip proposal came about because Senator Paul Simon, while staying in a hotel, saw some of *The Texas Chainsaw Massacre* on Spectravision and confused it with broadcast."

Spectravision was a pay cable service that could only be accessed through a credit card, usually as part of the billing in hotels. In other words, it was virtually impossible for a kid to stumble upon a Spectravision movie accidentally.

Painstaking and repeated explanations to Simon and his staff that his experience had absolutely nothing to do with network television, or even conventional cable TV, did not seem to get the point across. "He couldn't distinguish between the box and what came out of the box," recalls Dr. Weinman. "And his staff refused to acknowledge the distinction as well."

A series of meetings on the V-chip ensued, first with Simon and other members of Congress, later with top representatives of the Clinton administration. All embraced the gimmick.

Dr. Weinman, as executive vice president of standards and practices, was NBC's chief spokesperson and strategist on dealing with government pressure. She recalled, "The conversations were tautologies. They were truly going around in circles. It was 'whose definition?' Good violence versus bad violence."

Simon focused on graphic violence because it supposedly led to real violence. But Janet Reno, who has admitted that she did not own a TV set prior to becoming attorney general, was concerned about violence that wasn't graphic enough. Sanitized violence, she believed, could mislead kids into underestimating the consequences of violent behavior.

"The more we talked," Dr. Weinman recalled, "the more frightful it was in terms of who gets to decide on the definition of what is or is not deemed as violent entertainment."

Advocates of the V-chip, like others who have attacked entertainment media over the years, insisted that there were numerous scientific studies that "proved" a connection between television and antisocial behavior. In fact, there is a vast range of scholarly disagreement on the subject.

No respected scientist would argue that smoking has not been shown to cause cancer. But a number of academics and researchers question the validity of studies suggesting that television causes violence. Jib Fowles of the University of Houston dissects many supposedly scientific studies in great detail in *The Case for Violence on Television*. Civil liberties authority Marjorie Heins does the same in *Not in Front of the Children*, which in 2002 won the American Library Association's award for the best book on intellectual freedom.

In November of 2000, Fenton Earls of Harvard and Jonathan Freeman of the University of Toronto, among others, debunked the TV/violence research in a thoroughly investigated *Rolling Stone* article by Pulitzer Prize–winner Richard Rhodes.

These and other scholars and journalists conclude that the much-publicized studies linking TV and violence lack credibility because they are based on completely artificial testing environments. Moreover, a phenomenon called researcher expectation makes subjects, particularly children, tend to want to give researchers the answers they are looking for.

In some studies, those exposed to supposedly violent TV clips actually showed less aggression than control groups. One study even showed that exposure to *Sesame Street* and *Mr. Rogers' Neighborhood* tripled aggressiveness in preschool kids.

"It's lousy science," says Dr. Weinman dismissively. "Kids watching a cartoon and then loudly saying 'pow, pow' is neither a reliable nor valid finding that television violence causes real-world violence."

Ultimately, government officials admitted there is no proof that violent entertainment causes violent behavior, but they said there is a "correlation," a conclusion that is worthless in showing cause and effect. There is also a correlation between being admitted to the hospital and dying.

Violent people may be disproportionately attracted to violent entertainment. But that does not mean that the entertainment itself makes them violent. Millions of people watch violent movies and live nonviolent lives. In Japan, extremely graphic violence is a staple of television. Japan has a very low rate of violent crime.

Dr. Weinman was frustrated by congressional staffers who refused to consider research that contradicted their biases. "A good deal of shoddy academic work was heralded by people in government," she said. "One particularly egregious study stated that the most violent program in the year the study took place was *Laugh-In*'s twenty-fifth anniversary show."

The whole endeavor, she said, was undermined by the refusal to even look at the effects of television news. She said, "Every piece of legitimate research showed that if there was a truly problematic effect, it was a result of kids watching real news, especially young children watching during the five o'clock to six o'clock local-news time period, when producers often follow the maxim 'if it bleeds it leads.'" But, Dr. Weinman said, politicians and their aides shied away from stirring up the ire of journalists.

During that period, at a dinner with television executives, Vice President Gore remarked, "TV violence is like salt. Salt doesn't hurt most people, but for a few it was bad for their health." President Clinton had been working from a similar arrogant assumption when he suggested that entertainment executives tailor their shows and recordings based on their possible impact on the most emotionally damaged and vulnerable members of the audience.

Television executives were repeatedly frustrated when they tried to talk specifics with congressional aides. Dr. Weinman recalls, "I would ask them to give me an example of five shows that they thought were violent, so I could get a flavor of what they wanted blocked. And they'd be silent, so I'd say, 'Tell me four, tell me three, tell me two.' And they literally would say, without any embarrassment, 'Well, I don't really watch much TV.' They were unable to give any examples of any specific shows that they deemed violent."

In February, the Telecommunications Act of 1996 was signed by President Clinton, mandating V-chips for half of all TV sets with thirteen-inch screens or larger sold after June of 1999, and all sold after June of 2000. The networks agreed on a ratings system that they hoped would conform to V-chip capability.

Within a few years, the failure of the plan was clear. In July of 2001, the Kaiser Family Foundation released a survey showing that only 17 percent of parents who had one of the new TV sets and 7 percent of all American parents used the V-chip, despite widespread publicity from the networks and parents' publications. And there were very few calls to an 800 number set up for anyone who wanted to complain about programming. Says one network executive, "This was strictly a creation of the Beltway."

Shortly after I interviewed her for this book, Dr. Weinman called me to add a thought. "There were hundreds and hundreds of hours spent by very intelligent people on the V-chip. Instead of all that effort being made for political expediency, that combination of government officials and TV producers could have done *something* that was actually helpful," she said mournfully.

The liberal snobs inside the Washington Beltway did not let up on their attacks on popular culture. Senator Joseph Lieberman and others complained when NBC moved the time slot of the popular TV sitcom *Friends* from 9 P.M. to 8 P.M., when more children presumably would be awake. *Friends* is filled with sexual innuendo among its young adult characters, but it is far from graphic in either its images or its language.

"We got virtually no complaints about *Friends* being at eight o'clock," said NBC's Dr. Weinman. "If there was a news interrupt or an Olympics interrupt in regular programming in that time frame, you could get as many two thousand to three thousand phone calls complaining that regularly scheduled shows were pre-empted. So it's not as though people who wanted to contact the networks to complain about programming couldn't figure out how to do it."

Political scientists can do a far better job than I can in evaluating President Clinton's first term, but it seems almost impossible to find a rational description of it. To his partisans he was a genius who saved America's economy. To the right he was an incarnation of the worst aspects of the sixties. To many on the left his presidency was, as Harry Belafonte says, "a betrayal" because of his failure to get universal health care, his uncritical support of big business interests, his mostly moderate judicial appointments, and his lukewarm support for civil liberties. Belafonte laments, "We invested in Clinton and he helped put the knife into liberal character, and liberal minds."

To me, Clinton was what he always said he was: a political moderate, more progressive than recent Republicans and less so than liberal Democrats. Although I share a lot of the progressive critique of Clinton, there is no denying that on some crucial cultural issues he made a huge positive difference. No previous president acknowledged the gay and lesbian community the way Clinton did, and his actions, big and small, helped break down an ugly and immoral wall of prejudice. And most significant, when affirmative action for minorities and women was under assault by both conservative forces and middle-of-the-road Democrats, Clinton guaranteed it for another generation with his impassioned and effective speech in which he said, "Mend it, don't end it." It was no accident that African Americans became one of Clinton's most loyal group of supporters, and it reflects on Clinton's best side.

After losing the 1996 presidential election, the would-be moral leader Bob Dole began appearing on TV and in print ads as a spokesperson for the newly available impotence drug Viagra. With his newfound image as a virile older guy, Dole then appeared in a Pepsi commercial sitting next to a hound dog and watching sexily dressed teenage pop singer Britney Spears dance and gyrate suggestively.

As the commercial ended, Dole glanced up at the screen, then at his dog, and said, "Down, boy."

# CHAPTER 9

# Clinton's Second Term

> *Said the Speaker Skeleton, you won't sign the bill, Said the Presidential skeleton, yes I will.*
>
> –Allen Ginsberg, "Ballad of the Skeletons"

I N MY PROFESSIONAL LIFE, I got lucky again when Russell Simmons and Lyor Cohen, the co-owners of Def Jam, chose to become affiliated with Mercury. That gave us an immediate presence in rap through artists such as LL Cool J.

The success we had with Def Jam and Joan Osborne gave me the chance to fulfill a long-held desire to produce some spoken-word records. Poetry and other spoken-word albums sell a limited amount but cost very little to produce, and I like to think of them as a way of connecting the record business with literary tradition.

The first release was from Paul Krassner, the longtime editor of the *Realist* and one of the founders of the Yippies. Krassner had been a hero of mine since high school.

Then came Timothy Leary. Tim and I had been friends for more than a decade, and when he learned that he was dying of cancer, he said he wanted to record as much of his last days as possible. We agreed. I visited him often in that period. We did audio recordings of deathbed interviews, and Danny Schechter shot them for a home video.

It's always painful when a friend dies. Not being able to call Tim on the phone or drop by to listen to him chat with excitement about some new technology or some old feud is an irreplaceable loss. But the way Tim handled his death, with equanimity, humor, and feistiness, was inspiring and underlined for me the depth of his spiritual core. One day, about a month before he died, I was with him when he called William Burroughs at his home in Kansas. I sat as Leary listened to Burroughs talk for a few minutes, only getting in a few grunts.

After he had hung up, Tim said to me, "Jesus, if there was one person I thought I could count on to be unsentimental it was Burroughs, and here he is blubbering away like a child." Tim's face was emaciated by illness, but he grinned at me with a wry sparkle in his eye.

Tim was reviled by drug warriors and was arrested dozens of times. But he saw psychedelics as a consciousness-expanding sacrament and thought they should be taken only under supervision. He never advocated hard drugs like heroin or cocaine or amphetamines. I didn't agree with everything Leary said or did, but I grew to love him personally. I think he was much more of a force for good, and for enlightenment, than for bad.

Of all the great people he had met in his life, Leary had told me, the greatest was Allen Ginsberg. I reconnected with Allen after seeing him perform his poem "Ballad of the Skeletons" with members of the Patti Smith Group for Tibet House at Carnegie Hall. The poem, an impressionistic commentary on the Clinton era, included the couplet:

Said the Middle Kingdom skeleton, we swallowed Tibet
Said the Dalai Lama skeleton, indigestion's what you get.

I thought the ballad was one of Allen's most successful mixes of poetry with rock, and Mercury recorded Allen chanting it with musical help from Paul McCartney, Lenny Kaye, and Philip Glass. Sophisticated about the limits of radio freedom, Allen made me a "clean" profanity-free version as well as the full-length "dirty" version. Allen asked many of his artist friends, such as David Hockney and Julian Schnabel, to do drawings for the packaging. We released it on Bill Adler's Mouth Almighty imprint.

Allen Ginsberg had helped create modern culture and remembered in detail his early battles. Neoconservative Norman Podhoretz had attended Columbia at the same time as Ginsberg and Jack Kerouac. Allen recalled, "I was the editor of the Columbia literary magazine and refused to publish Podhoretz's poetry. He was a terrible poet."

Later, when *On the Road* and "Howl" were published, Podhoretz viciously denounced the Beat movement.

"All through the years," said Allen, "he's attacked us, and over these many years, every time I need to debate an idea, I argue with him in my imagination. I'm going to call him and thank him for having been a kind of spiritual teacher over so much of my life, representing a force that sharpens my arguments and commitment."

Allen, a devout Buddhist, actually did try to get in touch with Podhoretz. In his memoir *Losing Friends*, Podhoretz boasts that he refused to return Allen's call because he could not forgive him for the "damage" he'd done to American culture. Soon afterward, Allen was dead.

Tom Freston and Judy McGrath of MTV were both huge Ginsberg fans. A low-budget video of "Skeletons" was directed by Gus

Van Sant, and MTV played it for many weeks. At the time of Allen's death, we were planning an "Unplugged" concert that would feature Bob Dylan and many others who owed so much to Allen.

The recording, which was to be Allen's last, gave the great poet a connection with yet another new generation of rock fans. We also released spoken-word recordings by Burroughs, Jim Carroll, and Spalding Gray, among others.

On the more commercial side, Mercury ushered in a new generation of teen pop with Hanson, who sold more than 10 million copies worldwide of their debut album, propelled by the song "Mmmm Bop." Hanson was the first group I worked with that my kids personally appreciated.

When Hanson played *Saturday Night Live*, both Lisa Marie Presley and Caroline Kennedy brought their kids to rehearsal to get the group's autographs. I got a huge kick out of knowing that a group that I helped launch meant something to the grandchildren of John F. Kennedy and Elvis Presley.

Another notable success was the acquisition of half of Phil Walden's Capricorn label. Walden, who had managed Otis Redding and the Allman Brothers, had signed some great new rock bands. We quickly got two of them, 311 and Cake, to platinum.

In May of 1997, two controversies involving popular culture and free speech collided at an ACLU dinner in Los Angeles.

Gloria Steinem and several other feminists objected to our honoring director Milos Forman for his film *The People vs. Larry Flynt*. Steinem felt that the film glamorized a vile pornographer whose *Hustler* magazine debased women, pointing out that he had once run an illustration of a woman's body going into a meat grinder.

Forman grew up in Communist-controlled Czechoslovakia and had a deep personal and emotional commitment to free speech. To him, the movie was about the First Amendment. He also found the attack aesthetically baffling. "Why," he wondered, "would portraying a character be described as glamorizing him?"

Flynt's character, played by Woody Harrelson, did many unsympathetic things and comes across as a morally flawed and deeply unhappy person. But his victory in the Supreme Court over Jerry Falwell's libel suit was a landmark decision for freedom of the press.

In fairness to Steinem, Forman did choose to give Larry Flynt a cameo role and included him in a lot of the film's publicity, somewhat undercutting his argument that it was not the man but free speech that the film was celebrating. Nonetheless, Ramona Ripston and I considered Forman to be a major and serious artist and saw the film as a rare dramatic depiction of an important First Amendment fight. Free-speech advocacy often involves defending the rights of people whose views are repellent. From a practical standpoint, we also knew that honoring Forman would attract financial support from the film industry.

The second dispute, a related one, was the most bizarre. Courtney Love had starred in the film as Larry Flynt's wife, and I asked her to present the award to Forman. Courtney delivered a thoughtful and moving speech about free speech and about what Milos Forman meant to her. After Forman accepted his award, a young man with a British accent walked confidently onto the stage and started railing about how hypocritical it was for Courtney to talk about free speech when she herself was so uncooperative with the press.

It became apparent to me that the speaker was about to bring up the crazy Internet rumors that Kurt Cobain had not committed suicide but had been murdered. Knowing how depressed Kurt had been in the days prior to his death, I have zero respect for this theory. But most important, I didn't want Courtney subjected to this painful diatribe about her late husband after she had been gracious enough to appear at the dinner. I ran onto the stage and shouted at the intruder, "You're not part of the program, get off of the fucking stage." He immediately walked away.

I later found out that the man was filmmaker Nick Broomfield, who was working on a documentary called *Kurt and Courtney*. The scene at the dinner is included in the movie, accompanied by his self-righteous narration about the paradox of a free-speech organization stifling speech. Broomfield's simplistic attack ignores the fact that the First Amendment does not give anyone the right to rudely crash a private event and seize the microphone.

In late 1997, Polygram increased my responsibilities, promoting me to chairman of the newly created Mercury Records Group. The group included Motown Records and the Polygram classical labels, as well as Def Jam and Mercury Nashville. Early the following year, Phillips, the Dutch electronics company that owned 75 percent of Polygram, announced it would sell it to Universal. It took most of the year for the deal to go through, and I did my job in the midst of uncertainty.

Two of my personal signings to Mercury were Lucinda Williams and Shelby Lynne, both strong, fearless, sexually frank singer-songwriters whose records had not done very well commercially. Lucinda, a critical favorite who had never sold more than 75,000 albums, had been a longtime legal client of Rosemary's. For months, I had heard Lucinda's completed but unreleased album *Car Wheels on a Gravel Road* on Rosemary's car stereo. The album had been recorded for Rick Rubin's American Records but rejected by his two distributors, Warner Bros. and Columbia Records.

To my ears, the songs on *Car Wheels* were powerful, and some of them had strong potential commercial appeal. I also thought the production, by Steve Earle, made it more musically accessible than her previous work. We bought the album from Rubin and released it on Mercury, and it became a hit. *Car Wheels* eventually sold over 500,000 copies, making it Lucinda's first gold (500,000 units sold in the United States) album. It won a Grammy Award for best contemporary folk album.

Shelby Lynne's *I Am Shelby Lynne* also went gold and won a Grammy. She was named best new artist, despite the fact that she had been making records for over a decade.

The most successful project was Shania Twain's superb country album *The Woman in Me*. Shania's previous album had sold 7 million copies, making her the biggest female star in country music. We promoted *The Woman in Me* to a pop audience as well, and it sold over 20 million copies worldwide.

On the classics side, we focused on Andrea Bocelli, who became the first operatic tenor since Pavarotti to sell over a million albums. But perhaps the most interesting, enlightening, and fulfilling work I did involved Motown.

Polygram had been unhappy with Motown's profits ever since it acquired the label in the early nineties. Motown's chairman, Clarence Avant, and I were asked to find a new president. Clarence suggested movie producer George Jackson, and I immediately agreed. George and I had become friends in Los Angeles where he had co-produced such films as *New Jack City* and *Krush Groove*.

Until I worked with George Jackson and Motown I had not fully realized how meaningful the company was to the African American community. To me, Motown was the source of classic pop and R&B music, and its recordings by Diana Ross, Marvin Gaye, Smokey Robinson, the Temptations, and others were America's answer to the Beatles and Rolling Stones in the 1960s.

In the African American community, however, Motown was also a symbol of black entrepreneurship. Founder Berry Gordy was one of the preeminent African American business success stories of the era, and certainly the most prominent one in the entertainment business.

Diana Ross held a dinner at her home welcoming George Jackson to Motown, and sitting next to Berry Gordy I felt that I was with a historical figure as significant as Jackie Robinson.

George and I made many appearances in front of young mostly African American audiences who wanted information about entering the entertainment business. Intellectually, I had long understood the terrible legacy of racial discrimination. But I had not realized until then how close to the surface the feelings of vulnerability of young African American men and women are, many of whose parents were blocked from avenues to business success that many whites take for granted.

In the middle of trying to help George and Clarence revive Motown, I was asked to get involved with a racial contretemps at Polygram.

In a deposition, Polygram executive Eric Kronfeld was asked about the criminal record of a black employee. Kronfeld went off on a bit of a tangent, decrying the American criminal justice system for its treatment of blacks, and stated that ex-convicts were so common among black men of a certain age that it was hard to hire a black staff without including some with criminal convictions.

In the cold light of a written transcript, taken out of context, Kronfeld's remarks could be interpreted as saying that most black men were criminals. An excerpt was quickly e-mailed and faxed around the country, and public pressure began building on Polygram to disavow Kronfeld's statement and fire Kronfeld.

Kronfeld made a public apology. He was strongly defended by Clarence Avant, known as the "godfather of black music" because he was a key advisor to most senior black music executives, including Quincy Jones. But fallout from the deposition was so great, and the underlying emotions so bitter, that the issue kept getting bigger. One afternoon, I was asked to join top Polygram executives and Clarence Avant in a meeting on the problem with Jesse Jackson.

An outside litigator hired by Polygram warned that Jesse Jackson was a "hustler" who was there to try to shake the company down, but I told my colleagues that my experiences suggested otherwise, and asked them to keep open minds.

After listening to our side of the story, Jackson suggested that Polygram as a company should apologize, and he suggested that Clarence Avant be given a seat on a largely ceremonial company policy board. We agreed. Jackson issued a statement that he was satisfied with the solution, and the furor died down. Jesse Jackson never asked Polygram for a dime.

In 1998, the Mercury Records Group led all its competitors in over-the-counter sales. Despite our success, in early 1999 the new owner, Universal, dismantled the group and spread its companies over various new divisions. George Jackson and I were among the Polygram executives who were asked to leave.

On April 20, 1999, two students at Columbine High School in Littleton, Colorado, opened fire with assault rifles on students and faculty. They killed twelve students and one teacher before turning the weapons on themselves.

Initial media reports suggested that the Columbine killers were fans of rocker Marilyn Manson, leading a Denver concert promoter to cancel a scheduled Marilyn Manson show. It soon was revealed that Eric Harris and Dylan Klebold didn't even like Marilyn Manson. They thought the band's music was "wimpy." There was, as it turned out, not the slightest evidence of a connection between the entertainment tastes of Harris and Klebold and their murderous behavior.

Similarly, Jim Carroll, author of the semi-autobiographical novel *The Basketball Diaries*, was attacked because of a scene in the movie version of the book—Leonardo DiCaprio portraying Carroll, is shown having a dream in which he imagines killing kids and a teacher at school. Carroll is my wife's first husband and a close family friend. Nonviolent and socially conscious, Carroll was devastated by the attacks and asked for my advice on dealing with the media.

"When CNN shows the clip, they edit out the context that shows it's a dream," Carroll told me. His pain and frustration showing on his face, he said intensely, "Artists have nothing to do with the deranged actions of a few celebrated nutcases. The guy who shot John Lennon, Mark David Chapman, loved *Catcher in the Rye*. But how many millions of people have been helped by that book or by mine to feel less isolated, less alone, relieved to know there is someone else out there who understood how they feel?"

Although there was no evidence that the Columbine killers liked or even ever saw *The Basketball Diaries*, the film had been mentioned by a killer at a similar incident in West Paducah, Kentucky. In the wake of Columbine, MGM withdrew the home video.

President Clinton, under siege because of the unfolding Monica Lewinsky scandal, ordered the Federal Trade Commission to investigate entertainment marketing practices. And Senator Lieberman renewed his attacks on teen-oriented films, saying, "None of us wants to resort to regulation, but if the entertainment industry continues to move in this direction and continues to market death and degradation to our children and continues to pay no heed to the real bloodshed staining our communities, then the government will act."

Meanwhile the annual National Rifle Association convention went on as scheduled in Denver, a few miles from Columbine. NRA president Charlton Heston proclaimed, "We cannot, we must not let tragedy lay waste to the most rare, hard-won right in history...the right to bear arms."

In the spring of 1999, I started an independent company called Artemis Records in partnership with Michael Chambers, who had produced several movies, including *Kids*, and started a small heavy metal label. Our first album release, in the fall of 1999, was *Somewhere Between Heaven and Earth* by singer-songwriter Cindy Bullens. The album was a tribute to her daughter, who had died of Hodgkin's disease at the age of eleven. A most remarkable expression of love and grief, the album has become a cult treasure for people who have lost loved ones. Some of the Columbine families e-mailed their thanks to Cindy when the album was released and wrote about it on their websites.

Other early Artemis releases included gold albums from rapper Kurupt and the female heavy metal band Kittie, and new recordings from Steve Earle, Rickie Lee Jones, and Warren Zevon.

During the late 1990s, the music business was rocked by the Internet. Start-up companies such as MP3.com and Napster tested the limits of copyright law by providing free access to thousands of recordings. The RIAA, representing major record companies, sued to stop this practice. I kept Artemis out of these disputes. On one hand, we certainly needed strong copyright laws to protect our releases, as did all intellectual property businesses. On the other hand, we were an independent label and I didn't want us associated with the rigid approach of the majors. We often experimented with the Internet in ways the majors wouldn't; for example, by releasing songs to publicize albums and producing Internet radio shows.

I had gotten to know Rabbi Michael Lerner, founder and editor of *Tikkun* magazine, when I lived on the West Coast. Started during the Lebanon war, *Tikkun* importantly gave voice to American

Jews who disagreed with Israel's policy and who identified with the Israeli peace camp. My attraction to *Tikkun* was also based on Lerner's analysis of American politics. I admired some of his insights about the American left, particularly the belief that spirituality could and should be a part of the way progressive ideas are expressed. Much as some of us had implored the left to learn from Ronald Reagan's media savvy, Michael urged progressives to respect the spiritual yearnings addressed by organizations like the Moral Majority.

Michael and his colleague Peter Gabel, both of whom had been Berkeley radicals in the sixties, tried to make connections between modern politics and what they saw as the best qualities of the sixties.

I disagree with Lerner and Gabel about some civil liberties issues. Michael and Peter are die-hard supporters of free speech. But they feel that excessive focus on such civil liberties as gay rights and the rights of the accused (as in the O. J. Simpson case) can tear apart a sense of community. In this respect, Lerner and Gabel are similar to the communitarian intellectuals who had influence on President Clinton.

I feel that these communitarians have it exactly wrong. The fight for civil liberties, as I have experienced it, is about championing the rights of other people, about supporting those with whom we may have little in common. It creates community. Principles like freedom of religion, freedom of speech, freedom from racial and sexual discrimination, and the right to a fair trial are connections that everyone in a free society can plug into.

However, Michael Lerner always relished debate, and I greatly respect his voice. In 1997, Michael asked me to become publisher of *Tikkun*. With the magazine based in San Francisco, he was looking for funding and editorial input from New York. By coincidence, my father, Victor Goldberg, was getting a little restless in his job as associate publisher of the *Nation* but was still eager to stay involved in progressive causes.

From 1997 to 2000, my dad and I were co-publishers of *Tikkun*, and ran a small editorial office out of New York. We got pieces from Mary Gordon, Nick Von Hoffman, and Michael Tomasky. Jack Newfield did a series of interviews with Mario Cuomo, Frank Rich, Budd Schulberg, Jesse Ventura, and his old nemesis Ed Koch.

I usually tried to inject a civil liberties spirit into the magazine that was otherwise lacking. For example, when gay activists around the country urged a boycott of sponsors of Dr. Laura Schlesinger's TV program because of antigay remarks she had made, I opposed the boycott. I can't stand Dr. Laura Schlesinger's self-righteous, narrow-minded, and bigoted concept of morality. But the ACLU, for good reason, has always opposed boycotts intending to block ideas in the media, whether the target is books, movies, or TV shows. Seductive as such campaigns are, when one is wounded by something in the media, the result is a narrowing of "safe" subjects for discussion, and such a narrowing ultimately always serves the status quo and dampens the possibility of progressive change.

Progressives were disappointed with much of Clinton's second term, as they had been with his first and for the same reasons: too much concern with the interests of the superrich, and too little concern with civil liberties. On the other hand, he adroitly stymied the scary reactionary agenda of Newt Gingrich and Tom DeLay in a way that other, less media-savvy Democrats would have had difficulty doing.

The Washington response to the Monica Lewinsky scandal mirrored a lot of the disconnect between politics and culture that I had previously observed. Large majorities of Americans were more appalled by Kenneth Starr's persecution of Clinton than by

Clinton's sins. Yet most Washington politicos and pundits, including many nominal Democrats, sided with Starr. The public be damned.

Although we were never part of Bill Clinton's campaigns, Rosemary and I did get invited to White House Christmas parties during the last two years of his presidency. The president and I never discussed anything of substance, although he chatted in a friendly way with our son, Max, then six and rather shy.

I attribute the White House invites to our friend Sidney Blumenthal, the Clinton advisor who was required to testify in the impeachment trial. Sid has always rolled his eyes at my complaints about liberal snobbery, but he is no snob himself. His son, also named Max, interned at Mercury one summer and later became an accomplished rap producer.

Meanwhile, Clinton himself continued to mix liberal snobbery with a more positive attitude toward the entertainment business. Not long after he'd demanded a Federal Trade Commission investigation into marketing practices in the film, video game, and music businesses, he and the First Lady appeared at Walden Woods in Massachusetts to celebrate a remarkable accomplishment by Don Henley, one of the strongest voices against liberal snobbery and culture bashing.

Early in the nineties, Henley had been outraged to learn that real estate developers planned to build an industrial complex in the woods that Thoreau had immoralized in *Walden*. Many environmentalists considered Walden Woods to be the birthplace of their movement. Having been inspired by Thoreau in his college years, Henley impulsively called me and Betsy Kenny of Norman Lear's office to accompany him on a visit there. We were all transported by the beauty of the woods, as Thoreau had been a 150 years earlier. Henley began a quest to buy the land as a public trust and to build an environmental museum there.

Over the next few years, Henley raised $18 million, the bulk of it by staging benefit concerts with a number of musicians, including his former group, the Eagles. In 1998, I was at the dedication ceremony for the Thoreau Institute and the surrounding ninety-six acres of protected Walden Woods with Betsy Kenny, now Betsy Lack, and her husband, then NBC president Andy Lack. At the time, Washington pundits and politicians, including many so-called liberals, were pounding Clinton on Monicagate, misreading the attitude of the public, much as they did on popular culture. President and Mrs. Clinton, who attended the ceremony, were radiant in describing the importance of Thoreau's legacy. President Clinton was at his best, joking about the irony of walking in pristine woods while trailed by a TV camera. As the president drew connections between the world of art, philosophy, and the environment, Lack looked at me with a shrug of his shoulders and a rueful smile as if to acknowledge that the president, who his own correspondents were relentlessly belittling, could still rise to an occasion such as this with an effectiveness and eloquence rare in public life.

In the spring of the presidential election year of 2000, I was asked by the Creative Coalition to attend a meeting with Joseph Lieberman, Republican senator Sam Brownback of Kansas, and conservative moralist William Bennett, who had been drug czar in the George Bush administration. Besides my disagreement with Bennett about pop culture, I have a deep moral aversion to the war on drugs. If today's drug laws had been in force when I was arrested in the late sixties, my life would have been ruined by imprisonment. Millions of poor people who do not have access to good lawyers languish in prisons for nonviolent drug crimes despite ample evidence from other countries that treatment of drug abuse as a medical problem instead of a criminal problem creates far less social chaos.

About twenty of us from the entertainment business packed into a conference room at HBO's New York offices, including NBC's Roz Weinman, legendary film industry spokesman Jack Valenti, TV and film producer Steven Haft (*The Dead Poets Society*), and Creative Coalition president William Baldwin, the actor.

I first met Joe Lieberman in 1988, when he was asking for money for a run for the Senate. To my lasting regret, I responded to the argument that the Democrats would have a better chance of controlling the Senate if Lieberman defeated Republican Lowell Weicker. I gave Lieberman $250. Thus, in a tiny way, I was complicit in the defeat of Weicker, who was notably sensitive to civil liberties, and the victory of cultural conservative Lieberman. Beneath his affable demeanor, Lieberman has a self-righteous, intolerant, Puritanical streak. "Hollywood is a place that doesn't understand piety," Lieberman once said.

Lieberman led off the meeting at HBO by invoking Columbine and asked, in his scratchy, folksy voice, how we would feel about overall standards for all entertainment, similar to the very strict ones in the movie business from the 1930s to the early 1960s. Lieberman expressed his vision, shared by Bennett and Brownback, for the creation of universal ratings for films, television shows, video games, and recordings with a set of standards that all parents could use.

Billy Baldwin asked me to respond first, and I pointed out that music, films, and video games were totally different forms of communication and did not lend themselves to similar types of categorization. As to "standards," people of goodwill often disagreed about subjects like sex and violence in entertainment. I gave, as an example, Oliver Stone's *Natural Born Killers*, which many social critics had accused of glorifying violence. To me and many others, it was a black comedy satirizing the news media's infatuation with violence.

I cited *Natural Born Killers* in part because I was sitting next to one of its stars, Juliette Lewis. She reiterated that the film was a satire and then pulled out research indicating that all of the murderers in the previous eight schoolroom shootings, including Columbine, had only one thing in common. It was not their taste in entertainment. All of the young killers had been given prescription drugs for psychological and behavioral problems. Lewis pointed out that millions of young children are on these drugs, and cited studies showing that 1 percent of kids taking them could have psychotic reactions. The explosion of violence in schools had come at the same time as the indiscriminate increase in the use of such drugs.

Lieberman had received large campaign contributions from pharmaceutical companies. His wife, Hadassah, had formerly worked for Pfizer, which made some of the mood-affecting drugs used to treat kids. He refused to acknowledge Lewis's comment and acted as if she didn't exist.

None of us agreed with Lieberman, Brownback, and Bennett on universal ratings. "That's off the table," said Haft firmly. But many of the entertainment people said they shared the concern about the state of the culture and welcomed a dialogue.

As the meeting was breaking up, Bennett, who surrealistically has claimed to have dated Janis Joplin, tried to play the part of the affable Washington hipster. He started riffing about the music of Buddy Holly. I quickly left. I couldn't stomach schmoozing with the architect of the war on drugs. I have some standards.

# CHAPTER 10

# The 2000 Election

## Ralph Nader, Joe Lieberman, and Eminem

IN THE SPRING of 2000, Ralph Nader asked for my support in his run for the presidency. I had long admired him for his public interest work, and there was no question that he was willing to speak about the environment, economic justice, and other issues that would otherwise be slighted or absent in the national campaign. However, Nader's self-righteousness in recent years had begun to grate on me. He seemed to feel that his approach to any problem was the only possible choice for a moral person.

Famously out of touch with culture, he

*There is a swelling sense that much of our culture has become toxic. That our standards of decency and civility are being significantly eroded by the entertainment industry's shameless and pervasive promotion of violence, sex and vulgarity, and that traditional sources of values in our society such as faith, family, and school are in a life and death struggle with the darker forces of immorality.*

—Senator Joseph Lieberman, *In Praise of Public Life*, published in September 2000 had said in a recent interview in the *Nation*, "Television watching teaches children that violence is the preferred solution to life's problems. They are taught to value cheap sensuality in everything from sex to self-image to food and they become addicted to entertainment that shortens their attention span." When I complained about this outburst, Nader, who has no children of his own, told me he thought kids would grow up better "if they performed their own versions of Eugene O'Neill plays or *Romeo and Juliet* instead of watching movies or TV."

"Ralph," I responded in frustration, "I've seen two O'Neill plays in the last year and they were filled with alcoholics and depressing monologues. *Romeo and Juliet* ends with a murder and suicide. Frankly, I'm much happier that my kids have memorized large sections of *Austin Powers*." It was clear from the dead silence on the other end of the line that Nader had no idea what *Austin Powers* was.

When Nader again parroted the conventional wisdom about violence and popular culture, I got angry and yelled, "You don't know what you are talking about, and you're needlessly alienating millions of young people who might support you."

"I do know what I'm talking about," Nader yelled back, and hung up.

In April, before the presidential campaign had really heated up, ABC News announced that movie star Leonardo DiCaprio, who was chairman of Earth Day 2000, had interviewed President Clinton for a network special on the environment. Columnists ridiculed the idea, and ABC News stars Sam Donaldson, Peter Jennings, and Diane Sawyer were widely reported to be furious that a mere movie star had been assigned to interview the president.

ABC News president David Westin, apparently intimidated by the snobbish Washington media, backed away. He characterized the interview as merely a brief and unplanned chat, just part of a walk-through in which Clinton showed DiCaprio how the White House had been made environmentally friendly.

Ken Sunshine, who handles DiCaprio's PR, told me at the time, "This is such bullshit. I have e-mails from ABC specifically asking about the interview and scheduling it." It quickly became known that ABC had spent hours setting up cameras for a lengthy interview and had submitted questions to the White House ahead of time. At a Washington correspondents' dinner, Clinton got a big laugh by twitting Westin with "It's not the mistake that causes problems, it's the cover-up."

In May, Rosemary and I hosted a fund-raiser at our house for Hillary Clinton in her race for the Senate. One of our co-hosts was Ken Sunshine. In the midst of a successful evening of schmoozing with people who were delighted to meet her, including our children, Katie and Max, Mrs. Clinton made a point of saying, "I'm glad that President Clinton spoke to Leonardo DiCaprio."

However, ABC had used only a brief fragment of DiCaprio's interview with the president, depriving them (and the Democrats) of the chance to reach a younger audience on environmental issues. Inside-the-Beltway snobbery had prevailed once again.

In early August, about a week before the Democratic National Convention, Al Gore named culture basher Joseph Lieberman as his running mate. Lieberman had publicly castigated Clinton about the Monica Lewinsky scandal, and naming the Connecticut senator to the ticket was widely judged as part of Gore's campaign to distance himself from the president. Voters were suffering from "Clinton fatigue," according to influential pundits and campaign consultants.

Elite Washington's misreading of the public's feelings about the Clinton scandal fatally infected the Gore campaign from the beginning. The public consistently showed that they detested the self-righteousness of Clinton adversaries like special prosecutor Kenneth Starr and Henry Hyde, the Republican chairman of the House Judiciary Committee. The heavy-handed moralism of the Gore-Lieberman campaign may have calmed the anxieties of some anti-Clinton swing voters, but it probably hurt more than it helped with millions of Americans who were much more appalled by the excesses of the president's enemies than by anything Clinton had done.

Lieberman turned off other voters with his incessant references to his orthodox Jewish faith, which became so extreme that even the Anti-Defamation League, which was formed to fight anti-Semitism, criticized him for making religion a litmus test of political virtue. Many civil libertarians felt like feminist Ellen Willis, who wrote in Salon.com that she was supporting Ralph Nader specifically because she was so turned off by Lieberman's excessive religiosity. "He's a Christian rightist in Jewish drag," she wrote, and slammed both Lieberman and Gore for "pandering to religious and moral conservatives."

Gore made his antipathy for popular culture a major part of his 2000 campaign. In his acceptance speech at the Democratic National Convention, Gore said, "To all the families who are struggling with things that money can't measure, like trying to find a little more time with your children or protecting them from entertainment that you think glorifies violence and indecency, I want you to know: I believe we must challenge a culture with too much meanness and not enough meaning."

Of course, he left open the question of just who was to decide the difference between meanness and meaning.

During the convention in Los Angeles, Congresswoman Loretta Sanchez had scheduled a fund-raiser at the Playboy Mansion. Christie Hefner, CEO of *Playboy*, has raised millions of dollars for the Democratic party and its candidates over the years. Because of the moralistic tone that Gore wanted for his convention, enormous pressure was put on Sanchez to cancel the event. A still-outraged Hefner told me later, "They told her that Al Gore would not campaign for her, and that if he were elected he might campaign for a primary opponent in future elections, and that she could be stripped of her committee positions and party leadership roles."

Representative Patrick Kennedy, Ted Kennedy's son, announced that the fund-raiser "totally contradicts what our party stands for in terms of equal rights and civil rights for all people, respect for human dignity of every individual."

*Playboy* has long been a part of mainstream American popular culture and has consistently taken strong stands over the years for civil rights and civil liberties.

"Months earlier," Hefner told me, "Patrick Kennedy had raised thousands of dollars at my house for an Illinois House candidate. How come that was okay, but suddenly it was immoral for a Latino congresswoman to do the event at the mansion?"

Further to the left, there still seemed to be little connection between generations. Antiglobalization protesters, mostly young, demonstrated in front of the convention. They were largely ignored. At the same time, older dissidents had convened a "Shadow Convention" to focus on issues ignored by the major parties. I participated, and I was inspired by the concern with poverty and the war on drugs. But after several elders went on about the need to create a "movement," one of the younger *Tikkun* staffers suggested that they drive a few blocks to where the antiglobalization protesters were being harassed by police. The leftist elite nodded politely and stayed where they were.

After Al Gore announced that Joe Lieberman was going to be his running mate, Nader called again. He gleefully asked, "How do you feel now that Gore has picked the arch critic of entertainment as his running mate?" I told Nader I agreed with him about many issues but I was worried about his effect on the outcome of the election.

Nader told me, as he would many others, that his goal was to get 5 percent of the national vote, enough to funnel millions of dollars in federal financing for the Green party in the next election. He said his plan was to pick up most of his votes in large states where he would not affect the outcome: the Republicans were a shoo-in in Texas, and the Democrats were sure to win in New York and California. So progressives and young people in those three states, the largest in population, could vote for Nader without affecting the outcome. It was a well-thought-out argument that he had obviously repeated many times. He faxed me a Molly Ivins column calling for progressives in locked-up states like Texas and New York to vote "with their hearts" for Nader, while voters in key swing states vote "with their heads" for Gore.

Ralph Nader assured me he would not be campaigning in swing states.

Right after Labor Day, the Federal Trade Commission issued a report criticizing the marketing of violent entertainment. The key point of the study, which had been commissioned by Clinton after the tragic shootings at Columbine, was that entertainment rated unsuitable for children was marketed through media whose audience included many children.

Gore, Lieberman, and Clinton immediately condemned the entertainment companies. The day the report came out, Gore said on the *Oprah Winfrey Show* that if he were elected he would give the companies six months to "clean up their act," and if they did not, he would consider action by the federal government. His wife, he said, had been "successful in convincing the recording industry to use warning stickers when material is inappropriate. We're going to try to persuade the companies to abide by what they said they would do."

Intriguingly, Republican presidential nominee George W. Bush was silent—as supporters in Hollywood like producer Jerry Weintraub did not hesitate to point out.

At that point, much of the furor about popular culture focused on the white rapper Eminem. His album *The Marshall Mathers LP* was full of profanity and flaunted sexist attitudes toward women and lyrics that offended many gays: "My words are like a dagger with a jagged edge/ that'll stab you in the head whether you're a fag or lez," he rapped.

There was a vigorous debate among music critics about the album. Some, such as R. J. Smith in the *New York Times,* argued that Eminem had crossed a moral boundary with his lyrics. Many critics, however, praised the album as a brilliant evolution of rap and saw Eminem as a wisecracking ironist who used exaggeration in a humorous way to make a point.

In *Spin* magazine, rock and roll/country legend Johnny Cash praised Eminem and pointed out, "The biggest-selling song of the nineteenth century was a song about a bandit and an outlaw and a killer. It was called 'The Ballad of Jesse James.'

"Those themes," he said, "have carried through up until now. I watched Elvis go through it—people saying, 'You're leading our children to hell.' I've been hearing it all my life. But I have yet to hear anyone take it seriously and actually shoot a man in Reno just because my song said so."

I empathize with those who feel that when gays are still physically attacked in America, lyrics such as Eminem's can be inflammatory. But Eminem is a legitimate artist, one who populates his songs with many characters, some clearly unsympathetic, to express conflicting ideas. His songs do not have the ugly, leaden quality of Guns N' Roses' late-eighties lyrics cursing "niggers and faggots." Elton John, the most successful openly gay recording artist, praised Eminem's album and performed the song "Stan" with Eminem on the internationally televised Grammy Awards.

Teen culture has always included male adolescent misogyny, but it has also empowered women to express themselves in important ways. It is hard to think of any feminist culture that reached as many young women as the Lilith Fair tours of 1997–98, with the passionate songs of dozens of artists like Sarah McLachlan, Jewel, and Alanis Morissette, and it's impossible to imagine a code of content that would eliminate Eminem's sexist lyrics but give Alanis and Ani DiFranco the freedom, honesty, and frankness that created their intense connection with their audience.

Following the release of the FTC report, congressional hearings were hastily convened for September 13 by the Senate Commerce Committee, chaired by Republican senator John McCain. I was asked to testify, along with the RIAA's Hilary Rosen and Strauss Zelnick, the CEO of BMG's Music Division, a major recording distributor.

We met ahead of time at the law office of David Kendall, a senior partner in the venerable D.C. law firm of Williams and Connolly, which the RIAA had on retainer. Kendall is an expert on First Amendment law but is best known as President Clinton's impeachment lawyer. I was excited to meet the guy who had cross-examined Kenneth Starr.

Kendall was neat in appearance, with perfectly coifed brown hair and slightly graying sideburns. He radiated the physical energy common to many successful people. He turned out to be a master schmoozer, far more vibrant than his stoic, dour, Monicagate TV persona.

Kendall's office displayed fascinating impeachment memorabilia: photos with the president, a framed *Washington Post* front page with the headline "Clinton Acquitted," a framed copy of the actual roll call of the impeachment vote, the "uncomfortable chair" he sat in as counsel for the president at the trial.

When Kendall listened to us talk, he shut one eye, appearing to concentrate intently, as if whoever was speaking were the most fascinating person he had ever met. There must be something in the water supply of Washington that enables its powerful people to do that so convincingly.

Other framed memorabilia identified Kendall as having served as a federal marshal in Oxford, Mississippi, to help enforce the Voting Rights Act. There was also, to my puzzlement, a *National Enquirer* front page revealing that Liberace had AIDS. Kendall explained that he had long represented the *Enquirer* and although it had been a "tough decision," he had advised them to run the story.

The Washington gossip about the hearing at which we were testifying, according to Kendall, was that Senator McCain had scheduled it to give committee member Joe Lieberman another positive media hit. The Arizona Republican had lost a bitter battle for his party's presidential nomination to George W. Bush and was said to be willing to do almost anything to undermine Bush, even while professing to support him.

"The Bush people are furious," Kendall said. They had pressured McCain into including as a witness longtime culture basher Lynne Cheney, the wife of the Republican vice presidential nominee. At that point in the election, national polls conducted by the *Wall Street Journal*/NBC and the *New York Times*/CBS both showed Gore and Lieberman overtaking Bush and Cheney.

Kendall drew my attention to an editorial in that morning's *Washington Post*. It remarked, "When it comes to children, movies and violence it has always been hard to tell whether the H stands for Hollywood or hypocrisy. You have studios and recording companies piously invoking their cultural integrity and First Amendment rights as they peddle stuff with no discernible redeeming virtues. You have the movie theatre chains pretending they can't control the teens who buy tickets to PG-rated films at the multiplex and then stroll in to watch R-rated movies. And you have politicians like Al Gore whose sensibilities on the matter seem to depend on whether today is devoted primarily to soliciting money from the moguls or votes from everyone else."

The *Post* seemed to be suggesting that everyone in America except entertainment moguls—"everyone else"—hated the records and movies and TV shows that had mysteriously become so popular, or at least hated the way the records were sold. Perhaps the editorialists should have checked with the paper's music, TV, and film critics, who often gave their highest praise to the edgy works that had inspired the furor in the first place, including recordings clearly directed at a youthful audience.

Or perhaps they should have polled their readers.

"Seventy-four percent of people surveyed by the FTC are happy with the current record company parental-advisory labeling system," Kendall stressed. "That's in the FTC's own report."

But, he said, "The *Post* is very important here." I rolled my eyes and suggested that the intellectually inbred community in Washington that was so sure the public agreed with it on entertainment had also been certain that the American people wanted Clinton impeached. Kendall smiled and said, "I always used to laugh when people discussing Whitewater would talk about what a small community Arkansas was, as if this town isn't just as incestuous."

As the time to leave for the hearing approached, Hilary Rosen, who as RIAA president thoroughly understands the nuances of

power, warned us to "expect AK-47 attacks from the dozen con-
gresspeople who are speaking before you testify.

"Republicans want to outbid Democrats in attacking Hollywood," she said. "You guys are concerned with what you're gonna
say. The senators only care about what *they're* gonna say."

As we walked to the Hart Senate Building, we ran into Massachusetts Democratic representative Ed Markey, one of several congressmen who were slated to testify. Hilary, who is well connected
on Capitol Hill and exudes far more humanity, passion, and humor
than the typical lobbyist, asked jokingly, "Where are you going—
don't you want to speak and beat us up?"

Markey smiled and said, "I'll be back—there's so many people
speaking I don't want to sit through all of it. It's gonna be like Mo
Udall used to say—'everything's been said but not everyone has
said it.'"

The main hearing room was filled with media and witnesses,
approximately 150 people in addition to most of the 23 members
of the committee. Joe Lieberman was nowhere to be seen.

McCain, in a blue shirt and red tie, had recently recovered from
surgery for skin cancer and wore a bandage on the slightly swollen
left side of his face. He read an opening statement, quoting the
FTC report: "Individual companies in each industry routinely market to children the very products that have the industry's own
parental warnings or ratings with age restrictions due to their violent content."

McCain cited ads for R-rated movies that ran on TV shows such
as *Dawson's Creek* or *The Simpsons,* whose audience is mostly kids
under seventeen. He then made it clear that he was miffed that
only Jack Valenti, president of the Motion Picture Association,
would be there to represent the movie industry.

"There'll be much said today, but thundering silence will be heard from motion picture executives," he proclaimed. "By some uncanny coincidence, every single studio executive was either out of the country or unavailable . . . Their hubris is stunning."

Praising those of us from the music and video game businesses who had agreed to testify, McCain announced, "I want to make clear that neither this report nor this committee intend to make the case for censorship. We make no threat against the First Amendment. It is not my place to pass judgment on the products of your industry." According to McCain, it was all about the marketing, a point that was quickly lost.

White-haired Ernest ("Fritz") Hollings from South Carolina was the ranking Democrat on the Commerce Committee and the first of a long roll of speakers. His pink face was mottled with age and he walked slowly and stiffly. Hollings was one of the few who had been on the committee in 1986 for the hearings on rock lyrics. He informed us in his deep southern drawl that hearings about violence and TV had first been held in the early fifties, and that between 1960 and 1999, "this Committee itself has had twenty hearings" on similar topics.

Hollings pitched what he saw as a solution to the half century of wrangling: the Safe Harbor bill, initially proposed in 1995, which would forbid "excessive gratuitous violence" from nine in the morning until nine at night. Hollings said the practice was "proven and tried and true in Europe and Australia and down in New Zealand. They don't go into school down in Australia or in countries in Europe and shoot up the student body."

Hollings's remarks were completely unrelated to the FTC report and the purpose of the hearing, as just stated by McCain. He mentioned nothing about marketing practices. Nor did he mention that people in the countries he cited watch the same movies and TV shows and listen to the same music as Americans.

They are, however, subject to much stricter gun control laws than Americans.

Oversized easels displaying lyrics from Dr. Dre's "Chronic 2000" and Eminem's "Kill You" were brought out for an attack on the record business by Republican Sam Brownback of Kansas, Lieberman's frequent sidekick. Excerpting the most offensive lyrics from rap or rock songs has been a favorite tool since I first started in the business. I, too, cringe at reading some of Eminem's words out of context: "I invented violence, you vile, venomous, volatile bitches...," but context is everything in analyzing the actual meaning of art and entertainment.

John Kerry, a liberal Democrat from Massachusetts, was the only senator who seemed to be living in the same country that I did.

"Let's not assume the sort of pontificating role," he said. "Elvis Presley was unacceptable at periods of time. James Dean and *East of Eden* reflected alienated young people. Alienation among young people is something that's historical, part of adolescence. I think we ought to ask ourselves up here why so many kids reflect the kind of life they reflect. Why are so many kids out of school in so many communities in the afternoon with no parents at home? Why are there no after-school programs? Why is it that so many children are growing up at risk in this country at a time when we're the richest nation on the planet? If you want to empower parents to be able to make some of these choices, parents need to also be able to be home and be with their kids."

Kerry was a Vietnam vet who protested the war when he returned to the United States, and he had developed an unexpected friendship with McCain, the former prisoner of war. With his chiseled cheekbones and lush, Kennedy-esque salt-and-pepper hair, Kerry looked like a movie star. He had been on Gore's short list for vice president before Lieberman was chosen. Had he been the running mate, I doubted this hearing would be occurring. The election might have turned out differently as well.

Tennessee Republican Bill Frist announced that he had three teenage children, ranging in age from thirteen to seventeen. Collectively, he said, they would "go to at least fifty movies this year, watch probably over five hundred hours of television, and probably listen to over a thousand hours of music.

"Much of what the boys are exposed to in music and in the movies is simply vulgar and violent...the impressions that it leaves I am absolutely convinced will affect them as individuals, in their emotional life, in their spiritual life, their happiness, their degree of fulfillment in the future." A Senate hearing, it seemed to me, was a rather impersonal way to communicate with his kids. (In 2002, Frist became the senate majority leader.)

Senator John Ashcroft of Missouri is a dour and chinless fellow. (Ashcroft was soon to be defeated for reelection, losing to a dead man, former governor Mel Carnahan, who had died in a plane crash weeks before the election. Carnahan's wife, Jean, was appointed to fill his seat and Ashcroft was then appointed attorney general by President Bush.) Ashcroft quickly rehashed the FTC report one more time for a sound bite on TV back home. "If the industry does not police itself and young children continue to be targets of violent promotional material," he threatened, "then government should target the industry with false and deceptive enforcement actions."

The most flamboyant looking committee member was John Breaux, a centrist Democrat from Louisiana. He wore square glasses, a silver-gray suit, a yellow tie, and a daringly dark blue shirt. He looked a little like Jon Voight. I had first met Breaux in the late eighties at a fund-raiser at Don Johnson's house in Aspen. One of six Democratic senators on hand to raise money, Breaux told me he wanted to avoid getting his picture taken with Johnson because the folks back at home might not like seeing their representative hobnobbing with the star of *Miami Vice*.

Breaux said, "We have helped parents have tools to ensure their own children are protected, V-chips and rating systems. Are parents using those tools? Information I have is that ninety percent of the children tell us their parents have never discussed the ratings with them. How does Congress address that problem?" He did not dwell on the possibility that parents were not discussing the ratings because they did not perceive that there was a problem.

Although Utah's Orrin Hatch gave the ritual condemnation of violence in the media, he clearly understood more about the creative process than did most of his colleagues. The conservative Republican writes songs and had struck up an unlikely friendship with Marilyn Bergman, the famously liberal president of ASCAP, an organization that collects and disburses money to songwriters.

"It is clear you cannot regulate decency or legislate taste," Hatch said. "Some want to target Hollywood, but what in Hollywood are we targeting? Are we angry with those who gave us *Saving Private Ryan*, *The Patriot*, and *Schindler's List*? All of those movies are rated R for violence, and could not have been made in their present form under the movie code that prevailed until the sixties, and that some legislators wanted us to return to."

Like Donny Osmond, whose testimony in the eighties against a ratings system was partly inspired by experience with religious prejudice, Hatch is a Mormon. "Do we only object to the work of those with whom we have no cultural or personal connection?" Hatch asked. "As one who has written gospel music only to be told it was unacceptable because of my religious faith, I have seen both sides of this debate on a personal level."

At this point, Senator Lieberman walked in. Popping flashbulbs confirmed that he was the star of the hearing. Lieberman waved at several of his colleagues and walked across the room to give a friendly arm-grab to Republican congressman Henry Hyde, who had fought so hard to remove President Clinton from office.

Hyde, appearing as a witness, began his testimony by reading the "toxic culture" passage (it's quoted at the beginning of this chapter) from Lieberman's brand-new book, *In Praise of Public Life*. Lieberman broke in with a chuckle and said, "Thanks for the promotion, Henry." I wanted to throw up.

As he often did, Lieberman launched his culture-bashing diatribe with a reference to Columbine, "a psychic breaking point for our country." The tragedy in Colorado, said Lieberman, "was a warning that the culture of carnage surrounding our children may have gone too far and that the romanticized and sanitized visions of violence that our children are being bombarded with by the media have become part of the toxic mix that has now turned some of them into killers." "Culture of carnage" became the featured catchphrase for Lieberman's sound bite on the evening news.

Barbara Boxer, a liberal Democrat from California with a lot of support in Hollywood, changed the tone dramatically by focusing on what she considered to be the real causes of violence among young people. Quoting statistics from the National Institute for Justice, she compared Windsor, Ontario, in which there were 4 firearm murders in 1997, with Detroit, which had 354. Windsor and Detroit are only a few miles apart and essentially share the same electronic media. The same movies and television shows are shown and the same recordings are sold in both places. But Detroit has much more poverty, and many more guns, some of which would not be legal in Canada.

Senator Boxer pointed out that by far the biggest predictor of violence in young people, according to the NIJ, is an abusive father. She cited an FBI report that was critical of entertainment marketing but noted that it also looked askance at gun advertising aimed at the young and at Eddie Eagle, the NRA mascot.

A rumpled picture of the earnest bureaucrat, FTC chairman Robert Pitofsky was asked by McCain for an analogy between the marketing of entertainment and the marketing of tobacco. Pitofsky replied, "The harm from smoking is more documented I suppose. Also selling tobacco to kids is illegal. Selling violent movies and rap lyrics to kids is not illegal. And there's the First Amendment. There's no First Amendment protection to market cigarettes," the FTC chairman concluded mournfully.

After Lynne Cheney lambasted Eminem, it was my turn. I was part of a panel with Strauss Zelnick and three video game spokesmen. I went first. The lights were a bit brighter than I'd expected, but I could see that McCain, Hollings, and Brownback, at least, were listening.

I outlined my background in the record business and said, "I am speaking not only as a longtime record executive, but also as a father of a ten-year-old girl and a six-and-a-half-year-old boy. I do not believe either government or any entertainment industry committee has any business in telling me and my wife what entertainment our children should be exposed to."

McCain nodded in approval as I continued:

"The United States is a diverse country with hundreds of divergent religious beliefs, ethnic backgrounds, regional traditions, and opinions about art and entertainment. Unlike the visual media, the record business is being asked to categorize and label groups of words. For the same reason there is no ratings system for books, or for that matter congressional testimony: With one narrow exception, it is virtually impossible to rate words."

At the beginning, I found myself gasping for breath in nervousness. My anxiety at testifying before the Senate was abated, in part, by McCain's body language. He never lost eye contact and continued to nod at some of my remarks, as if he agreed with me.

"What kind of system," I asked, could "distinguish between the words 'I want to kill you' said in an affectionate, sarcastic, or ironic way and those same words being used literally? Song lyrics are by their nature impressionistic and are often used symbolically. No one really thought that the words 'killing me softly with his song' referred to murder.

"The one exception are the so-called seven dirty words, and for fifteen years, record companies, including my independent company Artemis Records, have been placing 'parental advisory' stickers on albums that have a lot of curse words."

The stickers, I pointed out, were strictly advisory, and contrary to recent statements by both President Clinton and Vice President Gore, record companies had never suggested there be an age limit on who could buy the records—that was up to parents.

"We placed such a sticker on our current album *Spit*, by the heavy metal band Kittie, because the teenage girls in the band use several curse words over the course of the album. There is nothing illegal about this, and I and critics across the country and the half a million people in the U.S. who have bought the album are morally comfortable with it as well. I know that there are many Americans who are offended by curse words and don't want children exposed to them. However, those people have no moral or legal right to impose such a standard on my family or the millions of other Americans who, like George Bush, are comfortable with cursing."

There were a few laughs, and a few groans. A recent news story had revealed that the Republican presidential candidate had called a *New York Times* reporter an "asshole."

"I respect the fact that many parents don't want their kids to watch R-rated movies," I said, "but I prefer a deeper analysis of each movie. I recently recommended the R-rated *Erin Brockovich* to our ten-year-old daughter, Katie, who is a passionate feminist and environmentalist, because I had seen the film and knew the rating was because of cursing. Others may disagree, but this country will cease to be free the day that one group of parents can tell all other parents how to raise their children.

"Song lyrics are not literal. Listening to the blues often makes people happy. Angry weird songs often make adolescents feel less lonely and more connected to other kids. Millions of these teens and young adults feel ostracized when politicians and academics who obviously have no real understanding of their culture make sweeping generalizations about their entertainment, conveniently overlooking the fact that literally every generation has embraced entertainment with sexual and violent themes. Gangsta rap is the direct descendant of the gangster movies of the thirties and forties, the TV westerns of the fifties, and critically acclaimed films like *The Godfather*."

I looked at McCain, who still seemed to be following every word intently. He nodded encouragingly.

"Mr. Chairman, I don't like every record. Spike Lee criticizes much of the rap culture in his new movie *Bamboozled*. Criticism and moral argument is appropriate and an integral part of the entertainment culture. In an Internet world, there will be ever-increasing ways for parents to find like-minded groups who can advise them on entertainment through the prism of their own particular values. However, so-called self-regulation achieved by political intimidation is the equivalent of censorship."

At the word "censorship," McCain's expression changed from friendly to grim. I took a sip of water and plowed ahead.

"It has become commonplace to assert that popular culture is popular against the wishes and values of its fans. But popular culture gets that way precisely because the balance of consumers—not record makers, not rule makers, but everyday people—enjoy it.

"Mr. Chairman, make no mistake, their tastes, their values, and their morality are under assault every bit as much as the entertainment executives who occupy the hot seat today.

"Washington is a culture of legislation and policy. Asking the FTC or the Washington media or the Congress to analyze popular entertainment makes about as much sense as going to Hollywood to restructure Medicare... Washington political leaders are out of touch with the real dynamic of the ways young people process entertainment and condemn youth culture. The only result of demonizing pop culture is to drive millions of young people away from politics. In the last Congressional election in 1998, less than 17 percent of eighteen to twenty-five-year-olds voted... I believe that fifteen years of youth culture entertainment bashing in Washington has greatly contributed to alienation and apathy on the part of young people from politics."

I paused for a moment and peered through the bright lights at McCain before I concluded with, "Mr. Chairman and members of the committee, please help to stop this trend of pushing young people away from politics."

Strauss Zelnick followed, also identifying himself as a parent and acknowledging that "Certain of the messages that pervade our society make it difficult to teach our children the difference between right and wrong." But he stressed that "many of our artists legitimately comment on the problems of our society."

At the end of our testimony, McCain said, "Obviously Mr. Goldberg, in his statement, and Mr. Zelnick to a lesser degree, view this as some sort of coercion or censorship, I do not."

He asked the two of us to "engage in a little colloquy."

"Since I would feel free to interrupt you," he said, "please feel free to interrupt me." I shook my head vehemently, indicating I had no intention of interrupting John McCain. But he said earnestly, "Seriously, I think that's the only way we can have an honest exchange of views here, because I am concerned about some of the things you stated in your testimony."

McCain's personal charm is so strong that even from a distance, up on a rostrum, he is a highly seductive figure. Somehow, he made me feel that he had been hanging on my every word. He now said, "First of all, Mr. Goldberg, I think that young people are not involved in the political process simply because they don't believe they're represented here."

McCain, who had fought a long battle for campaign finance reform, blamed "special interests and big money" for making young people think they were not represented in the political process.

But I had a different point to make: "There are no young people testifying today. There are no groups of fans or consumers that have been invited."

McCain responded, "Well, I would be glad to do that, but we were reviewing a study of marketing practices as opposed to purchasing principals." Perhaps sensing that this is a dubious distinction, McCain added, "But I do agree with you. Perhaps we should have more young people come and testify before Congress. But I'll tell you what a lot of them would say: 'It doesn't make any difference because I couldn't afford the five-hundred-thousand-dollar-ticket fund raiser.'"

Moving to labeling, McCain said he believed people have a right to know the contents of a product before buying it. Why, then, did I seem to view labeling as censorship?

"We label albums with curse words," I said. "That's exactly what we've been doing for fifteen years..."

McCain jumped in, saying he was talking about more specific recommendations. Couldn't we say something was not suitable for audiences of a certain age?

I replied that there were no universal criteria.

"A fourteen-year-old in one family, the parents may not want exposed to material that in my family, maybe we do. We have no idea how to further categorize words. I do agree with making all of the words available for parents who want to read them, subject to the copyright owner's permission to do so. But I don't understand what criteria could be used to create additional categories. Book publishers don't do it, magazines, newspapers don't. Words don't lend themselves to those kinds of categories except for profanity, which we already label."

McCain said, "I frankly recoiled at the lyrics Senator Brownback put up there. Isn't it pretty clear that something like that should be labeled? I want to emphasize, Mr. Goldberg...I can't speak for other members of this committee, I don't want to resort to censorship. We want to try to remove and eradicate a problem that's been identified by a respected agency of the government. Did you want to respond?"

"The Eminem album is stickered," I replied. "A lot of people like it anyway. And I realize that everybody here didn't like reading those lyrics isolated, disconnected from the music, disconnected from context, and you might hate hearing the whole album, even after meeting the artist. But millions of people like it, and in a free society, what do you do about that except tell your opinion? I think you also have to recognize that young people have different language that they use, different symbols, and have a different feeling about this. Most young people I know feel that this is a humorous record not a violent record. You may disagree with them, but it might be good for you to hear their point of view, the actual fans of the music, instead of assuming how they interpret it."

Although McCain and I failed to find a meeting of the minds, I found his attempt at actual dialogue, even in the context of a public hearing room, more substantive than any conversation I'd had over the years with Democrats.

It was during the same time period that Artemis had its biggest and most unexpected hit with a song that was featured in a G-rated movie for kids. Steve Greenberg, who had worked for me at Atlantic and Mercury, had always been a big supporter of a relatively obscure Bahamian world-music group called the Baha Men, and when he played me their raucously joyful "Who Let the Dogs Out," I jumped at it. The recording would become almost ubiquitous in the fall and winter on the radio and as a sports anthem, played at countless baseball, basketball, and football games. It really exploded after it was used in the popular children's movie *Rugrats in Paris*. We sold over 3 million copies of "Who Let the Dogs Out," which helped Artemis achieve the ranking of the number one independently distributed label in the United States for 2000.

Jack Valenti called to congratulate me on my testimony. In his sonorous Texas drawl, Valenti said with typical hyperbole, "You spoke truth to power. They're not used to hearing it." He reassured me with the voice of experience, "Don't worry, after Election Day things will be different."

Valenti's sanguine view was echoed by Jann Wenner, the publisher of *Rolling Stone*.

"There's not going to be any censorship," Jann told me. "I've spoken to Tipper about it."

Wenner and VH-1's John Sykes put together an impressive fund-raiser for Gore that included performances by Sheryl Crow and Jon Bon Jovi. An issue of *Rolling Stone* came out close to the election with a passionate endorsement of Gore by Wenner and an interview in which Gore quoted the Dylan line, "He not busy being born is busy dying," that Jimmy Carter had used twenty-four years earlier.

Following the Senate hearing, I debated Jerry Falwell on a talk show co-hosted by Democratic power figure and former Clinton counsel Paul Begala. After the show, I asked Begala if he thought that the Democrats' obsession with culture bashing hurt them with young voters.

"I don't think so," said Begala. "I think the reason young people don't vote is because the issues of government don't affect people until they're married and have children." I pointed out that this has always been the case, but that younger voting had been precipitously declining in the last decade. "Well," said Begala, "there were bigger issues, like the Vietnam War."

Of course, the Vietnam War ended in 1975. More to the point, when Jesse Ventura ran a campaign for governor of Minnesota that was fueled by pop culture and straightforward language, youth turnout skyrocketed.

As the 2000 campaign droned on, Rosemary and I became more and more disenchanted with Gore. We resented it that Democrats made sure that Ralph Nader (and for that matter, Pat Buchanan) could not participate in and broaden the scope of the televised debates. We decided to go with our hearts, as Molly Ivins had suggested, and support Nader in New York, where Gore was leading in the polls by twenty points.

We introduced Nader to Patti Smith, and she appeared with Eddie Vedder of Pearl Jam, Ani DiFranco, Michael Moore, and others at a sold-out Nader rally in mid-September at Madison Square Garden. In his speech, Nader connected his campaign with the spirit of our No Nukes concerts twenty-one years earlier. The next night, we held a fund-raiser for Nader at our house, which was co-hosted by Tim Robbins and Susan Sarandon, among others.

By the middle of October, however, I and many other Nader supporters were having second thoughts. He had broken his promise not to campaign in swing states. Reportedly, he was persuaded by Green party leaders that he needed to swell his vote total to get the 5 percent needed to nail down matching funds.

Democrats, finally waking up to the fact that Nader was a factor, dispatched venerable leaders of the party's left wing to urge their followers not to vote for him. The Reverend Jackson called and lectured me that Strom Thurmond and Jesse Helms were "licking their chops at the idea of Bush in the White House and all of the appointments they'll control."

I told Jesse that I felt that older Democrats were coming home to the party in swing states, even if they didn't particularly care for Gore, but that Nader was drawing huge crowds on college campuses. Young people were not moved by the middle-aged surrogates like Gloria Steinem and Jackson himself that the Gore campaign was sending out. Nader was articulating strong positions on the environment, on labor, on poverty, and on trade that were not even being discussed by Bush or Gore.

Over the course of the presidential debates, Gore managed to make it literally impossible for most voters outside of Washington to understand the differences between him and Bush. The most memorable thing that came out of the debates were the *Saturday Night Live* parodies. Darrell Hammond's devastating caricature of Gore, simultaneously stiff and sneaky, reminded people of everything they didn't like about him, whereas Will Ferrell's George W. Bush seemed like silly fun.

"How can you change anything if you don't understand TV?" Michael Moore regularly admonished the left. His TV show *The Awful Truth* and his films *Roger and Me* and *The Big One* had given more mass exposure to progressive ideas than the rest of the alternative media combined. His very active website had helped galvanize public opposition to the impeachment, earning the thanks of both Gore and Clinton. Like me, Michael had decided to support Nader's campaign as a way of broadening the national debate.

"I figured Gore would win by ten points," Michael said to me in wonder as Election Day grew near, and the pollsters declared the race too close to call. "The economy is terrific," said Moore. "The public opposed impeachment. Gore was supposed to be this great debater, facing an idiot. I never thought Gore would lose all of the debates and that it would be this close."

Moore is a charismatic speaker who often appeared with Nader at rallies, but he refused to campaign with him in swing states. He tried unsuccessfully to get Nader to stop it, and called everyone he knew in the Gore campaign, trying to find a way to bridge the gap.

Moore told readers of his website that he could understand why Nader supporters would vote for Gore in swing states. Nader supporter Ani DiFranco urged young people in swing states to vote for Gore.

"Maybe Gore could say that he'd be in favor of Ralph being included in debates for the next election," Michael suggested as Election Day drew near. Instead, Gore chose to completely ignore Nader and never referred to him, nor to the millions of people who followed him and voted for him.

Steve Earle, who records for Artemis, tried to encourage his fans at least not to vote for Bush. A longtime and active opponent of the death penalty, Steve and director Amos Poe made a music video of "Jonathan's Song," a farewell to a condemned man Steve had gotten to know in Texas. While Steve's lament played in the background, the video showed the faces of over 300 people executed in Texas while George W. Bush was governor.

The Sunday before the election, Barbra Streisand called me,

explaining in her earnest, New York accent, the real policy differences between Gore and Bush. I agreed with her. So did many people who'd been attracted by Nader at the beginning. The problem wasn't the middle-aged left, or the old left. The problem was young voters who didn't watch C-SPAN or read the editorial pages, people for whom the *Saturday Night Live* caricatures of Bush and Gore rang true.

I asked her to support Moore's efforts to get Gore to acknowledge Nader, but she said she no longer had any input to Gore's campaign. I told Barbra that Lieberman and Gore's attacks on popular culture hadn't exactly helped with young people. Barbra asked me plaintively, "Aren't they doing things on college campuses?"

The answer was, too little too late.

A major reason Gore lost in 2000 was a very severe case of liberal snobbery. With his unwillingness or inability to communicate in ordinary language ("Dingell-Norwood"?), his shrill attacks on popular culture, his selection of a running mate even more sanctimonious and elitist than he, and his obsessive need to distance himself from President Clinton, Gore turned off millions of voters he could have attracted.

Conservative Democrats and some pundits implausibly blamed what they called Gore's "populist" message for driving away swing voters. This theory totally ignores the voters who swung between Nader and Gore. Even if Gore occasionally said something that could be taken as populism, his style and affect remained hopelessly elitist. Gore had none of the common touch of true populists such as Ross Perot or Jesse Ventura. On the contrary, he always seemed like a lecturing professor, while Bush was able to portray himself as the solid voice of common sense next door.

Gore's dramatic drop in the support of younger voters alone cost him the election. The statistics are clear. Among voters aged eighteen to twenty-four, Clinton defeated Bob Dole, the archenemy of popular culture, by 19 percent in 1996. In 2000, Gore and Bush, who was not identified with attacks on youth culture, equally split 9 million voters in the eighteen to twenty-four category. If Gore had retained the Democratic margin among young voters from the previous election, he would have added almost 2 million votes to his national margin. That would have tipped the balance his way in several swing states (including, of course, Florida), and he would have won the electoral college and thus the election decisively.

Although I think Ralph Nader was too cavalier about his effect on the outcome, blaming Nader misses the point. Most people who voted for Nader had made up their minds that they didn't want to vote for Gore or Bush.

Rock the Vote registered over 500,000 eighteen to twenty-one-year-olds at rallies around the country in 2000. Mario Velasquez, Rock the Vote's executive director, told me shortly after the election, "Young people were obviously not part of the Gore-Lieberman campaign strategy. For months we had events on college campuses where representatives of Bush and Nader would come, but not from the Democrats. Finally, the last few weeks of the campaign, when their polls showed the appeal of Nader to young people, Gore sent people, but by then it was too late." Not only was Gore hostile to youth culture, he made scant reference to issues that would move young people. There was almost no reference to the great moral purpose of politics, the ability of government to help the most disadvantaged, to create ladders that can lift people out of poverty or despair. There were no misgivings about a drug war that landed hundreds of thousands of people in jail for the same crime Gore himself admitted to having committed in his younger years. Gore, who had genuine passion about the environment and who had written a book about it, almost never mentioned the issue in his campaign, and on those rare occasions when he did, he failed to draw clear distinctions between his positions and those of Bush.

Judy McGrath, president of MTV, spoke of a similar failure. "We had a great relationship with Clinton, but it was almost impossible to get Gore to do anything on MTV. When he finally came on, the most telling moment for me was when a black kid with dreadlocks held up a copy of the Mos Def album and explained how there was a side to rap that was socially conscious and that many young people such as himself combined their belief in music with their politics."

Mos Def is a politically oriented rapper who has never been criticized for misogyny, violent lyrics, or any of the usual catalogue of sins. "Instead of hearing what the kid was saying," Judy said, "Gore totally ignored his comment and used it to lecture him on how women would feel about the word 'bitch' in songs, an answer that had nothing to do with what the kid was saying. He just squashed him. And our audience."

CHAPTER 11

# The Media Marketing Accountability Act

I N THE BATTLE FOR FLORIDA that followed the 2000 election, the Democrats made some of the same mistakes that had plagued their campaign. Stiff, sour-visaged Warren Christopher was not a compelling spokesperson, and David Boies, the brilliant litigator, took courtroom arguments and put them on TV, lecturing the public in colorless legalisms. He came across as what he is, a shrewd lawyer, reinforcing the Republican message, "They're trying to steal the election." Democrats certainly could have said the same thing.

The Republican spokesman, former secretary of state James Baker, spoke in coherent, media-friendly sound bites that rallied the troops.

The Democrats virtually ignored a potentially powerful story line, the disenfranchisement of black voters. The Gore forces seemed anxious to keep the Reverend Jesse Jackson and other black advocates at a distance, and to rely on the lawyers and the courts. In the months that followed, Democrats studiously avoided the circumstances that led to Bush's "victory" in Florida. Two years later, when a group of first-time filmmakers released the documentary *Unprecedented* outlining the systematic exclusion of African American voters in Florida in 2000, many Democrats wondered why the case had not been made at the time.

Gore won several hundred thousand more popular votes than Bush. As Rick Hertzberg pointed out in the *New Yorker*, Gore could have used this fact as the basis to give monthly speeches on behalf of the plurality of Americans who had voted for him to criticize Bush's policies when he disagreed with them and advocate his own. Instead, Gore disappeared from public life for almost two years.

On the morning of April 18, 2001, Senator Joseph Lieberman came to another Creative Coalition meeting. This one was on the third floor of the imperial office building of talent agency CAA on Wilshire Boulevard in Los Angeles.

Around thirty-five actors, producers, and directors filled the conference room. The many actors included Richard Schiff and Bradley Whitford, whose show *West Wing* was already providing millions of Americans with a fictional Democratic alternative to the new Bush administration. Also present were columnist Arianna Huffington and Tom Hayden, who was in the midst of an unsuccessful runoff for election to the LA City Council. I was the only person from the music business.

Lieberman made an unpretentious entrance accompanied by a single aide. In the wake of the election, and the widespread feeling among Democrats that it had illegitimately been decided by the Supreme Court, even I felt some goodwill toward the defeated Democratic candidate for vice president. Lieberman quickly, however, reverted to type.

"Since I was out here to speak on foreign policy at USC," he said in a casual tone, "I thought I'd meet some people from the entertainment business to continue a dialogue. Entertainment became a source of concern to me when I walked by the TV set and my then-five-year-old daughter was watching *Married with Children* with my then-seventeen-year-old son. I had no problem with my seventeen-year-old watching it, but I did remove my five-year-old.

"A society expresses itself through stories," he said. "Culture affects us. Social scientists seem to say it affects behavior. I never say it causes violence, teen pregnancy, sexually transmitted diseases, but that it contributes. Kids are affected, especially vulnerable children are affected.

"Can we do better?" he asked plaintively.

Lieberman said that a new Federal Trade Commission report on entertainment marketing would be issued imminently.

"I've said I'd introduce legislation to empower the FTC to have authority to enforce ratings issued by companies," he said. He did not again refer to legislation at the meeting. Instead, he asked us to focus on a paper he distributed on "media literacy," which was basically about learning how to understand, analyze, and use modern mass media. It was filled with feel-good generalities.

Actor Daniel Stern, who teaches a media literacy course to ninth graders and has enormous passion for it, spoke up excitedly, "I was in the *Home Alone* movies, and kids came up to me to ask if heavy objects really hit me in the head." But, Stern admonished,

"Regulation is a slippery slope. Education is the key. But it takes money, Senator."

Lieberman appeared flummoxed. He said he wanted foundations and charitable groups to sponsor and teach media literacy, not the federal government. Seeing the disappointed looks in the room, he added, "The typical way we do this is to give incentives to states—maybe that's a good idea."

*Pulp Fiction* producer Lawrence Bender, a host of the meeting, adroitly changed the subject by reading an article detailing how TV news had exaggerated violence in society and had been unfair to minorities in covering crime. He was obviously not calling for censorship of TV news but trying to create some perspective on violence and the media.

Lieberman sighed and said, "I've noodged TV. It's harder to do because news is local." Quickly returning to movies, he said, "We need to limit or educate or inform the public regarding violent intake." I cringed at the implications of the innocent-seeming word "limit."

Boaz Yakin, in his mid-thirties but appearing younger, with his look-of-the-moment stubble and short hair, said, "I am the director of *Remember the Titans* for Disney, as gentle a movie as you could want. I'm sure you would want children to see it." The film, which stars Denzel Washington, is the achingly sincere, true story of a black football coach taking over a previously all-white team in the South in the early 1970s.

"We got letters from Saudi Arabia, saying they really wanted to release the movie there," Boaz recalled. "But they asked us to make some changes, including removing scenes showing crosses, showing short skirts on girls, and scenes of males and females holding hands. When we got the letters we all laughed and said to ourselves what a fucked-up society they have. We think that because we have freedom here. I see freedom of ideas as a way to protect me.

"I was educated at a Yeshiva. I was brought up in an insular, narrow way. A rabbi there told me black people were inferior because they were descendants of one of the sons of Noah—he called them *schvartzes*. When I finally met a black person he was Catholic and he told me that he had been taught that there was a special place in hell for Jews."

Lieberman interrupted to quip, "a very special place."

He got a laugh, but Yakin wasn't done. Lieberman was well known as a strong advocate of funding religious groups to provide a variety of social services, including schooling. Boaz said, "You want to give money to religious institutions like these to teach. What are they going to teach? I was able to expand my mind by reading William Burroughs and Henry Miller, whose works were once banned, because of the way they dealt with complex issues that I had to work through as a human being. Who will be teaching this media literacy? What if they're bigots? I believe in letting all the ideas be expressed, and the best ideas will win. Sometimes someone crazy will shoot someone and have liked a movie—that's the price you pay for a genuinely stronger society. This is about fear of ideas, fear of real communication."

There was dead silence. The room belonged to Boaz, and Lieberman didn't want to take him on. "Given the choice of freedom or limitation, I'd always choose freedom," Lieberman claimed.

Lieberman complimented the MPAA ratings system as a good basis on which to build more "consumer information." Producer Tom Baer interjected, "Don't be so enthusiastic about ratings. *Billy Elliot* is an R, and I'd like every nine-year-old to see it."

Arianna Huffington agreed. In her thick Greek accent, she told Lieberman that she and her husband had two kids, aged eleven and thirteen. "I don't want less choice, I want more choice," she said. "I insisted they see *Traffic* and *Erin Brockovich*. *Traffic* has changed debate on the drug war." There was much nodding in approval.

I took a turn. "Senator, first, thanks for a more collegial approach compared to confrontational."

"I'm sooo glad you appreciate it," interjected Lieberman, his voice dripping with sarcasm.

I kept going. "As a Democrat, I am concerned that young people are turned off to voting. They feel politicians of both parties attack what they think is their culture. We didn't think Woodstock was Warner Bros. culture, it was our culture. Democrats have lost the edge they had with younger voters, from a nineteen-point margin in 1992 to zero in 2000."

Lieberman implausibly replied, "I didn't know those numbers," and had no comment on how to motivate young people to participate.

Toward the end of the meeting, Richard Kind, an actor in the TV series *Spin City*, began railing at Britney Spears, declaring that her revealing outfits were a bad influence on young teenagers. I suggested that Britney Spears's image might be empowering to pubescent girls, and that her lyrics were substantially less risqué than those of the previous decade's female icon, Madonna.

"Well, I wasn't too crazy about her, either," the actor countered.

"What about Janis Joplin?" I asked.

Kind, who was born in 1956, looked at me with misty eyes. "I loved Janis Joplin," he said.

I said that I loved Janis Joplin too, but reminded him that Joplin posed for nude photos, cursed like a sailor from the stage, and was an unapologetic drunk and druggie.

In the elevator to the lobby, Lieberman said to me sarcastically, "My thirteen-year-old daughter will be so thrilled that you defended Britney Spears."

The next day, under the headline "Senator Joe Lowers Boom on H'wood," the *New York Post* reported, "Lieberman claimed Hollywood has failed to police itself so he'll introduce a bill allowing the FTC to fine companies that direct explicit films, music and video games toward young audiences." That was certainly a lot more information than Lieberman had given us directly the day before.

Lieberman, the story continued, "feels the movie industry hasn't done enough and the music business has done nothing."

On April 24, the Federal Trade Commission released a new report on entertainment-business marketing. The report charged, "The Commission found advertising for explicit content-labeled music recordings routinely appeared on popular teen advertising programming. All five major recording companies placed advertising for explicit content music on television programs and magazines with substantial under-17 audiences, in some cases more than 50 percent under 17."

One particularly surreal part of the report was a criticism of record companies for advertising stickered albums on the World Wrestling Federation's *Smackdown*, which features scantily clad, insanely aggressive men and women screaming vitriol and pretending to knock the living daylights out of each other. Thirty-six percent of the program's audience is under eighteen, it turns out. Well, at least they could be protected from rap music.

Two days later, three Democrats—Joe Lieberman, Senator Herb Kohl of Wisconsin, and, shockingly, Senator Hillary Clinton of New York—formally introduced the Media Marketing Accountability Act of 2001. It would expand FTC authority to crack down on businesses that engaged in "false and deceptive advertising practices." Senator Clinton explained, "If you label something as inappropriate for children and then go out and target it to children, you are engaging in false and deceptive advertising."

The proposed new law would require record companies and film studios to have "an age-based rating or labeling system" with more teeth than the traditional movie ratings. And the FTC would be given authority to decide if "advertising or marketing is... directed or targeted to minors." In practice, the FTC could decide which music and movies could be mass marketed and thus, by and large, which ones would be released. The bill would, in essence, have criminalized the marketing and sale of most rock and rap albums to kids under seventeen.

Jack Valenti, head of the Motion Picture Association of America, attacked the bill with unusual intensity: "The bill defiles the Constitution. There's a difference from putting labels on cereal boxes and Hershey bars. You're dealing with Supreme Court–ordered protection. The bill will be dead on arrival at the first federal court to hear it. What's next, books, newspapers?"

I called Valenti to congratulate him on his comments and I told him that Lieberman had dissed him at the Creative Coalition meeting, complaining about his resistance to supplying more detailed information in film ratings. Valenti sighed.

"I know," he said. "I refuse to attack him by name publicly, though. I say Joe Lieberman is my friend, he and I just clash on this issue. I'm a staunch believer in the First Amendment, and I thought he was, too."

I asked Valenti if he'd pointed out the First Amendment implications of the bill to Lieberman, and he sighed again. "When people get very religious and they believe their course of action is sanctioned by a higher authority, there's not much you can do to communicate with them—left, right, whatever," Valenti pointedly concluded.

Uncharacteristically irate, Valenti kept fuming. "And Hillary Clinton," he said. "She's a lawyer. How could she say that labels are appropriate for foods and forget that there's a First Amendment?"

I called Chuck Schumer, the other Democratic senator from New York. "I'm against it," said Schumer. "If I say anything publicly now, it would look like I'm picking a fight with Hillary. The media is constantly harping on our supposed rivalry. If it ever comes to a vote, I'd be against it and speak against it—it's ridiculous. But don't worry, the bill is not going anywhere."

Jerry Nadler, a staunch First Amendment supporter and the congressman whose district includes our Greenwich Village neighborhood, agreed. "The bill isn't going anywhere, so what difference does it make?" The implication is that the whole process was grandstanding to make some Democrats more politically palatable to culturally conservative swing voters. But the effect of that symbolism cuts more than one way. To me, the "difference" that congressional rhetoric makes in cases like this is to further alienate young people and fans of pop culture from politics in general. I believe that the cost of such alienation in terms of creating nonvoters and third-party voters is far greater than any gain for Democrats.

Washington gossip had it that Lieberman had spent a lot of energy trying to get a Republican senator to co-sponsor the bill, but that Orrin Hatch and John McCain, among others, had declined. Valenti told me that Senate majority leader Trent Lott saw the legislation as a PR vehicle for Lieberman's national aspirations, and that he would make sure that no Republican signed on as a co-sponsor. None did. Thus, for those paying attention, Republicans came across as less snobbish and less elitist than Democrats.

A conservative columnist for the New York Post was one of the few media pundits to attack the legislation. Andrea Peyser wrote, "It's much easier to target Hollywood and Nintendo than to suggest that guns should be removed from the reach of already damaged and emotionally disturbed kids. It is much easier to blame rap music for violence than it is for some parents... to sit down with kids and discuss the lyrics they've heard. Censorship is easy, which makes it popular. Trouble is, it's doomed to failure."

While the controversy was building, I had a business meeting with Ray Daniels, a big Canadian rock manager. He told me an anecdote about one of his clients:

"With the Matthew Good Band, at the request of Wal-Mart in the United States, we had to change the title on the package of *A Boy and a Machine Gun* to *A Boy and* followed by three dots. In Canada we can say what we want on the album cover, but you can't buy guns in the same store. At Wal-Mart, you can't have the word 'gun' on an album cover—but they sell actual guns!"

In June, the Creative Coalition issued a statement condemning the proposed legislation as a violation of the First Amendment and urged Senators Lieberman, Clinton, and Kohl to withdraw their support. Among those signing were actors Robin Williams, Ben Stiller, Lauren Bacall, Chevy Chase, Bo Derek (who publicly campaigned for George W. Bush), Olympia Dukakis (cousin of the former Democratic presidential nominee), Hector Elizondo, Richard Belzer, Harvey Fierstein, and Kathleen Turner. Ron Reagan signed it, as well as Jane Alexander, head of the National Endowment for the Arts under Clinton. Creative Coalition president William Baldwin went on television news shows to oppose the bill.

Responding to a Creative Coalition letter, President George W. Bush straddled the issue with a note from his ranch in Crawford, Texas: "I believe that government must be engaged but restrained. I will take your views into consideration in the coming months."

In the spring of 2001, powerful black record executive Russell Simmons organized a rap summit, both to defend rap and to move it in more socially responsible directions. Dozens of rappers and record executives attended, along with several members of the

Black Congressional Caucus, Minister Louis Farrakhan, Martin Luther King III, and Harvard professor Cornel West.

Simmons, one of the founders of the seminal rap label Def Jam, with his shaved head and his stand-up comedian's sense of timing, had become the best-known rap impresario. He set a balanced tone for the meeting.

On one hand, he said, "I want to defend forever the right of rappers to say 'fuck the police.' We have to be able to comment on and express our lives just like every other group and every other generation."

On the other hand, Simmons called for rappers and executives to take a closer look at lyrics, particularly those involving women. "I know the relationships a lot of you have with your wives," he said, "so why talk like a pimp? If this culture is about truth, then tell that truth as well."

Russell Simmons also was a key player in a meeting between Hillary Clinton and several of us who had enthusiastically supported her run for the Senate, and who were particularly annoyed at her co-sponsorship of the Lieberman bill. Simmons's wealth and his house in East Hampton had given him access to New York's elite, yet he always kept in close touch with "the street" through the rappers who congregated around him. He was and is an indispensable link to young African Americans for black political leaders, and for white ones, like Hillary Clinton, who courted the black vote. Hillary Clinton was one of the few white politicians with any currency among African Americans, and Simmons was concerned that she would lose some of that.

We met at Senator Clinton's Manhattan office. She was ebullient, and looked striking in an orange pants suit. She quickly addressed our reason for being there. "I didn't realize how culturally divisive this bill would be. It was just after that terrible election and I wanted to be supportive of Joe. But this is a different time now. I thought we would build on the progress we made in the White House. We got a lot accomplished—such as the V-chip—and you all supported that."

I stared at her blankly. The only people who "supported" the V-chip were TV networks, and they were coerced into it.

"The bill is not going anywhere," she assured us. "There are no Republican co-sponsors. Joe sees the world in a different way than I do, but I can't offend another senator—it's a very small body."

Echoing her husband's remarks years before, she talked about kids at risk and turned to me, recalling her encounter with Katie and Max at the fund-raiser at our house the previous year. "I saw you with your kids and could feel the relationship you have with them," she said. "What's scary is a lot of parents aren't there or aren't doing their job. To these kids entertainment becomes a co-parent."

Russell Simmons demurred. "If you were a kid with nothing in your head, the DMX album would be a positive influence. When he listens to the devil he goes to hell. When he talks to God he goes to heaven. DMX is a profound American poet—his lyrics will be taught some day like Shakespeare." Senator Clinton's staff took notes. I hoped that at least one of them eventually listened to a DMX album.

I explained that 80 percent of the music targeted by the FTC came from black artists. During the election, Senator Clinton had been interviewed by Angie Martinez of Hot 97, the number one hip-hop station in New York, and the station aired the interview repeatedly with obvious pride. Now Senator Clinton was aligning herself with attacks on the culture that the station celebrated. The racial undertone of attacks on hip-hop was so obvious that Hot 97 had created sarcastic "bumper" spots with a voice in an echo chamber intoning "Warning! Explicit Negroes."

Simmons, who had arranged the Hot 97 interview, told the Senator, "I'm not worried about this bill personally. I'm not going to jail. My artists are going to make the music they want. When there are political attacks it actually helps us. I make more money."

Simmons laughed, and then his face grew serious and he spoke with emotion directly to Hillary Clinton: "I don't want you associated with this. I don't care what Lieberman says—but you shouldn't be against youth."

Clinton responded, "I don't relish the role I'm in now. Chelsea was horrified that I supported this. She was saying to me, 'what about country and western songs with lyrics about killing,' and so on... She has told me about media literacy in Canada and I asked her to get more info on it from the Internet. Maybe that's a positive area." Clinton sighed wearily. "I'm going to talk to Joe."

On our way out, Russell said to me, "She sure was nice, but basically we got nothing, right?" Russell indeed was right.

On July 24, all of us from the meeting got a faxed letter from Senator Clinton that had all the hallmarks of a form letter that had been sent to thousands of constituents. Citing Columbine and the FTC report, she wrote, "Since we met, I spoke with Senator Lieberman again about these issues. As I have explained to you and many others, I view the Media Marketing Accountability Act as a measure of last resort."

I sent a reply, saying, "The carefully balanced approach that you and President Clinton employed in the past is very different from the radical step embodied in the legislation proposed by Senator Lieberman...there is no question that the Media Marketing

Accountability Act would involve the heavy hand of government in regulating the marketing of entertainment in a way unprecedented in the United States or any western democracy."

I cannot imagine how to explain to a young rap artist that his or her words couldn't be marketed to teenagers, but that the exact same language and concepts in more traditional literary packages were free from restrictions. I was gratified when an umbrella publishing group called the Media Coalition came together to fight the bill. Its members included all of the major book and literary organizations, and large associations of book and magazine publishers, distributors, and sellers.

In late July, hearings began on the Media Marketing Accountability Act in the Senate Committee on Governmental Affairs, chaired by Joe Lieberman. Republican senator Fred Thompson of Tennessee expressed the sharpest criticism of the bill. "We can't keep our vital national security secret," said the Tennessee senator, a sometime film and TV actor. "You think we'll keep entertainment out of the hands of kids?"

Russell Simmons was initially refused a slot to testify, but Lieberman eventually gave him some time, after several witnesses complained about the bizarre exclusion of African American voices. The essence of his testimony was laid out succinctly by Simmons in a *New York Times* op-ed piece on August 3.

"Hip-hop," Simmons argued, "is an important art form, really the first new genre of music to emerge since rock and roll. To condemn it without understanding it is irresponsible. To disregard its huge audience is arrogant. To deny its power and artistic merit in an attempt to silence it is downright dangerous ... If the government can target young African American artists for censorship, no one's freedom of expression is safe.

"Studies created by government bureaucrats and papers prepared by academics can only go so far," he wrote. "At some point, to truly understand the anger, profanity, joy, humor, and celebration of hip-hop you have to go to the artist."

I and many people in the entertainment community have supported Al Gore and Bill and Hillary Clinton and others whose views on art, entertainment, and free speech diverge from our view of the world, and if electoral logic called for it, I would do so again. However, I would never under any circumstances support or vote for a ticket with Joe Lieberman on it. Not only is he one of the most conservative Democrats with a national profile, but his self-righteousness about religion and venom toward popular culture would make him a serious threat to a free and intellectually diverse American society if he were to gain more power.

**CHAPTER 12**

# September 11

I WAS IN THE MIDDLE of writing this
book when planes crashed into the World Trade Center and the
Pentagon. For weeks after September 11, 2001, the wind would
occasionally blow smoke north from the devastated ruins of the
Trade Center into the Greenwich Village neighborhood where my
family lives. Like almost everyone in New York, I knew several
people who died on September 11. I shared the sense of stunned
horror, anger, and fear that so many Americans felt in the weeks
following the attack. Even if we could have forgotten, our children
regularly reminded us with their fearful questions about the newfound sense of peril that accompanied their lives.

On TV, David Letterman and Jon Stewart wept, and Larry King
asked Jerry Seinfeld without irony, "When will it be okay to be
funny again?"

A month later, the tragedy was still haunting New Yorkers, as
became clear at a panel on Music in the Time of War at the annual
conference of college radio programmers and music professionals
sponsored by the CMJ music network. The panel, which I partici-

pated in, was chaired by *Village Voice* music editor Bob Christgau, who has probably listened to and written about more rock and rap records than anyone else in history.

Christgau sobbed during his opening remarks, and said that because of his grief for the deaths of September 11 he was having a hard time listening to new music. *Newsweek* music writer Lorraine Ali, an Arab American who had been in Cairo during the attack and had been temporarily assigned to write about reaction in Arab countries, also spoke of how difficult it was for her to imagine going back to writing about music.

I said I felt that the voices of people in the arts needed to be part of national conversations in times of emergency or tragedy. But I also felt that we in the music business needed to be sensitive to the physical and emotional horror and pain wrought by the killing of thousands.

Radio programmers told Artemis Records that they didn't want to broadcast a song by our group Sugarcult because of the phrase "everybody is blowing up the neighborhood." The band didn't hesitate to rerecord a new phrase. The reference had clearly been to teenage partying, but they could certainly understand how it now could be construed as insensitive.

Similarly, The Strokes, who my wife Rosemary represents, eliminated a song on their debut album on RCA that referred derisively to New York policemen. These changes didn't seem like censorship to me, but were made by artists themselves in recognition of a radically changed context.

But cultural reactionaries couldn't wait to take advantage of the tragedy. On Pat Robertson's *700 Club*, Jerry Falwell said that the destruction of the World Trade Center was God's punishment to America for "feminism, gay rights and groups like People for the American Way and the ACLU." The attack had an effect, but not the one Falwell intended. The ACLU experienced the greatest membership increase in its history in the months following September 11, growing from about 250,000 members to around 350,000. In October, we organized the first LA-style fund-raising dinner for the New York Civil Liberties Union, honoring Nickelodeon president Albie Hecht and film director Ang Lee. It was the most successful fund-raiser the NYCLU ever had.

Susan Sontag wrote a thoughtful and thought-provoking piece in the *New Yorker* in which she mentioned that President Bush's reference to the terrorists as "cowards" seemed an odd way to describe people willing to die in flames for their beliefs. Conservatives, who had long hated Sontag, attacked her as if she were urging support for Osama bin Laden.

Bush's use of the word "coward" was also mocked by Bill Maher, host of the TV show *Politically Incorrect*. Maher was sternly rebuked by White House press secretary Ari Fleischer, who said, chillingly, "Now is a time when people have to watch what they say." With happy visions of blacklisting dancing in their heads, conservatives convinced a few sponsors to pull out of *Politically Incorrect*, but they soon were replaced. ABC did fold the show the following summer, but its ratings had been low for some time.

Liberal snobs also jumped at the chance to use the national crisis to advance their pet cultural theories. Singer-songwriter Paul Simon wrote in the *New York Times* that the tragic deaths at the World Trade Center were "ameliorated" by what he anticipated as a forthcoming decline in "violent entertainment." I found it quite extraordinary that Simon would be on a hobbyhorse about entertainment violence. The last time I had seen him was during my brief tenure as chairman of Warner Bros. Records. Simon spent much of our lunch together expounding on his passion at the time, the forthcoming Broadway musical *Capeman*. It was the story of an infamous murderer of the 1950s.

But the great majority of the American public had no appetite for conservative cultural obsessions. Clear Channel, the Texas-based company that owns more music radio stations than any other—at this writing, about 1,200—dispatched a memo listing 200 songs that might be offensive in the wake of the tragedy. The list ranged from all work by the political rock band Rage Against the Machine to many long-popular songs with lyrics that could now be interpreted differently, such as Peter, Paul, and Mary's "Leavin' on a Jet Plane" and John Lennon's "Imagine."

The outcry at the reported banning of "Imagine" was enormous. What was the "inappropriate" line—the one that says "Imagine all the people, living life in peace?" or the one that asks us to "Imagine there's no countries?" In the wake of widespread criticism, not a single executive at Clear Channel would admit to having had anything to do with the memo. "Imagine" quickly became one of the most frequently played songs on the radio, including stations owned by Clear Channel. When celebrities raised hundreds of millions of dollars for families of the victims of September 11 in a national telethon, Neil Young's performance of "Imagine" was generally considered to be the emotional and artistic high point of the event.

To me, the most striking symbol of the adverse relationship between critics of popular culture, liberal or conservative, and most of America came at Madison Square Garden in late October 2001. The occasion was the nationally televised "Concert for America." Six thousand policemen and firemen and their relatives were invited to sit in the best seats. Many rock stars from the sixties and seventies performed. Much of the audience that night consisted of white ethnics, union members, and working families, exactly the kind of swing voters political consultants say are swayed by cultural conservatism.

Artists such as the Rolling Stones and Billy Joel, performing songs that had been filled with alienation and anger when first recorded, touched some kind of emotional chord in the audience, transcending many cultural differences. The passionately applauding audience seemed to represent a much bigger slice of America than the one that resided in the imaginations of either Jerry Falwell or Joe Lieberman.

Then Hillary Clinton was introduced. She was loudly booed.

Yet the same people applauded rapper Jay-Z, who had recently pled guilty to assault, and cheered the publicly gay musicians Elton John, Peter Townshend, and Melissa Etheridge.

"Why I Love !?!?! New York," a short film by director Kevin Smith that consisted of profanity and bleep-filled interviews, was met with enthusiastic cheers, as was the appearance of Howard Stern, whose suggestive radio broadcasts have led to countless fines over the years from the FCC.

So what motivated those who booed? My guess is that it was a combination of factors. Some of the men in the audience just didn't like strong women. Some were economic conservatives, and many, I suspect, perceived Senator Clinton as a politically correct liberal snob.

Meanwhile, George W. Bush's brilliant political advisor, Karl Rove, met amid much fanfare with film industry leaders to discuss ways that Hollywood could support government policy in the war on terrorism.

CHAPTER 13

# 2002—
# The Beat Goes On

I N THE MONTHS AFTER SEPTEMBER 11, terrorism
remained a real threat. Escalating violence between Israel and
the Palestinians was not only a tragedy to people who lived in
the region but a reminder of the vulnerability of any society. The
Bush administration's approach to the threat of domestic terrorism
was debated by both the left and right. American corporations
experienced a series of scandals that helped plunge the stock market into a dramatic decline. The environment, health care, and the
drug war continued to have a real effect on the day-to-day lives of
Americans.

These were important issues, some of them profound. For people
like me, it was a moment when a progressive critique of conservative
assumptions was vital. Yet the cultural overlay in which political discourse was formed continued to weaken both Democrats and the
political left. The progressive agenda still suffered because huge
chunks of America's population were turned off to politics.

My business again bumped up against these forces in the reaction to Cornel West's CD *Sketches of My Culture*. I first met Cornel through *Tikkun* editor Michael Lerner, with whom he'd written the wonderful book *Blacks and Jews*. After my father and I became publishers of *Tikkun*, Cornel had co-hosted an event for the magazine at our house. With his three-piece suit, retro Afro haircut, and eloquent theatrical speaking style, Cornel is the epitome of the "public intellectual," balancing serious academics with mass media communication skills.

To my dismay, Cornel had indulged in some left-wing culture bashing in his book *The War Against Parents* written with Sylvia Ann Hewlett, in which they stated, "The entertainment media has moved from celebrating to denigrating parental role and function...Hollywood feeds off psychobabble, narcissistic individualism and market-driven hedonism." I respectfully but strongly criticized those passages in *Tikkun*. I feared that Cornel might be less than friendly when I encountered him again, but when we talked about it many months later, he shrugged it off. He had developed some friendships with rappers such as Chuck D and KRS-One, and when he spoke at the rap summit he balanced criticism of sexism and homophobia with deep respect for hip-hop's place in the history of American and African American culture.

In the spring of 2001, while on leave from Harvard, Cornel played me an album he and his brother Cliff had just finished recording called *Sketches of My Culture*, which Artemis released later that year.

*Sketches* is a concept album that includes R&B instrumental tracks, a little bit of singing, and rap, as well as West's poetic and charismatic monologues on subjects ranging from the heroes of the civil rights movement to the sweet soul music of the 1970s. While the album recognizes the artistry and relevance of hip-hop culture, one of its songs, "N Word," urges young rappers to stop using the word "nigger."

The connection of spoken word and contemporary music on the album reminded me of Allen Ginsberg's best recordings. Although Cornel hoped that some rap fans would learn about African American traditions from his album, it seemed more likely to me that older black audiences would learn from Cornel the connective tissue between the civil rights generation and the hip-hop scene.

In October 2001, Henry Louis Gates, chairman of the department of Afro-American Studies at Harvard, hosted a "welcome back" lecture and dinner for Cornel in conjunction with the release of the album at the Kennedy School of Government at Harvard. Cornel combines a keen intellect with a preacher's emotional range and is a compelling public speaker. The lecture hall was packed with close to a thousand students. Ironically, Cornel used the very colloquialism he criticized on his album, referring to September 11 as "The niggerization of America," explaining that "all Americans now know what it feels like to be hated, and to feel unsafe." Blacks, he suggested, could teach other Americans how to persevere in such circumstances.

At a time when there was an American consensus about rebuilding infrastructure in Afghanistan, Cornel mused, it seemed appropriate to marshal political will to rebuild infrastructure in America's poorest neighborhoods as well. At a time when working people such as firemen, postal workers, police officers, schoolteachers, and emergency workers were correctly being acknowledged as heroes, there was a political opportunity to push for higher pay for such workers, a long-held progressive goal.

I found myself wishing that Cornel's ability to see a progressive opportunity in the tragedy could be translated to the general media environment.

At a dinner for Cornel after the lecture hosted by the Afro-American Studies department, there was an emotional and bitter-sweet feeling in the room because Cornel's doctors had detected a resurgence of prostate cancer. Cornel would take another leave shortly to have an operation. Although the prognosis was good, I found it impossible not to worry about the forty-seven-year-old professor's future, and to appreciate his contributions in a more vivid light.

This combination of personal vulnerability and extraordinary value to his colleagues and students made Cornel's encounter the following week with the new Harvard president, Larry Summers, all the more odious. West and Gates and most of the Afro-American department at Harvard had joined the university under Summers's predecessor, Neil Rudenstine, and Cornel was summoned to a meeting with the new president.

Summers, like West, was an academic prodigy and was in his late forties. He had been one of the youngest tenured professors in the history of Harvard and had most recently been secretary of the treasury in the final months of the Clinton administration.

Cornel told me of a very confrontational meeting. Cornel said that the new Harvard president admitted he had never read any of West's sixteen books, but he nevertheless attacked them as lacking academic gravitas. He had never listened to *Sketches* but attacked Cornel for "embarrassing" the university by having recorded a CD. "To ignore the medium of musical recording," Cornel told me afterward in disgust, "is like living in the nineteenth century and ignoring the cultural significance of the novel."

Summers also criticized Cornel's activism on behalf of Bill Bradley and Ralph Nader and his recent public appearance with Reverend Al Sharpton when the latter was released from jail following a protest over military bombing of the Puerto Rican island of

Vieques. The Harvard president suggested that Cornel had missed classes to engage in activism. The charge was patently false. Cornel had not missed a class in eight years and had done all outside activities at times that didn't conflict with his classroom schedule. Summers could easily have discovered this information. It appeared to Cornel that Summers was trying to smear him for contrived academic reasons rather than directly confront him ideologically or culturally.

News of the dispute broke on the front page of both the *New York Times* and *Washington Post* in early January in articles that singled out *Sketches* as a primary reason for Summers's unusual attack on an eminent professor.

Many political conservatives were cheered at the attack on Cornel for ideological reasons. However, many liberal snobs joined in because of their implacable bias against his populist style. Journalists who supported Summers repeated the false charge that West had missed classes and claimed that Summers was really worried about "grade inflation"—a concern that too many professors gave out too many A grades. But why single out West for a conversation on that topic when scores of Harvard professors had the same tendency? In *Harper's* magazine, Shelby Steele nastily suggested that West's role at Harvard was to relieve "white guilt," but West's following on campuses around the nation as well as at Harvard consists primarily of young black academic stars. Cornel's real sin to liberal snobs is that he himself is not a snob. He insists on making connections between classical philosophy and theology and modern colloquialisms and issues. He is a challenge to the snobs' need to feel that they are better than average people, and his embrace of a populist medium like music epitomizes it, which is why the CD became such a flashpoint.

I don't mean to denigrate the importance of traditional academia, but it seems to me that in the overall fabric of culture there is a place for a few intellectuals who also have a commitment to communicate complicated ideas to a broader public. One would think that lovers of knowledge would rejoice in the notion that a wider public can connect with wisdom, not feel diminished by it.

Cornel waited until April, a couple of months after his successful prostate operation, to formally announce his departure from Harvard and his renewed affiliation with Princeton. As Cornel traveled around the country promoting his CD he spoke brilliantly on many R&B radio shows, effortlessly connecting, for example, current events, the ideas of Aristotle and Christ, and the art of John Coltrane or Lauryn Hill. There is no other academic in the United States with the gift for reaching such large numbers of people. It said something about Harvard that Cornel West taught there, and it says something about Harvard that he no longer does. And it is another sad footnote to the recent history of the Democratic party that it is a liberal snob from the Clinton administration who is responsible.

Reactionaries tried to grab political and cultural space in the wake of September 11. The American Council of Trustees and Alumni, formed in the mid-nineties by Senator Lieberman and Lynne Cheney, issued a report that listed the names of academics along with statements they made questioning the Bush administration in the wake of the World Trade Center attacks. "College and university faculty have been the weak link in America's response to the attack," the report hysterically concluded.

William Bennett, in his post–September 11 book, *Why We Fight*, a fierce defense of George W. Bush's military policies, also attacked various college professors by name and incongruously bemoaned that "some Americans have ended up tolerating, protecting or apologizing for evil—like those rap songs or those movies" that Bennett disapproved of. The very title *Why We Fight* was culturally savvy on Bennett's part since it had been the name of the group of films that director Frank Capra made at President Roosevelt's request to explain to American soldiers the purpose of World War II. Unlike Bennett, Capra never portrayed his fellow Americans as the enemy.

In July, cultural conservatives in the American media turned their rhetorical guns on Artemis artist Steve Earle because of his song "John Walker's Blues," which was part of his album *Jerusalem*.

Steve Earle was the first artist I signed when I started Artemis. His combination of artistic brilliance and political consciousness reminded me of Bonnie Raitt and Jackson Browne. Steve has been a passionate anti–death penalty activist. Although Steve lives outside of Nashville and uses country, bluegrass, and blues in his music, he is not a "country" artist as defined by current country music radio. A leader of a subgenre called "alt-country," or Americana, Steve has drawn an audience composed primarily of rock fans of artists like Bruce Springsteen, Tom Petty, or Lucinda Williams.

After September 11, Steve wrote several songs for his album *Jerusalem* that had a political tinge, including the prayer-like title song and "John Walker's Blues," a poetic first-person musing on the thought process of the young American who joined the Taliban. In the know-nothing tradition of other distorted attacks on entertainment, some right-wingers claimed that the song was "glorifying" Walker. Steve Gill, a talk radio host in Nashville, said that Earle was "in the same category as Jane Fonda and John Walker and all those people who hate America." Both Fox News and CNN had Gill debating music critics about Steve's patriotism and artistry.

Steve was on vacation in Europe when the controversy broke but had done an interview about the album for our press kit in which he said clearly: "I do not condone what Walker did. Funda-mentalism, as practiced by the Taliban, is the enemy of real thought and religion, too." The song, a minor-key lament sung in Walker's voice, begins, "I'm just an American boy, raised on MTV/And I've seen all those kids in the soda pop ads/But none of them looked like me/So I started lookin' around for a light out of the dim/And the first thing I heard that made sense was the word of Mohammed, peace be unto him." The lyric is subtly sarcastic when it refers to Walker's delusion that he was doing God's work: "Allah had some other plan/Some secret not revealed/Now they're drag-gin' me back with my head in a sack/To the land of the infidel."

To my ears and those of the music critics around the country who scoffed at the attacks on the song, "John Walker's Blues" is obviously in the folk tradition of songwriters getting inside the head of crimi-nals such as Bruce Springsteen's songs in the voice of criminals on *Nebraska*, Johnny Cash's "Folsom Prison Blues," and Steve's own "Jonathan's Song." Earlier in American history there were popular songs about such criminals as Pretty Boy Floyd, Jesse James, and Stagolee. Jackson Browne leapt to Steve's defense, telling *Entertain-ment Weekly*, "It's a beautiful song, a very soulful thing to do."

The authoritative voice of American conservatism, the editorial page of the *Wall Street Journal*, devoted a long editorial to an attack on Earle headlined "Terror Tune—A Country Song Celebrates a Man Who Betrayed His Country." The smug author, Collin Levey, wrote of Earle, "His apologists seem to have taken a rather watery line of defense: If you look at the body of Mr. Earle's work, you'll see he regularly sings from the perspective of society's rejected without necessarily endorsing their actions. That's an interesting tack, and one frequently employed by gangsta rap aficionados. Their violent use of misogynistic lyrics are said to simply hold a mirror to life in the streets. Uh-huh." The *New York Times* soon thereafter published an editorial comparing Steve's song favorably to other post–September 11 songs, and critical response to the album was overwhelmingly favorable. Its first-week chart position of number fifty-nine was the highest Steve had ever attained.

Meanwhile, Eminem's new album, *The Eminem Show*, released in the summer of 2002, was easily the best-selling album of the year. Its opening song, "White America," included the lines "Fuck you Ms. Cheney, fuck you Tipper Gore, Fuck you with the freest of speech this divided states of embarrassment will allow me to have." Eminem's sold-out "Anger Management" tour began with a montage of video excerpts of Cheney, Lieberman, and C. Delores Tucker from the Senate hearing where I had testified. *The Eminem Show* became, by a wide margin, America's number one best-selling album for the year 2002.

Was the vast segment of American society who enjoyed these entertainments really less moral than William Bennett and the staff of the *Wall Street Journal*?

In the summer of 2002 Robert Shogan, a *Newsweek* and *LA Times* political writer, published a book called *War Without End: Cultural Conflict and the Struggle for America's Political Future*. Shogan's well-written and researched book reflected the Washington media's conventional wisdom about the cultural tensions with which I've been involved. According to this narrative, the protests of the 1960s galvanized the religious and cultural right, who in turn have driven American politics in recent decades. Referencing Gertrude Himmelfarb's book *One Nation, Two Cultures*, Shogan refers to "one culture shaped by the 1960s...permissive, secular and bent on individual gratification," and "the other, drawing its beliefs from the 1950s and earlier decades...God-fearing, moralistic, and devoted to traditional values, particularly the importance of the family."

Of course, this formulation is a cartoon of two nonexistent cultures. Many on the cultural left are religious. The civil rights and peace movements emerged from churches. Believers in Eastern religions are not "secular." Nor is there any evidence that cultural conservatives love their families more than other Americans.

Shogan, echoing establishment Washington's obsession with the Monica Lewinsky scandal, hypothesized that Al Gore lost the 2000 election because of his association with Clinton. Amazingly, in a sixty-page analysis of that election, Shogan never mentioned Ralph Nader or the 2.5 million people who voted for him! The ludicrous inference is that the Nader voters as well as the Bush voters were motivated by a reaction to Monica Lewinsky and not by the issues championed by Nader, such as the environment, corporate corruption, and campaign finance.

Counterintuitively, Republicans seemed more comfortable with popular culture than their Democratic counterparts. Bush's secretary of the treasury Paul O'Neill completed a trip to the poorest nations in Africa with U2 lead singer Bono. Secretary of State Colin Powell did an interview on MTV in which he talked about subjects as diverse as foreign policy and AIDS. Without embarrassment or overt reproach from the administration, Powell endorsed the use of condoms as a health measure. CNN covered Attorney General Ashcroft's rendition of his own patriotic song "Let the Eagles Soar," and Ashcroft appeared on the *David Letterman Show* punctuating his theories about how to fight terrorism with a performance on the piano of the Beatles "Can't Buy Me Love."

In the spring of 2002 there was a piece in the *Daily Sun* by former Reagan and Bush speechwriter Peggy Noonan about the MTV series *The Osbournes*. Describing Ozzy Osbourne's visit to the 2002 White House Correspondents Dinner, Noonan wrote of Ozzy: "His presence was so electric that wherever he and his entourage walked, they eclipsed all in their wake. President Bush in his remarks mentioned Osbourne's hit 'Sabbath Bloody Sabbath' and quipped, 'Ozzy, Mom loves your work.' Afterwards when Ozzy suggested that the President wear his hair in magenta-tinged locks, the President yelled with affection 'Second-term Ozzy.'" The easy embrace of Osbourne by a Republican president and pundit was a marked contrast to the distance that most progressives and Democrats create between themselves and far less controversial entertainment figures.

I encountered a classic bit of leftist cultural tone-deafness in response to a book I edited with my dad, Victor Goldberg, and TV and film producer/director Robert Greenwald. In addition to various Emmy-winning TV movies, Robert had directed the Abbie Hoffman bio-pic *Steal This Movie*, and Artemis had produced the soundtrack, with sixties songs covered by Bonnie Raitt, Sheryl Crow, Steve Earle, and others.

Our book was called *It's a Free Country: Personal Freedom in America After September 11th*. It was an anthology with a foreword by Cornel West and pieces by several ACLU officials, as well as Michael Moore, Michael Ratner, and others. A well-meaning leftist activist e-mailed me that many of her friends loved the galleys of the book but suggested we change the subtitle because the words "personal freedom" were associated with conservatives. That, of course, was exactly the point! Why should wonderful words like "responsibility" or "personal freedom" be hijacked by the right wing?

Although I don't pretend to know why the left has drifted away from populism, especially as it relates to mass communication, I keep coming back to my own generation, the baby boomers and their weird political and cultural alienation from younger generations.

In the spring of 2002 an old friend, Jim Steyer, published a book called *The Other Parent*, about the effect of entertainment media on children. I met Steyer in 1988 when he started the

California-based children's advocacy group Children Now and asked me to join the board of directors. Jim taught law at Stanford and had started a TV production company, JP Kids, whose biggest success was *The Famous Jett Jackson* for the Disney Channel.

*The Other Parent*, which includes an afterword by Chelsea Clinton, has many important insights about how America could treat its children better, rooted in many of the policies he advocated at Children Now.

However, the book also contains the now familiar litany of attacks on pop culture, such as convoluted attempts to connect violent-themed entertainment to the Columbine murders. With misguided baby-boom nostalgia, Steyer wrote, "Before our mass media culture became so explicit and so pervasive, before large media companies began to realize huge profits by pushing sex and sensationalism, things were different."

The fact is that there has never been a time when violence was not part of the media. I grew up in the 1950s when network television's primary genre aimed at kids was the TV western. These were televised dramas in which guns were always used to solve problems, with titles such as *The Rifleman, Wanted Dead or Alive*, and *Have Gun Will Travel*. Also popular were crime shows such as *The Untouchables*, and *Dragnet*, or the legal drama *Perry Mason*, in which a murder was depicted every week. I did not know any boys in the Republican Westchester suburb where I grew up who did not have toy guns.

As I grew older and became fascinated with the culture that my parents had grown up in, I found that the male icons of the 1930s and 1940s, Humphrey Bogart and James Cagney, had become famous playing gangsters. Subsequent generations have given the highest awards to gangster-themed drama such as *The Godfather*, and *The Sopranos*.

Admittedly, the fact that "things have always been this way" is not a serious moral argument. There were decades in which racial segregation and sexism were the status quo as well. If there is a serious moral argument that entertainment is bad for kids or adults, it should be given weight, but the same people who attack teen culture are completely comfortable with the violence of their own generation's entertainment.

The same generational double standard exists about sex. In May of 2002, *U.S. News and World Report* had a cover story "Teens and Sex," with the breathless bullet points "They're Starting Earlier" and "The Growing Health Risks." In an article in *Extra* magazine, which critiques mass media, Mike Males debunked the middle-aged newsweekly's alarmism. He pointed out that the birth rate among ten- to fourteen-year-olds is lower than in 1950, and that sexually transmitted diseases (STD) are at the lowest level among boys ages ten to fourteen since 1958 and at the lowest among girls of that age since 1972, according to the Centers for Disease Control report on STD 2000.

I don't deny that sexual behavior has a moral component. Pregnancy is one of the most important events a human can experience and should never be considered lightly. And nobody denies that there are profound health consequences to sex that kids should be aware of. What I don't get is the bizarre notion that baby boomers handled these issues better than today's young people. As Males wrote, "The junior high sexual revolution happened 30 to 40 years ago and kids have gotten much safer since." He pointedly concluded, "The main danger to young girls remains older men."

As to comparisons between baby-boom teen entertainment and today's, let's not forget that the Woodstock movie, the biggest youth culture phenomenon of its time, showed rock fans parading around nude and smoking pot and featured Country Joe and the

Fish chanting the letters F-U-C-K. What contemporary artists are more overtly sexual than Jimi Hendrix or Janis Joplin? John and Yoko posed nude on an album cover. The Rolling Stones posed in drag on the single sleeve of "Have You Seen Your Mother, Baby, Standing in the Shadows?"

What is it with liberal baby boomers? Is it guilt about drugs and sex? Is it, for some, a sense of failure because of the lowered economic performance of so many compared to their parents? Is the baby boomer's angst somehow connected with Vietnam? Is all the adulation for "the greatest generation" causing generational self-esteem problems?

Instead of more studies on teenage behavior, maybe we need studies of why middle-aged people turn on teenagers. For parents who treasure the cuddly and relatively safe years of young childhood, the inevitable independence and risks of adolescence are understandably frightening. And it's not just the kids who keep getting older. We miss our formerly unlined faces and smaller pants size. We don't like being older than most celebrities, older than most cops, older than all athletes, and now older than many presidential candidates. We don't like seeing an increasing proportion of obituaries of people younger than us. We don't like colonoscopies or mailings from the AARP. Sometimes we're jealous of those fellow baby boomers who are at their peak of power, and other times we're fearful we'll be pushed into early, unwanted retirement. But these pressures and others do not give us the right to attack or dismiss younger generations.

As media critic and author Jon Katz wrote in *Wired* magazine, describing the avid young users of the Internet that he calls the "digital nation": "They share a passion for popular culture—perhaps their most common shared value, and the one most misperceived and mishandled by politicians and journalists. As much as anything else, the reflexive contempt for popular culture shared by so many elders has alienated this group. For much of their life, these young people have been branded ignorant, their culture malevolent. The political leaders and pundits who malign them haven't begun to grasp how destructive these perpetual assaults have been, how huge a cultural gap they've created."

We baby boomers seem to have a hard time knowing our place in the world. Sometimes it seems we have an inability to acknowledge that we, the "youth generation," are middle-aged. I'm all for staying vigorous as long as possible, but that's no reason for us to confuse ourselves with actual young people.

To turn our aspirations and anxieties into hostility toward the younger generation is morally wrong and, for progressives, politically wrongheaded.

# CHAPTER 14

# War Clouds, the Midterm Election, and the Democrats' Downward Spiral

> *Where have we betrayed ourselves? We're sitting here like deer numbed in the brightness of oncoming headlights of catastrophe.*
>
> —Harry Belafonte, explaining his frustration with the Democrats and the political left in the wake of the Bush administration's plans for war in Iraq

A FEW MONTHS BEFORE the 2002 election I opened an envelope from the Democratic Senatorial Election Committee (DSEC) to find an invitation to a fund-raiser, featuring Senate majority leader Tom Daschle. The entire front page of the mailing consisted of the following quote: "Never before in modern history have the essential differences between the two major political American parties stood out in such striking contrast, as they do today." The quote was from former president Franklin Delano Roosevelt and dated 1945. It seemed to me a terrible commentary on today's Democrats that they had to go back to the 1940s to evoke a contrast with Republicans.

The differences between the parties were indeed vivid fifty-seven years ago in the wake of the New Deal and during the end of World War II. The Democrats' problem is that unlike the way it was during the late 1940s, the differences between the parties *today* are not clear to many of their own supporters, not to mention nonvoters, Nader voters, and swing voters.

One Democrat who seemed to get this was Senator Jon Corzine of New Jersey, who wrote in a note to me convening a meeting to support the Century Foundation, a progressive think tank: "In my view, progressives must do a much better job of competing with conservatives in the areas of education, research and publicity." Corzine lamented the lack of progressive counterparts to Charles Murray, William Bennett, Irving Kristol, Abigail Thernstrom, Dinesh D'Souza, Lynne Cheney, and others.

I listened over lunch at the Harmonie Club with Century Foundation president Dick Leone, several dozen progressive funders, academics, and activists, as Corzine explained, "When I speak against privatization of Social Security on the floor of the Senate, the response comes first from the Cato Institute and Heritage Foundation followed by editorials in the *Wall Street Journal*. Then they have organs like the *Washington Times* and Fox News and Rush Limbaugh, and we have nothing to compete with that and we don't have enough coherence."

Arthur Schlesinger Jr., former aide to President Kennedy and one of America's leading historians, spoke next and pointed out that September 11 discredited those who demean government. "Ronald Reagan in one of his inaugural addresses said that government was not the solution to problems, government was the problem. That idea wouldn't be so popular today."

Schlesinger also commented on one of my pet obsessions, the presence of so many good-looking young conservatives on cable news outlets. "Does this mean that young people are becoming reactionary? Do these young fogies speak for their generation?" he rhetorically asked.

In fact, conservatives are a small minority of young people, but their leaders recognize the value of young faces and have successfully cultivated the few available to them. There seems to be no corresponding mandate from progressive organizations or from the Democratic party to develop young leaders. The *Nation* and the *American Prospect* are two periodicals I actively support and occasionally write for, but neither of them employs a regular columnist in his or her twenties or early thirties who could represent progressive ideas on TV the way Tucker Carlson, Ann Coulter, and dozens of others do for the conservative movement.

Senator Corzine said that the big liability of the left is a failure to "stay on message." I reminded him that Al Gore was incredibly disciplined in 2000 as he repeated his description of the Bush tax proposal as a "risky scheme" and the need to protect Social Security in a "lockbox" so many times that it became fodder for TV comedians. Richard Gephardt in the House and Tom Daschle in the Senate had "message teams" on a few maven-approved issues. The problem, as I see it, isn't a lack of superficial PR technique, but the failure to make a deeper level of connection with a wide constituency who could feel and express what "progressive" means in their bones with the same level of intensity that conservatives have had in recent decades.

As the meeting was breaking up I asked Senator Corzine if his vision included the mobilization of young people. He winced empathetically, "I've asked about that. But no consultant in Washington can do anything to reach young people. Bob Schrum and his team are the best—the best! But they say that it can't be done!" I assured him that organizations like Rock the Vote and candidates like Jesse Ventura and Clinton in 1992 and Nader in 2000 have proven that it indeed can be done to some extent, but not with national spokesmen like Joseph Lieberman.

Culture bashing receded from political discourse following September 11, but tone-deafness was in full bloom. By the early summer of 2002 it was clear that the Washington consultants for the Democrats had determined that "swing voters" could be swayed by focusing on prescription drug benefits, protecting Social Security, and warning of the impact of Bush economics on the stock market. These were all perfectly valid issues, but again most Democratic candidates had deliberately avoided issues of interest to younger voters and to many other parts of the Democratic base. There was no overarching moral vision of the appropriate role of government, a role that could have been articulated vividly after September 11. There were little or no references to poverty, to public financing of political campaigns, or to national service. There was no questioning of the drug war nor any passion about the environment.

This all took place against the backdrop of a Democratic strategy in the years leading up to the election in which consultants treated all messages as if they were in the last stages of a hotly contested election. Instead of looking at long-term opinion growth, they were focusing year-round on the sliver of "swing voters" who represent approximately 10 percent of those who actually vote. No attention was given to the half of the eligible people who choose not to vote. Far too little attention was given to issues that inspire emotional intensity on the part of activists who can influence media and turnout. Even among "swing voters" the assumption was that they are undecided because they are centrist on every issue. In fact, many such voters have strong convictions but can't figure out which party's candidate represents their views. If one were to dig down and read every detailed position paper of the Democrats, in many cases one would find that there were indeed significant differences from Republicans. For someone like me, who places importance on judicial appointments, and who closely follows the Senate debates, it was not difficult to root for a Democratic Senate. But it was not at all surprising to me that most voters who follow the popular media had no idea what Democrats stood for.

Democratic strategists seem to have assumed that any reference to September 11 would automatically benefit Republicans. Instead of offering a much-needed debate about security and foreign policy, they naïvely tried to avoid the subjects that were uppermost in the minds of most Americans. As Arthur Schlesinger had pointed out, the Democrats had traditionally been the party that stressed the need for collective action via government. Why hadn't there been a more aggressive government action to protect harbors, train stations, and nuclear power facilities? Why was it so important to the Bush administration to prevent new union members from being minted in a department of homeland security that the Republicans were willing to put off the creation of such a department? These were not esoteric challenges but ones that could have put Democrats at the emotional heart of the concerns of most Americans. Instead, most Democrats robotically repeated concerns about "prescription drugs" as their advisors had directed as if all other issues were irrelevant.

I couldn't understand why the Democrats weren't calling for energy independence. It seemed obvious to me that oil affects our relationships in the Middle East, where so much terrorism originates. Moreover, Bush and Cheney both have oil industry backgrounds. Progressive publicist David Fenton suggested that a goal of energy independence could be a progressive goal similar to President Kennedy's commitment to get a man on the moon. Neither Democrats nor environmental groups in Washington sparked to the idea, although around the same time EMA, the environmental group started by Norman and Lyn Lear, produced a public service spot calling for energy independence featuring movie stars Gwyneth Paltrow and Cameron Diaz. But a few airings of the spot were not sufficient to create political traction. Hollywood can be a wonderful echo chamber for political leadership, but it cannot be a substitute for it.

Why assume that Republicans had the unique ability to prepare the nation for future attacks? September 11 had occurred on the Republicans' watch. No one was held accountable for security lapses. Senate Democratic leader Tom Daschle had enormous moral authority on the subject of fighting terrorism because his office had been the target of an anthrax attack. Yet Daschle mysteriously avoided debating the Bush security policy and rarely mentioned that the search for the anthrax criminals had turned up no suspects nor even any theories of the attack's source.

Another issue that Washington mavens avoided was the performance of Attorney General Ashcroft. Early in the year Bob Borosage, who ran a progressive think tank called the American Future, floated the idea to civil liberties groups and progressive Democrats that there should be a national campaign demanding the resignation of Ashcroft. Many progressives felt that Ashcroft had crossed the line on a number of important civil liberties issues and seemed oddly focused on unpopular cultural conservative issues. Weeks after September 11, when the nation was looking toward Washington for ideas about improving security, Ashcroft's Justice Department instead filed a lawsuit in Oregon to prevent implementation of a "right to die" law that Oregon voters had supported in a ballot initiative. For months Ashcroft had kept FBI agents focused on the drug war instead of the war on terrorism. Most absurdly, Ashcroft ordered covering for nude statues in front of the Justice Department Building. However, neither public interest groups nor progressive Democrats chose to make Ashcroft an issue.

As summer turned to fall, the Bush administration's push for a preemptive war against Iraq intensified. Bush chief of staff Andy Card implicitly acknowledged the administration's PR strategy when he told a reporter that "August is not a good time to introduce a new product," in reference to the timing of the planned initiative to convert the American public to support of a war. Bush was said to have insisted to his staff that the resolution authorizing a war against Iraq be "so simple that the boys in Lubbock can understand it." Given the awkward and jumbled response of those Democrats who opposed Bush's policy, it was obvious that the antiwar forces were not thinking anywhere near as effectively.

I recognize that there are many progressives, people who are passionately pro-environment, pro–civil liberties, and deeply concerned about poverty, who nonetheless agree with the Bush foreign policy relative to Saddam Hussein and Iraq. However, much of the Democratic support of Bush's foreign policy was said to be based on the dubious theory that by avoiding debate on the war, Democrats could get the focus of the nation back on the economy, which pollsters indicated was a better issue for the Democrats.

The conventional wisdom of centrist Democrats relative to Iraq was laid out by Senator Zell Miller of Georgia in a *Wall Street Journal* op-ed piece in October. Cleverly entitled "That 70's Show," the piece managed to get in the now fetishistic Democratic insult to entertainment stars who supported the party. Miller's thesis was that the failed McGovern campaign of 1972 was still, thirty years later, the key cautionary tale for twenty-first-century Democrats. Miller, who had been a delegate for Vietnam hawk Henry Jackson at the Democratic Convention in 1972, recalled smelling "tear gas mingling with marijuana smoke."

Miller opined that "the 'peace at almost any price' position is a loser for the Democrats," adding that "the extreme left will . . . put their money, their emotion, their Ms. Streisand's vocal cords" into an antiwar movement. Of course, no one on the antiwar side advocated "peace at any price." The debate was over whether or not to initiate an unprecedented preemptive war, and the most coherent arguments from the political world against war with Iraq had come from Republicans such as Brent Scowcroft, the national security advisor for the first President Bush, and conservative Democratic senator Robert Byrd of West Virginia. Miller advised Democrats to "respond with strength and boldness not with the same failed script that doomed us 30 years ago."

No national Democrat saw fit to remind Miller that the biggest "failed script" of the early seventies was the continuation of the Vietnam War itself, nor that a "message" tailored for conservative Georgia might not be appropriate for national Democrats.

Instead, national Democrats, as expressed through the views of House leader Richard Gephardt and Senate leader Tom Daschle, bought into Miller's argument and supported the president's request for authorization for a war against Iraq. Those Democrats who disagreed with their congressional leadership made speeches on the floor of Congress and dutifully voted against the bill, but none of them spoke at antiwar rallies or staged teach-ins or expressed themselves in a way that was comprehensible to most Americans. At a moment when the Bush administration was making a radical change in American foreign policy, Democrats allowed the Bush administration to decide that a preemptive war was morally and politically valid without so much as a spirited and detailed debate. Why would anyone other than lifelong Democrats be attracted to candidates of a party who so stubbornly refused to engage this crucial issue?

Al Gore, who had been eerily absent from the public stage since winning a plurality of votes for president, made one speech articulating reservations about Bush's plan for a preemptive war, but rather than expanding on his position, he hastily retreated from public debate on the issue. Hillary Clinton, like the Democratic congressional leadership, voted in favor of Bush's war authorization bill. Of those Democratic senators up for reelection, only the late Paul Wellstone, who was tragically killed in an airplane accident shortly before the election, voted against Bush. Wellstone was leading in Minnesota polls taken just prior to his death. When Minnesota Democrats picked former vice president Walter Mondale, he followed the lead of national Democratic leaders and avoided the issue of Iraq, emphasizing instead his detailed knowledge of Senate rules. He lost.

After both houses of Congress passed the resolution giving President Bush the authority to go to war with Iraq, *New York Times* columnist Frank Rich pointedly wrote, "Perhaps more than he intended, Tom Daschle summed up the feeble thrust of his party's opposition on *Meet the Press* last weekend when he observed, 'The bottom line is...we want to move on.' Now his wish has come true—but move on to what? The dirty secret of the Democrats is that they have no more of an economic plan than they had an Iraq plan."

As I mentioned in the introduction to this book, the Democrats in 2002 did such a poor job of defining their agenda that a *New York Times* poll published on the Sunday before the election showed that only 31 percent of the electorate thought that the party had "a clear plan for the country." What makes this heartbreaking for progressives is that there are plenty of excellent plans gathering dust in the offices of policy wonks in Washington. What was lacking was the political judgment to advocate progressive government, and what was present was a cultural myopia among political consultants that actively prevented Democrats from expressing a clear agenda.

On Election Day, the low Democratic turnout permitted Republicans to control all three major branches of government for the first time in several decades. As Clinton media advisor and CNN commentator James Carville lamented on election night, "A party that won't defend itself is not going to be trusted to defend the country." Not long after the election I spoke to Congressman Jerry Nadler, who represents the lower Manhattan district where my family lives and which also contains the site of the former World Trade Center. Although Nadler easily won reelection, he was deeply upset at the poor performance of Democrats nationally. Nadler is one of the most progressive members of the Congress, and unlike the Democratic leadership, he had voted against both the Patriot Act because of its civil liberties excesses and the Iraq war resolution. "The party did much worse than the election results showed," he said. Nadler pointed out that although the Democrats lost only a few seats, the overall vote for Congress was 47 percent for Democrats, several points less than in previous elections. Nadler, who had grown close to many relatives of September 11 victims, wanted the party to focus more on fighting terrorism, which he saw as a long-term struggle similar to the Cold War. He pointed out the failure of the administration to allocate money to protect harbors or follow other recommendations of commissions that had studied homeland security. "If someone is worried about their safety," said Nadler, "it's hard to get them to focus on their job opportunities or health care costs."

I completely agree that Democrats need to focus on safety and that Republicans obsessed with tax cuts are vulnerable on these issues. Democrats and progressives are as elitist and tone-deaf in their language concerning terrorism as they are on other issues. However, Nadler misses the fact that most Americans have no idea what the Democratic positions on the economy are. To the extent that concerns about economics, health care, corporate excess, or the environment motivated people, Democratic positions on those issues, even those of progressives like Nadler, were indistinct to most Americans because of the culturally parochial way in which progressives and Democrats had been discussing issues publicly.

With regard to young people, more focus on issues such as education, the drug war, and a moral vision of the future was required to motivate participation. An issue of the *Nation* ran some instructive letters from alienated younger people. "The apathy of Generation X comes not from the fact that we watched too much MTV but from a frustration over a lack of liberal leaders. No one is out there capturing the leftist imagination which has historically been infectious," wrote one reader.

Another reader suggested some tangible steps to take for 2004: "(1) Advertise on MTV to reach 16- to 18-year-old future voters...speak about gun control, a woman's right to choose and the environment. (2) Get celebrity spokespeople young people have heard of—Shaq, Jennifer Aniston, Vin Diesel. (3) Advertise in magazines like *Vibe* and *Seventeen*. Stress pure air and water and explain to a 16-year-old who will vote in 2004 what the air will be like when she is 50. (4) Have voter registration inserts in cosmetic products, X-box games and at mall food courts. Think outside of C-SPAN and MSNBC."

Not all of these ideas are practical, and there are many other good ideas. I would say a good start would be to pay attention to the full range of culture that connects with young people and address it in terms of both content and style. Not only will there be an increase in the turnout of younger voters, but the mysterious "teen spirit" energy that affects the entire culture will be reconnected with progressive goals. Fashion, music, and all other aspects of culture are affected by teens. So are politics, but in recent years that ripple effect has been the ripple effect of apathy.

As the likelihood of a war with Iraq increased, most Democrats stayed silent. Even those against the war kept their comments limited to the *Congressional Record*. "Didn't you hear Senator Boxer's speech against the war resolution?" asked a staffer who requested that I organize a fund-raiser weeks after the election. Since I wasn't tuning into C-SPAN at the instant she made her speech, of course I didn't hear it. I admire Senator Boxer, but if she or Nadler or other progressive Democrats are going to be effective, they need a mass media strategy that reaches millions of people, not a micromedia one that reaches only die-hard political junkies.

Given the limited outreach of such antiwar politicians and the journalists who agree with them, and given the appropriately limited appeal of obscure radical left-wing groups who expressed their opposition in weird nihilisitic diatribes, several artists tried to fill the vacuum. Woody Harrelson, who was appearing in the play *On an Average Day* in London, wrote a column for the *Guardian* in London with the headline "I'm Tired of American Lies," saying, "The warmongers who stole the White House have hijacked a nation's grief and turned it into a perpetual war on any non-white country they choose to describe as 'terrorist.'" Sean Penn spent $56,000 of his own money to take an ad in the *Washington Post* urging the president to stop a cycle where "bombing is answered by bombing, mutilation by mutilation, killing by killing. I beg you," Penn continued, addressing President Bush, "help save America before yours is a legacy of shame and horror. Sacrificing American soldiers or innocent civilians in an unprecedented preemptive attack on a separate sovereign nation may well prove itself a most temporary medicine."

Singer Harry Belafonte, who four decades earlier had been a key advisor to Martin Luther King, burst onto the media stage when he told a radio interviewer: "There were those slaves who lived on the plantation and there were those slaves who lived in the house. You got the privilege of living in the house if you served the master exactly the way the master intended to have you serve him. Colin Powell has committed to come into the house of the master." He later told Larry King that this applied "even more" to Condoleezza Rice. Powell called the remark "a throwback to another time and another place that I wish Harry had thought twice about before using."

Some progressives were upset with Belafonte because they felt that Powell was the senior official in the Bush administration urging military restraint and that he deserved to be supported, not undermined. However, the very fact that Belafonte's comment was racially charged is what gave it news value and what gave him a platform to go on numerous news and talk shows and discuss his reasons for opposing the war. When I called Belafonte to discuss the reasoning behind his statement, he said that he had not anticipated the attention his remark had received, but that he felt the controversy was a blessing because it created a "tiny opening to jump into this fray, to exacerbate the dialogue and get it into the arena of honorable debate."

David Fenton launched a campaign with "I want YOU to invade Iraq" posters and ads depicting Osama bin Laden in an Uncle Sam pose pointing his finger. The copy read "Go ahead. Send me a new generation of recruits."

Several antiwar newspaper ads appeared sponsored by the group Refuse and Resist with the headline "Not in Our Name," with a heavy emphasis on the voices of artists. The group staged a rally in New York whose speakers included Tony Kushner, Andre Gregory, Ed Asner, Danny Glover, Howard Zinn, Marisa Tomei, and Pete Seeger.

I do not suggest that these eclectic voices were in any sense a substitute for a conventional opposition. By definition, such renegade voices had rough, impolitic edges. There was a need for progressive Democratic leaders to play a role on the left, similar to that played on the right by mavericks like Jesse Helms and Newt Gingrich during the Clinton administration, or that played by senators like Wayne Morse and William Fulbright during the Vietnam War. There was a need for more conventional progressive public interest opposition to doctrines such as that of "preemptive war." But in the absence of such political leadership, the spontaneous mélange of unorthodox voices gave some clues as to how an opposition could be expressed.

Barbra Streisand remained the highest-profile progressive in Hollywood, raising $6 million for the Democratic Congressional Committees at a benefit concert at the Kodak Theater in Los Angeles. Streisand had long vocally advocated that Democrats be more aggressive in challenging President Bush and she opposed Bush's Iraq policy. Marilyn O'Grady, the Republican opponent to Long Island congresswoman Carolyn McCarthy, aired a TV spot saying, "The *New York Post* calls her Baghdad Babs, but Carolyn McCarthy calls her a contributor." This referred to a $1,000 contribution that Streisand had made to McCarthy in 1998. Despite the smear ad, McCarthy handily won reelection.

Liberal snobs in the media focused on some minor errors Streisand made in her remarks at the fund-raiser instead of the substance of her implicit critique of the Democrats' lack of clarity. Ultimately, however, it was the "professional" Democrats whose strategy for 2002 failed and the "Hollywood" push for a clearer and more principled Democratic message that proved to have been right. It wasn't just the Iraq issue; it was the whole political philosophy of obscuring differences between candidates instead of emphasizing them that diluted the credibility of Democratic candidates. Democrats lost control of the Senate, lost seats in the House, and overall had one of the worst performances ever for a party not occupying the White House in an off-year election.

Meanwhile in California, Arnold Schwarzenegger was made the official spokesperson for the popular and uncontroversial Proposition 49, which would provide $455 million for after-school programs for California schoolchildren. Proposition 49 easily won a majority vote. Shortly after Election Day it was reported that Schwarzenegger had hired several advisors from former Republican governor Pete Wilson's administration to explore the possibility of a run for governor of California in 2006.

**CHAPTER 15**

# To My Fellow Former Hippies

O NE OF THE BAD THINGS that happened to the left in the sixties was that the older left never really embraced the new left. Jack Newfield is now sixty something himself and a contributing editor to the *Nation*. Although older than most hippies, he was one of the founders of SDS, the most prominent radical group of the sixties, and is quick to criticize the excesses of the sixties. "Drugs replaced politics for a lot of people," he laments, and he cites such crazy and destructive excesses as Yippie leader Jerry Rubin's reference to Sirhan Sirhan, Robert Kennedy's assassin, as a "freedom fighter." But Newfield also acknowledges the many mistakes made by the older left-wing intellectuals and leaders,

*My self-image was as a young person. Up comes this younger generation. I think they are ignoring my sincere, honest and absolutely profound advice. And that struck at my self-image.*

—Socialist Michael Harrington as quoted in Jim Miller's book *Democracy in the Streets*, describing his confrontations with "new left" radicals in the 1960s.

many of whom had lived through harrowing conflicts with American communism and who wrongly feared that sixties protesters would be co-opted by communism.

Newfield pointed out to me that leftist nit-picking of progressive artists is not new. When Phil Ochs sang "Love Me I'm a Liberal" at a peace rally in 1965, the legendary radical journalist I. F. Stone missed the humor of the song, responded literally, and spoke out against Ochs and the song that had entertained the crowd, shouting, "There are good liberals and there are bad liberals. Liberalism is not our enemy."

In his memoir *Somebody's Got to Tell It*, Newfield recalls that in the early sixties, Socialist icon and intellectual Irving Howe attacked the young Tom Hayden at a debate, accusing him of insensitivity to communism. Hayden was also singled out by Socialist Michael Harrington, a close friend of Newfield's and author of the groundbreaking study of American poverty *The Other America*. During the drafting of the SDS "Port Huron Statement," the defining document of sixties radicalism, Harrington bitterly railed against the younger Hayden for being insensitive to the authoritarian evils of communism, ultimately causing a breakdown of relations between many of the older leftists and the student leaders. Newfield remembers, "I told Mike, we are rebelling against the void of the 1950s" but pointed out that Harrington's criticism indicated that he was still "living in the 1930s," reflecting the fact that the Communist party was virtually irrelevant to the "new left" of the 1960s.

Years later, both Howe and Harrington regretted their dismissal of the younger radicals. Their rejection left the new generation unsupported. It deprived them of wisdom and advice that might have helped them to avoid some of the destructiveness that tarnished the successes of the sixties progressive movements.

With or without recognition by major media and help from

either the Democratic party or name-brand progressive institutions, a new generation of progressives is emerging. Many leaders of the growing antiglobalization movement and critics of the Bush administration's foreign policy have names unknown to older activists. I hope they develop some thoughtful spokespeople and not just incendiary sloganeers. I hope they study the media and the broad American population and do not become content speaking only to each other. Mostly, I hope the progressive baby-boom activists reach out with generosity of heart and respect for the fact that without teen spirit, and without young leadership, vision, and energy, progressive agendas don't have a chance. There's no detailed road map on how to do this, but starting with the Hippocratic maxim of "do no harm," older progressives have plenty of ways of respecting and including younger leaders as equals. The process isn't particularly complicated, but it does require an act of will to step aside, which can be bruising to the ego, as Michael Harrington admits in the quote at the beginning of this chapter. Yet great things can come from such bruises.

Not only do veterans of the sixties have to defer, when appropriate, to youth, we also have to complete our own destiny. Baby-boom satirist Joe Queenan in his book *Balsamic Dreams* criticizes our generation for underachievement. But this is a form of cop-out as well. We're not dead yet! While supporting and reaching out to "teen spirit," we should also emulate the continued focus and passion of people like Harry Belafonte, who remains effective at age seventy-five, Jimmy Carter, who won the Nobel Peace Prize at seventy-nine, Ramona Ripston, who runs the Southern California ACLU well into her seventies, and many others. The final judgment of the sixties generation will come not now but in twenty or thirty years. We do not have the luxury of either resting on our laurels or wallowing in self-loathing.

The left as well as the right can learn to communicate so that "the boys in Lubbock can understand it." Unless it connects with a mass constituency, progressive politics is like the proverbial trees falling in a forest that no one hears. Professors and critics can and should have rarefied taste. Political activists must learn to speak the language of the people, not solely the "Latin" of the political elite. David Fenton points out that leftist public interest groups, even well-funded ones, invariably pay low wages and thus exclude large numbers of talented people. Admittedly, some pubic interest groups simply don't have the funding to pay decent salaries, but even the best-funded public interest groups on the left tend to keep salaries artificially low, as if commitment to progressive politics requires a vow of poverty. Among those who do commit to these organizations, most come from government or academia, and hardly any have background in business, and thus have little or no experience with advertising or PR techniques.

Fenton recalls speaking at a staff retreat of a big nonprofit environmental group to advise them on advertising and media strategy. "I said they should pick one or two communications campaigns a year and only do those. And take whatever you're going to spend and maximize it on that. And everybody in the room got really angry. They said, 'You're saying that someone would have to choose that one person's program is more important than another's.' It blew my mind." This is almost identical to the reaction I got several years earlier in discussing children's issues with progressive congressmen. Such self-indulgent refusal to adapt elementary PR axioms guarantees a minimal impact on public attitudes.

There are a few bright spots in the nexus of culture and politics that can help point the way. Michael Moore has consistently been able to combine progressive politics and advocacy with entertainment through his films, TV shows, and best-selling books. Cornel

West is undaunted by elitist criticism and takes his knowledge and ideas about philosophy, politics, and religion into every corner of society. Tom Hayden, forty years after helping to author the Port Huron Statement, eschews sixties nostalgia and reaches out to antiglobalization teenagers and Latino gangs. One exciting younger voice who has emerged is cartoonist Aaron McGruder, whose comic strip "Boondocks" delivers entertainment with a political subtext and whose lectures are fiery and inspiring.

*The Simpsons,* created by baby boomer Matt Groening, has been enormously popular for fifteen years and has a progressive political subtext as powerful as any entertainment in history. Several progressive writers have valiantly and often brilliantly tried to fill the vision gap, including Eric Alterman, Joan Didion, Barbara Ehrenreich, Rick Hertzberg, Jim Hightower, Arianna Huffington, Molly Ivins, Bob Kuttner, Michael Lerner, and Bob Scheer.

In the cable news world, James Carville and Paul Begala, the architects of Clinton's 1992 campaign, have been consistently cogent and coherent in articulating progressive ideas in the mass media, as have been *Nation* editor Katrina vanden Heuval, and the indefatigable Phil Donahue. In the traditional media world since September 11, *New York Times* columnists Thomas Friedman, Maureen Dowd, Frank Rich, and Paul Krugman have have been articulate and aggressive in questioning the Bush foreign and economic policies and have helped fill the vacuum left by the mostly weak Democratic political leadership and the frequently incoherent leftist critiques of the administration.

One morning over coffee, several months before his eightieth birthday, Norman Lear, the genius behind *All in the Family* and *Maude,* told me that over the course of several decades not a single organization or political candidate or public official had been seriously interested in his thoughts on anything, not even on how to communicate through television. As Norman was grumpily reflecting on this, he suddenly interrupted himself with a smile. "You know there was one guy who I could really talk to? Ronald Reagan. I had great meetings with him. He really listened to what I was saying and tried to answer. When I wrote him letters about the Christian right, even if he had other people write the responses, at least the responses were specific, not those form letters," he said. "Unfortunately," Norman laughed wistfully, "I disagreed with Reagan on just about everything, but ironically he was the one guy who actually engaged me."

"Most people in Washington, including those on the left," observes Sid Blumenthal, former aide to President Clinton, "love the idea of America, which is the ideals, the symbols, the monuments, and the history books, but they don't like actual Americans very much. Americans are those gross people who go to shopping malls and watch television."

This is another indulgence the left cannot afford. Bob Dylan's message of four decades ago still works: "You better start swimming or you'll sink like a stone, for the times they are a changin'."

Let's swim.